ENGLISHMEN AND OTHERS

ENGLISHMEN
AND
OTHERS

BY

A. J. P. TAYLOR, F.B.A.

Fellow of Magdalen College, Oxford

HAMISH HAMILTON
LONDON

First published in Great Britain, 1956
by Hamish Hamilton Ltd
90 *Great Russell Street London WC*1

PRINTED IN GREAT BRITAIN BY
WESTERN PRINTING SERVICES LTD., BRISTOL

CONTENTS

		PAGE
PREFACE		vii
1.	PROPHETS OF MAN	1
2.	WILLIAM COBBETT	7
3.	RANKE	12
4.	MACAULAY AND CARLYLE	19
5.	METTERNICH	26
6.	CAVOUR AND GARIBALDI	31
7.	PALMERSTON	36
8.	JOHN BRIGHT AND THE CRIMEAN WAR	45
9.	DIZZY	65
10.	THE USE OF MONARCHY	70
11.	ECONOMIC IMPERIALISM	76
12.	THE RISE AND FALL OF DIPLOMATIC HISTORY	81
13.	THE CONFERENCE AT ALGEÇIRAS	88
14.	HOLSTEIN: THE MYSTERY MAN	108
15.	THE SECOND INTERNATIONAL	114
16.	THE OUTBREAK OF THE FIRST WORLD WAR	119
17.	MARX AND LENIN	126
18.	TROTSKY	131
19.	THE GERMAN ARMY IN POLITICS	136
20.	HITLER'S SEIZURE OF POWER	139
21.	THE APPEASEMENT YEARS	154
22.	THE ALLIANCE THAT FAILED	157

23. FROM ISOLATION TO WORLD POWER 168

24. STUMBLING INTO WAR 171

25. MAN OF AN IDEA 174

26. THE TWILIGHT OF THE GOD 179

27. DEMOCRACY AND DIPLOMACY 184

PREFACE

I AM not a philosophic historian. I have no system, no moral interpretation. I write to clear my mind, to discover how things happened and how men behaved. If the result is shocking or provocative, this is not from intent, but solely because I try to judge from
the evidence without being influenced by the judgements of others.
I have little respect for men in positions of power, though no doubt
I should not do better in their place. Englishmen interest me most,
and after them Europeans. They may be all of small account now;
but their behaviour in the last century and a half is a subject of
some curiosity and even of some importance. These essays present
aspects of their thought and action in the period when they imagined, however mistakenly, that they occupied the centre of the
world stage.

'John Bright and the Crimean War' was first given as a lecture
at the John Rylands Library. 'Palmerston' appeared in *British
Prime Ministers*, published by Allan Wingate; 'Hitler's Seizure of
Power' in a volume on *The Third Reich*, commissioned by
U.N.E.S.C.O., and published by Weidenfeld & Nicolson. I am also
grateful to the proprietors, publishers, and editors of the *Manchester Guardian*, the *New Statesman and Nation*, *Tribune*, the
Listener, *The Times Literary Supplement*, the *Revue Historique*, and
the *Saturday Review of Literature* for permission to reprint material
which appeared in their columns.

A.J.P.T.

1

PROPHETS OF MAN

CHRISTIANITY has never enjoyed undisputed mastery of the civilized world. There have been heresies within the Church, and rivals without. These enemies accepted the same need for spiritual values and also looked for authority to another world. Now Christianity is the only religion in full vigour, holding a sustained body of doctrine which is adapted to modern conditions. Yet at the same time the Christian outlook is challenged as never before—the challenge not of an enemy, but of a sceptic. Enemies sustain each other; oblivion is the only doom. What is loosely called the religion of humanism threatens Christianity, and with it all established values, simply by not being a religion at all. Every age flatters itself by supposing that it is unlike any other. Our age has more justification than most for making this claim. Or perhaps it would be more accurate to speak of the age that is just ending. It seems unlikely that the age of reason and of liberal thought will last much longer. All the more need therefore to hail its achievement and to acknowledge its unique character—the only age in history when man believed in himself and deduced every principle from this simple, though unreal, creed.

Where did humanism come from? How did man—usually so fearful of the universe—reach this rare confidence in himself? The Renaissance certainly rejected the Christian view of the world as a vale of tears, and taught instead an enjoyment of this life. But there was no coherent creed in this outlook, certainly no moral doctrine. Indeed, the men of the Renaissance knew that they were wicked and resigned themselves to it. The investigator of humanism will find its origins elsewhere—in the English secular thinkers of the seventeenth century, and in Italian writers of a slightly later period, who seemed to develop greater wisdom in judging public affairs with every step that their own country took towards anarchy and incompetence. But few will dispute the claim of the French *philosophes* to be the fathers of humanism. It was they who worked out every aspect of this 'secular religion', until it took on precise definition in the Declaration of the Rights of Man and showed itself, less satisfactorily, in practice as the French Revolution. Their thought was deeply written into all our political assumptions until just the other day — written in so deeply that conscious analysis of it was rarely attempted. When Mr. Kingsley Martin first systematized the ideas of the *philosophes* twenty-five years ago, his book[1] stood alone in its association of thought and public affairs. Since then others have entered the field; and Carl Becker, in particular, described their Heavenly City in an essay of incomparable mastery. Experience has taught us some bitter lessons which even Mr. Kingsley Martin did not recognize in 1929; and his occasional criticisms now strike us as unduly timid. But a book which is deservedly reprinted twenty-five years after its publication has stood the test of time. It has passed beyond either praise or blame; and its very detachment from the controversies of the moment makes it more useful than ever for the serious student.

Mr. Martin did not attempt to write a history of ideas detached from events; and he was certainly right. Ideas grow out of each other in mathematics and perhaps even in some of the less abstract sciences. Humane studies depend on men, as their name implies; and even the most aloof philosopher reflects events more than he is willing to confess. Even here ideas have a life of their own, but only in the way that a plant has a life of its own so long as it is rooted in the soil. The historian of political ideas has to know about politics as well as about thought; yet there is nothing more difficult than a successful marriage of the two. History can so easily be made to prove anything. When ideas turn towards liberty, then events can be found which will display the resentment and discontent of the ordinary man. When ideals turn back to tradition and caution, then street riots will obligingly display the need for order. It is all very well to find the cause of French liberal thought in the Bastille or in the lost wars of Louis XV. Frenchmen had been exposed to arbitrary arrest for a long time; and many countries have lost wars without producing a Rousseau or a Diderot. Mr. Martin seems, in fact, a little weak on his history, perhaps because the practical background of the Revolution has been studied so intensively by French historians in the past few years. His book makes it a little clearer why the eighteenth century welcomed the *philosophes*, but there are still many puzzles to be explained.

On the other hand, Mr. Martin is eminently successful in applying

1. *French Liberal Thought in the Eighteenth Century.* By Kingsley Martin.

what is called here 'the great-man method'. He never forgets
that thoughts occur only in the mind of a single man. We can trace
the development of ideas and their influence on each other. We can
convince ourselves, with more or less success, that events stimulate
ideas in one direction or another. But these are all so many metaphors; and the historian must never lose sight of the fact that ideas
have no independent life. Men make ideas; and each man who
handles them contributes some twist of his own. Voltaire, for
instance, transcended all his contemporaries as a writer. It is not
surprising that he had a burning passion for freedom of expression
and a hatred of injustice. Otherwise he cared little for public affairs
and asked only to be left alone in tranquillity. Hence his practical
demand was for 'civil liberty'—a demand that could be as well
satisfied by a despot as by a parliamentary system, or perhaps
better. Rousseau, on the other hand, never appreciated liberty in
terms of toleration. He resented disagreement as a calculated slight
against himself and dreamed of crushing every opponent by the
steamroller of 'the general will'. No more dangerous idea has ever
been invented by a political thinker; and Rousseau would not have
hit on it if he had got on with others a little better. Again, more
generally, the outlook of the *philosophes* was determined by the
social circumstances in which it was conceived. The clever, rather
frivolous, society of the time demanded generalizations free from
all restrictions of time and place, yet did not expect these principles
to have much practical application. Even Rousseau took fright
when he was asked to prescribe for the immediate future of Corsica
or Poland. A cultured class, which was itself involved in government, would have favoured writers of a different sort, as a comparison with England shows. But it has been no bad thing for English
politicians to be sometimes goaded from outside by writers who
did not have to consider what their ideas would look like when
translated into a parliamentary Bill.

The original impulse towards humanism had, of course, a practical side. Mr. Martin suggests that secular thought began in
France with the revocation of the Edict of Nantes. This act, so
obviously damaging to the State, could not be condemned by
theological arguments. Instead it proved the danger of theology;
and the axe which was levelled against the universal Church fell
with equal weight against absolute monarchy. Louis XIV had
overstepped the unwritten limits of divine right; he had disregarded

the half-forgotten constitution of France. In recent years this criticism has received increasing attention. The French nobility have
been credited with a conscious desire to build a constitutional
monarchy round themselves; and Professor Brinton, joining hands
with Burke across the years, has condemned the Jacobins for destroying the smooth process of constitutional growth. Perhaps Mr.
Martin was wiser to limit this theme to a single sub-section of his
introductory chapter.

The other element which launched humanism was of a different
kind and more nearly an example of ideas breeding ideas. The
English scientific revolution of the seventeenth century started the
French off in their search for political science. If the universe could
be reduced to ordered rules, then human nature, too, could be
brought within a single pattern. The *philosophes* were the heirs of
Newton; and they sought, though without success, a universal law
of political gravitation. Nowadays we are ready to admit that even
the Universe has a history and odd quirks of character. Then a
timeless universe seemed to imply an equally timeless system of
politics. Perhaps the greatest single stroke of this scientific attitude
was the transformation of men into Man. The millions of individuals, each with their separate character, disappeared; a universal
simplicity, or even simpleton, took their place. Helvetius only
carried this view to its logical outcome when he held that every
child was a blank sheet of paper on which society could write anything it liked, and indeed that each individual could be turned into a
genius, if this were a desirable outcome. We still hold this view,
in spite of a century and a half of disappointments. Only the method
of putting it into practice escapes us.

The *philosophes* never questioned the importance of their task.
The traditional pattern of political society had failed; abstract
general rules could be discovered; and these rules, once discovered,
would prove easy of application. The first of these rules was liberty
—the greatest of natural rights. Indeed liberty was, in a sense, the
only natural right; for, once it was accepted, all other rights followed from it. Liberty meant security from oppression or from
unfair laws; it meant security of life and property and therefore also
of freedom of thought. Neither for Voltaire nor for most other
philosophes did it mean freedom to vote one government out and to
vote another government in. Nothing is more curious in these
daring thinkers of eighteenth-century France than their remote

aloofness from anything resembling action. They were engaged in manufacturing a religion, not in devising a political programme. It is common form nowadays to speak slightingly of the nineteenth-century German liberals, who worried over constitutional niceties when they ought to have been tearing the reins of power from the hands of the German princes. But were the French liberals of the eighteenth century any better? Would any one of them have made a tolerable *intendant*? The Jacobins learned politics the hard way at the end of the century. Power was thrust into their hands and they had to wield it, whether they would or no. A single sentence from Danton was worth a ton of the abstract speculations summarized by Mr. Martin; and one's heart goes out even to Robespierre, trying to govern a great country with the guidance of a few oracular utterances from Rousseau. Still, the creed had to be made before it could produce such remarkable results.

One *philosophe*, Montesquieu, claimed to be himself a practical man—and with some justification. He exercised a profession; he tried to deduce laws from history, not from abstract reasoning; and he ended by holding up the example of the British constitution. But, as Mr. Martin observes, he did not escape abstractions. He supposed that the past was all much of a muchness, and he deduced laws from wildly distant periods without any suggestion that time changes all things. In one way Mr. Martin is unfair to Montesquieu. The separation of powers, which Montesquieu discovered in the British constitution, had a great influence on the constitution-makers of the United States and on later European liberals. Mr. Martin, echoing the English historians of his day, declares that Montesquieu had got the British constitution all wrong. The separation of powers was a myth; Cabinet government and the party system had already superseded it. But of course it is Mr. Martin who was wrong twenty-five years ago. The executive was firmly in the hands of George III, as—in the United States—it was placed in the hands of George Washington; and the British Cabinet of the day no more disproved the separation of powers than the American Cabinet does now. Our historians would have saved themselves much trouble if they had realized that Montesquieu, as a contemporary, was a more reliable observer than Whig sentimentalists one hundred years later. At any rate, our historians have got it right now; and the practical Montesquieu is vindicated.

This theme, as Mr. Martin himself observes, takes us away from the main current of French thought. We return to it with Holbach and Helvetius—the most important, though not the most readable, of the *philosophes*. Important, first of all, because they became conscious materialists. Once you have shaken off Christianity, it is no use stopping halfway, though English agnostics have tried to do so. Better far to search for purely secular rules of behaviour. It was the great achievement of these two to discover, though by a different route, the utilitarianism of Bentham. If man is the only test, then the benefit of the majority becomes irresistible. Instead of our doing good to others, it is they who do good to us, the speculators, by being happy. Johnson foresaw the consequences and denounced them: bread and circuses or—in contemporary terms—the welfare state and dance music on the Light Programme. Why not? It is a more agreeable outcome than the Utopias of most philosophers. The answer to this frivolous query was already in preparation; and it dominates the rest of Mr. Martin's book. The answer was Rousseau—the philosopher first of anarchy and later of totalitarianism. To those of a detached temperament he must always appear a detestable mind, but unfortunately a mind of the first quality. Eighteenth-century France produced no writer of equal power; and perhaps there has been none since—Marx is academic, second-rate stuff in comparison. Rousseau invented democracy. He invented, first, the dogma that every man has an equal right to a say in government—a dogma there is now none to dispute. Thereafter he invented the further dogma that democracy alone has the right to silence its critics or opponents—a doctrine applied by the one-party State of the people's democracy and, with less ruthlessness, in the two-party State of our own. It was an odd ending to a movement of thought that had started with respect for the individual.

Mr. Martin is left with a good deal to tidy up. There is the doctrine of equality, embarrassingly in conflict with individualist economics—a puzzle that was to dominate the politics of the nineteenth century. There is the doctrine of Progress, finally enunciated by Condorcet under the most pathetic circumstances. The hunted politician in his garret, asserting the perfectibility of man, was a sad epilogue to this record of speculation. And yet an inevitable one. Men insist on believing in something; and, once revealed religion has proved false, what is there left to believe in except ourselves? The humanists hunted Man, as a dog chases its tail; and, by a sort of miracle, they sometimes caught him.

2

WILLIAM COBBETT

TROTSKY tells how, when he first visited England, Lenin took him round London and, pointing out the sights, exclaimed: 'That's *their* Westminster Abbey! That's *their* Houses of Parliament!' Lenin was making a class, not a national, emphasis. By *them* he meant not the English, but the governing classes, the Establishment. And indeed in no other European country is the Establishment so clearly defined and so complacently secure. The Victorians spoke of the classes and the masses; and we still understand exactly what they meant. The Establishment talks with its own branded accent; eats different meals at different times; has its privileged system of education; its own religion, even, to a large extent, its own form of football. Nowhere else in Europe can you discover a man's social position by exchanging a few words or breaking bread with him. The Establishment is enlightened, tolerant, even well-meaning. It has never been exclusive, rather drawing in recruits from outside, as soon as they are ready to conform to its standards and become respectable. There is nothing more agreeable in life than to make peace with the Establishment—and nothing more corrupting.

The Establishment made nearly all our history and nearly all our literature. But what of those outside, the nameless many? It is characteristic of their fate that even when they found a name for themselves as the Commons of England, this was at once appropriated by the most privileged assembly in the world. Not only anonymous, they are also silent: 'we are the people of England, that never have spoken yet'. Yet silent is the wrong word; inarticulate would be better. For outside the snug structure of the Establishment, there is always a vague movement—sometimes no more than a rustle, often a breeze, occasionally a real storm. But rarest of all are the moments when the sound becomes an articulate voice, pronouncing recognizable words. It is not enough to be risen from the people; the writer must still think as they do, though expressing himself more clearly. There was never a writer

of more impeccably popular origin, for instance, than D. H. Lawrence; but his spirit soon took on an alien tinge, and his later
inarticulate phase was not at all like public-house conversation.
Nor is it enough to have advanced or revolutionary ideas. Republicanism has often been aristocratic since the days of Algernon
Sydney; and our most revolutionary poet was the son of a baronet.
It is not really possible to rouse a working-class audience by
reciting either Shelley or Swinburne, though I have seen the experiment tried; the audience preferred Ella Wheeler Wilcox.

The spokesmen of the Commons of England can be numbered on
the fingers of one hand; they earn recognition even if they speak
only a few words. John Ball has to carry the Middle Ages almost
alone. We have to wait until the seventeenth century for a real
democratic movement, obtruding itself into the Civil War between
the King and the magnates. Our own preoccupation with social
questions has led us to exaggerate the importance of the Diggers;
and we perhaps fail to see that the more profound revolutionaries
are to be found in the religious sectaries. John Bunyan is the first
great English writer who owed nothing to the Establishment; and
Pilgrim's Progress is the most subversive tract ever written. For
Bunyan did not merely hate Vanity Fair; he rejoiced to be outside
it. This democracy made but a brief stir. After the battle of Sedge-
moor the people of England disappear from history for more than
a hundred years; and we shall never discover the subterranean
channels which perhaps connected the Independents of Cromwell's
time with the Radicals of Peterloo. Tom Paine was the first to
break the long silence; and broke it so effectively that he is still
frowned on by respectable historians.

He was followed by a greater writer, though an inferior thinker.
William Cobbett was the common man suddenly grown articulate.
Apart from a supreme gift of expression, he had nothing—no ideas,
no policy, not even the ability to get on with others. Cobbett was a
torrent of printed words. He began as a Tory; he became a radical
Reformer. Both political descriptions are irrelevant to his real outlook. He hated the Establishment—the Thing. At first he hoped to
escape from it by returning to an imaginary past; later he hoped
to destroy it in an equally imaginary future. But he was more concerned to strike against it in the present. His first appearance was
as a barrack-room lawyer, and he had always the popular taste for
litigation. He went to law with his printers, his partners, his

creditors, with great statesmen, finally with members of his own family. He was self-taught in law and in politics, as well as in writing; and always unshakably self-confident in his own cause. Not only did he know best how England should be run. He also knew best how houses should be heated, what crops should be grown, what clothes should be worn. The reader who is to enjoy his writings must accept unquestioningly that Cobbett is always right—as much in his obscure feuds as in great issues of public policy. Lord Sidmouth and the Botley parson; Sir Francis Burdett and Sir Robert Peel—all must be consigned to outer darkness. Cobbett was always being cheated; always battling against great odds; always being threatened with the majesty of the law—yet always turning up remarkably successful in no time.

The *Political Register* was the first popular newspaper. Its secret was to express, clearly and forcefully, what every labouring man obscurely felt. Cobbett's political programme was simple: government should cease to exist, and the Thing along with it. The National Debt should be repudiated—with some compensation to small holders; the army disbanded; the civil service wound up. Then taxes could be ended; and everyone would be prosperous. It is only our unconscious allegiance to the Thing which makes us think these ideas preposterous. In reality, they are the politics of every natural man. Andrew Jackson applied them almost contemporaneously in the United States with extreme success; the Capital Levy was a basic part of the Labour Party's programme, in the days when it was Socialist; and even to the present day the Swiss manage to be the best-defended State in Europe without an army in our sense at all. If we did not have to carry the incubus of the gentry, the clubs and bishops, *The Times*—Cobbett's 'bloody old *Times*'—and the public schools, we should be nearly as prosperous as Cobbett wanted us to be. Unfortunately, if you knock one Thing down, another bobs up. The United States and the Soviet Union both prove it in their separate ways.

Cobbett was against the Thing; he was on the side of the labouring people. This is far from saying that he had any idea of a new social order, or indeed of any social order at all. He thought that the farmer and his labourers, or for that matter the factory-owner and his workers, were on the same side. He, too, was a master and an employer. Though he refused to accept letters addressed to 'William Cobbett, Esq.', he always described himself in his

B*

writings as 'Mr. Cobbett'; yet, when he wrote to his farm-labourer, began abruptly, 'Marshall!' Attwood argued rightly that his insistence on an undiluted gold currency would retard the development of industry. Cobbett thought this all to the good. He always refused to admit that the population of England was increasing. He held that it had been greater in the Middle Ages and proved it by calculating how many people the village churches would hold if they were packed to the doors. He invented an extraordinary version of the past in his *History of the Protestant Reformation*. His *Advice to Young Men* is advice about how to have a good life without being associated with the Thing. Cobbett did not advise his young man to be educated at Winchester or to join the Fabian Society or to oppose sponsored television; in fact he did not give good advice for those who wish to become Labour Cabinet Ministers.

Yet it will not do to turn Cobbett into a popular saint. The Thing gets hold of you, even if you kick against it; indeed the Thing shows its greatest skill in rewarding its opponents. Cobbett became a respected and admired character even in his lifetime. Hazlitt canonized him as the representative Englishman; the Steam Intellect Society reprinted his pamphlets; and he ended as a Member of Parliament, put in by a wealthy radical mill-owner. His son, starting as a Chartist delegate, ended as a Conservative M.P., supporting Disraeli; and his descendants were pillars of Manchester conservatism. Cobbett always presented himself as a farmer, who had taken to writing as a side-line. Like most agricultural experts, he does not seem to have known much about practical farming. His various farms were no great success; and he made money, apart from journalism, by running a seedsman's shop in Kensington. *Rural Rides* is one of the greatest books written in English: but its title gives it away. It describes the visits of a town-dweller to the country, not the country seen and felt from inside; it is the hiker's pocket-companion. Anyone who tries to follow the advice of *Cottage Economy* condemns himself to a laborious life; and Cobbett himself got up early in the morning to write pamphlets, not to brew beer.

The contradictions of Cobbett are best shown in the parable of the Indian corn. Cobbett came back from America as great an advocate of maize as of democracy; and in subsequent years he put as much energy into preaching its virtues as into attacking the Thing. Maize is not a reliable or profitable crop in the English climate, as

Cobbett could have learnt from any practical farmer. It has never been grown extensively in our fields. But seedsmen produce a delicate variety for private gardens; and what Cobbett advocated as a staple food for the labouring poor has become an exotic delicacy at the tables of cosmopolitan epicures.

3

RANKE

THOUGH standards vary, greatness remains; indeed it is the true mark of greatness that it can survive changing standards. Shakespeare was great to Johnson; great to Coleridge; is great to us. Ranke was a historian of the same grandeur—great to his contemporaries, still great after the passage of a century; if not the greatest of historians, securely within the first half-dozen. Great as a scholar, great as a master of narrative, Ranke has the special claim of having achieved something more than his own work; he founded a school, the school of scientific historians, which has dominated all historical thinking since his time, even when in reaction against it. His wish to present the past 'as it really was' became, in the German phrase, 'a winged word'; one of those pregnant sayings which concentrate the aspirations and outlook of a generation. Indeed the past 'as it really was' can be put with Bismarck's 'blood and iron' as the two most important spiritual legacies left by the Germany of the mid-nineteenth century. A composite picture of the German character would have to include Ranke, just as it would have to include Goethe and Schiller on the one side, Hitler and Himmler on the other. Perhaps Ranke displayed even more clearly than these other representative figures the strength and achievement, also the weakness and the defects, of the German character.

The present revival of Ranke is not simply a publishing accident. The German interest in Ranke is one attempt among many to find normality and self-confidence among their own kind; it is also, however, one attempt among many to evade the responsibilities of the day, as Ranke evaded them, by a sort of political quietism— finding God in history in the hope that He will take the blame for everything that goes wrong. In his life, as in his work, Ranke remains full of lessons for the Germany of the present day and also for the historian in every country.

Ranke has one qualification which he himself regarded as essential for the study of a subject: there is plenty of material. His works stretch at unrivalled length on the shelves; and his life was as interminable as his works. Few historians have matured so young; none

other of the first rank has kept going, in full possession of his
faculties, until well over ninety. His first published letter is dated
1814, the last 1886. Both show the same gravity and self-confidence.
These qualities made Ranke a great historian. He never doubted
what he wanted to be and what he wanted to do. Though he was an
affectionate son and brother and, late in life, an affectionate hus-
band, he was dedicated to the study and writing of history, accepting without complaint the solitary existence which that involved.
He never sought guidance or instruction; when he met other historians, it was to discuss questions of organizing historical studies,
not to debate historical problems. He never troubled about criticism, except when this challenged the accuracy of his facts. Facts
were his guiding star, one might say his illusion. In a letter to his
brother Heinrich in 1831 he wrote:

> My basic thought is not to accept either one theory or another, not
> even the one which lies between them; but to recognize the facts, to
> master them and display them. The true teaching is in the recognition
> of events.

Forty years later, facts had become even more sacred. He wrote in
1873:

> The historian exists in order to understand the sense of an epoch in
> and for itself and to make it understood by others. He must keep his
> eye with all impartiality only on the subject itself and on nothing else.
> Through everything runs the divine order of things, which certainly
> cannot be precisely displayed, but is to be felt all the same. The signi-
> ficant individuals have their place in this divine order, which is identical
> with the succession of epochs; this is how the historian must compre-
> hend them. The historical method, which seeks only the genuine and
> the true, thus comes into direct contact with the highest questions of
> the human race.

Yet what were these facts which revealed the divine order of
things? Simply the documents which had survived by accident and
which jealous archivists allowed him to see. Time and again he
wrote to the archivists (or, when these proved stubborn, to their
official superiors, even to Metternich) for one more document, one
more 'fact', endlessly confident that with this extra 'fact' everything would at last fall into place and the divine purpose be revealed.
He supposed that in writing documents men record their motives;
he almost assumed that men wrote documents for the benefit of

historians. The supreme consequence of Ranke's doctrine was the belief, universal after the first German war, that if the archives were combed through an 'explanation' of our twentieth-century turmoil would be discovered. Nowadays we know better and read diplomatic history for purposes of entertainment. 'Facts' have crumbled along with the Newtonian system of the universe. Ranke would have been bewildered by a judgement essential to modern science: 'The person of the experimenter is himself part of the experiment.' Or, to put it in terms of the historian: 'Impartiality gives a more dangerous bias than any other.'

Though impartiality is impossible, accuracy is a different matter. An historian can copy a document accurately, though he can never give to it a full, final and lasting interpretation. Impartiality would not have carried Ranke so far, if he had not been accurate as well; and maybe he would not have been accurate without his worship of the elusive 'fact'. The present-day historian feels his mouth water as he reads of Ranke's three years in Italy, moving from one archive to another and seeing them opened for historical purposes for the first time. Ranke was then a little over thirty, perhaps the best time for an historian to engage in intensive research: old enough to know what he was doing, young enough to have energy and zest. We smile at the assiduity with which scholars nowadays get their foreign travel at other people's expense—a week at Monte Carlo at the expense of U.N.E.S.C.O., three months in America at the expense of some foundation, a trip round the world at the expense of Andrew Carnegie or Cecil Rhodes. Ranke did far better than his modest successors: he spent three years in Italy at the expense of the Prussian State. No historian without private means has ever had such a stroke of fortune. While in Italy he bought every manuscript and early printed book which might be useful to him for the Royal library in Berlin; on his return he borrowed them as long as it suited him—a convenient arrangement. For Ranke, though remote from the world, was not without worldly skill.

It is curious to trace, in his letters, Ranke's growing realization that the historian, especially of modern times, will do well to be on the right side of the authorities. There was no element of dishonesty in this; Ranke had been on the side of authority from the beginning. Though he wrote his letters on a desk that had belonged to Gymnastic-father John, and had always a touch of German romanticism in his private judgements, Ranke had no sympathy with the political enthusiasms which spluttered among German students after 1815. His religious convictions were deep; among these was a confidence in the divine mission of the monarchical State. He wrote of a speech delivered by Frederick William IV in 1847:

> I say definitely that I know nothing since the psalms where the idea of a religious monarchy has been expressed more powerfully and more nobly. It has great passages of historical truth.

Since this religious monarchy was a 'fact', Ranke was never troubled by any conflict between his devotion to 'facts' and his loyalty to the Prussian State. It never occurred to him that he might discover a fact discreditable to the Prussian monarchy; and sure enough he never did. Each year, in his old age, Ranke would produce a new volume of history 'as it really was'; and each year a copy of the new volume would be sent to William I with an accompanying letter, emphasizing that the volume was devoted to showing the religious mission of the August House.

Thus Ranke escaped from the problems of intellectual integrity which have troubled many academic figures. His nearest contact with it was in 1837, when the famous 'seven of Göttingen' protested against the abolition of the Hanoverian constitution and were deprived of their chairs. Ranke thought their action unnecessary; on the other hand, he refused to accept one of the vacant chairs. It may be wondered whether his refusal would have been so firm if the offer had come from the House of Hohenzollern. This is not to say that Ranke approved of all that happened in Prussia after 1862. His ideal king was Frederick William IV; and though he tried to turn William I into a pillar of European peace, he had difficulty in striking the right note with Bismarck. Ranke distinguished clearly between States and nations; and he regretted Bismarck's association, however equivocal, with German liberalism. He believed that a divine monarchy must keep finance and the army out of parliamentary control. Bismarck had done this in Prussia; but the Imperial constitution of 1871 made dangerous concessions to liberalism. It is not surprising that Ranke sought escape from Bismarck's policy by editing the letters of Frederick William IV to Bunsen—editing them, as he explained to William I, with the necessary discretion. Between Ranke and Bismarck there was never more than a watchful, doubting truce—a conflict of character rather than of

fundamental outlook. After all, Bismarck, too, was engaged in pre-
serving the August House (to his own later regret); and Ranke's
disciples, though not Ranke himself, had no difficulty in fitting
Bismarck into the divine order of things.

Though Ranke did not ignore domestic events either in history
or in politics, his consuming interest was in foreign affairs—the
domain of history in which the 'fact' is at once most attainable and
most elusive. Here, too, he found a divine order, but of a different
kind. Within the State the divine order rested on monarchical
authority; in the wider community of Europe it was expressed by
sovereign States acting to preserve their independence. Not that
Ranke was unconscious of the cultural links which held Europe
together; after all, he enjoyed a European reputation. He visited
Macaulay (though disapproving of the way 'in which he illumin-
ated the present by the past'); he was on intimate terms with
Thiers and had an important conversation with him at the height of
the Franco-German war; he appreciated Italian art in his rare
moments of escape from the archives. But these cultural issues
seemed to Ranke to have little to do with politics; or rather, he
regarded the conflict of States as an aspect of European culture.
Since he accepted the Prussian army as a special manifestation of
divine providence, he found no fault in war as such; he condemned
only wars fought to spread 'red republicanism' or to establish the
domination of a single Power on the Continent—in other words he
condemned wars fought against Prussia. For when one comes to
look for other monarchies which would display the divine purpose
they are difficult to find. Ranke was on friendly terms with King
Maximilian of Bavaria and even claimed that Maximilian, who
died in 1864, would have prevented the Austro-Prussian war. But
this was no more than a gesture of appreciation to a generous patron
of history; besides, the divine order in this case had a curious
origin, for the Kingdom of Bavaria had been created by Napoleon.

Austria was a different matter. Here, too, was an August House,
of indisputable historical character, and the traditional opponent of
revolution. So long as the Habsburg monarchy co-operated with
Prussia, it received Ranke's blessing; when it sought to overthrow
the divine balance between the two German Powers, Ranke discovered that Roman Catholic Powers did not understand the work-
ings of Providence. It was no accident that in the same year, 1865,
Ranke on a visit to England observed a revival of intolerant

Protestantism and was glad of it; 'for positive religion, which rejects the general flight into a vague liberalism, accords with my own beliefs'. Thus, the war of 1866 appeared to Ranke as a war of Prussian defence, meant to restore a divine balance which Austria had threatened to overthrow. Once Austria returned to co-operation with Prussia, she became again part of the 'God-willed' order. Beyond these two German Powers, one so full of defects, the monarchical system seems hardly to have extended. Ranke makes virtually no comment on Russia: only Bismarck understood that German destinies depended on what happened beyond the Vistula. Ranke saw catastrophe to the divine purpose in the French Revolution; though he spoke often of Franco-German co-operation he assumed that this could only follow a repudiation by the French of the revolutionary tradition—a sound judgement, as the story of Vichy shows. He welcomed the war of 1870 as a war both against Jacobinism and against Napoleonic imperialism; it was for him a war of the balance of power, a war of self-defence. This carried him far from the controversies of the nineteenth century. He told Thiers in October 1870: 'The King of Prussia is not fighting any longer against Napoleon, who is a prisoner, nor even against France as such; he is fighting the idea of Louis XIV.' Yet it is difficult to think of any monarchy more divinely appointed than that of the Bourbons. Here again the divine order turns out in practice to mean nothing more than increase of Prussian strength.

Worship of power was the creed which bound Germany together; it is a more repellent creed when decked out with phrases of Christian religion. Ranke's letters are a strange mixture in which love of Nature and sincere religious feelings are compounded with sycophancy towards the great and apologies for Prussian power. A reader of them turns almost with relief to those latter-day Germans whose orthodoxy did not shrink from straight brutality and dishonesty. Yet this feeling is as mistaken as the hero-worship of Ranke, traditional in German scholarship. Ranke was by no means a hypocrite. He was a man truly dedicated to his task. In his own words: 'I know that I am born to do what I am now carrying out, that my life has no other purpose. I must go on whether I want to or not.' And again: 'I'm content to know what I live for; my heart leaps with happiness when I foresee the joy that executing an important work will give me; I swear daily to execute it without departing by a hair's-breadth from the truth which I see.'

This dedication was a noble passion. But it rested on the assumption that others were dedicated to public duties as Ranke was dedicated to history. Ranke spoke of historians as priests; he regarded kings as the most sacred of priests. The State could never sin; and if it did, this was not his affair. This was the spirit of the learned classes in Germany which brought Hitler to power. Ranke and his followers were not National Socialists, not even their precursors. They were all dedicated men, simple and pure in their private lives. But they regarded the State, whoever conducted it, as part of the divine order of things; and they felt it their duty to acquiesce in that divine order. They never opposed; they rarely protested. Inevitably, therefore, they usually found themselves apologizing for what the State had done. If Hitler was merely the working-out of historical forces, then how could historians condemn him? Ranke had 'explained' the revocation of the Edict of Nantes; his successors 'explained' the gas-chambers. Nor can the Western world regard Ranke's political quietism with complacence. The English or American scientist who believes that he has discharged his duty to society by working devotedly in his laboratory evades responsibility as Ranke did; and will end in the same service of blind power. It is tempting to believe that government is a special calling and that the calling will always be of God. If history has any lesson it is that men should resist this temptation and should recognize that no member of a community can escape responsibility for its actions. The historian or the scientist does well to lead a dedicated life; yet, however dedicated, he remains primarily a citizen. To turn from political responsibility to dedication is to open the door to tyranny and measureless barbarism.

4

MACAULAY AND CARLYLE

CRITICS used to have a trick, now rather gone out, of matching two contemporary authors like prize-fighters in a ring. Dickens and Thackeray, Fielding and Richardson, Meredith and Hardy—there was not much sense in it. These contrasted pairs do not demonstrate anything except that it takes all sorts to make a world, especially the world of literature. They are a warning against taking any writer, however great, as typical of his age; there is always someone equally great who is his exact opposite. Macaulay and Carlyle were the two greatest writers of history in nineteenth-century England. It is all that they had in common. There are only two other historical works in English which can match Macaulay's *History of England* and Carlyle's *French Revolution* for literary and intellectual pleasure. It is not difficult to guess one, though it is unlikely that you will guess the other.

Though Macaulay and Carlyle were both great historians, they were not only historians, indeed not even primarily historians. Macaulay was a politician, Carlyle a prophet. This is not unusual. Most historians are amateurs in that they write in their spare time —nowadays the time that they can spare from teaching or administration. Paradoxically those who devote all their lives to writing are usually the most amateurish. Macaulay came to history as a journalist. I do not mean that he knew little history—many journalists know a great deal of history, and Macaulay's mind was stocked with historical information in a way without parallel. His mind ranged over the centuries. He could match the decline of the Moghul empire with incidents from the Carolingian eclipse; and in a single speech in the House of Commons he brought in Edward I and Constantius Chlorus, the Rump and the Plebeians of Rome, Socrates and Mr. Burke. But he used the past as Machiavelli and the men of the Renaissance had done: it was a storehouse of anecdotes and events, which illustrated the character of individuals. As an essayist his subjects were chosen for him by the books which he had to review. He took a theme; made up his mind about it; and wrote down his ideas fast, in time to catch the press. He had no time to hesitate; and there has never been a historian who doubted so little.

Politics reinforced the same habit. In politics there can only be one of two answers—Yes or No, For or Against. As an historian, too, Macaulay always chose his lobby and stuck to it. The complexity of history is very different. Time and again the evidence does not allow us to make a firm conclusion; and even when it does, we cannot say that one side was right and the other wrong—the two sides were merely different. We cannot even say that there were two sides. Parties and sects shade into each other; and the historian who is trying to recapture the past must often leave his reader with an impression of muddle and confusion. Macaulay never did this. He was always cocksure. He never doubted what had happened or which side was in the right. His characters were all drawn in black and white, the good very good, the bad very bad. Those who are not bad but whom Macaulay does not like turn out to be very silly. James II and those who supported him were villains; William III and the Whigs were enlightened statesmen who could do no wrong. This is, to say the least, a very simple view of human nature. But then Macaulay had a very simple outlook. He thought that the England in which he lived—the England of the Reform Bill—was as nearly perfect as a country could be; and therefore he found no difficulty in judging the past. The people and events that had helped to produce early Victorian England were in the right of it. Everyone else had gone off the rails. This 'Whig interpretation of history' comes in for a good deal of criticism nowadays; and it is suggested that Macaulay and his school only picked out the bits of history that suited their doctrine. As a matter of fact, all historians do that; and the most dangerous are the ones who do not realize how selective they are.

In any case I am not sure that Macaulay and the Whig view of history were all that mistaken. He thought that the British constitution was a unique display of political genius. But wasn't it? The revolution of 1688 was truly a Glorious Revolution. George Orwell once pointed out that in this country we do not kill each other for political reasons. Is there any other great community where this has ever been true? Those who criticize Macaulay either do not care about liberty, or they think that it can take care of itself. Macaulay was a good deal more sensible. Not only did he regard liberty as supremely important; he knew that it needs ceaseless defending. In recent years we have had a number of books on the eighteenth century which assume that profit and jobbery were the only things the Whigs cared about. They certainly cared about them a good deal; but I think that they also cared about parliamentary rights and the liberty of the subject. The father of Charles James Fox was the most corrupt of eighteenth-century politicians; it is more important that he himself was the founder of modern Liberalism. If men are to have a hero, it is better to find him in William the Deliverer than in Frederick the Great, though no one would have been more surprised than William III himself at this heroic role.

Macaulay's views did not make him a great historian. His unrivalled gift was his power of narration. No one ever told a story better. Tastes have changed. Now we want analysis, not narrative —what made things happen, not the record of events. You can see it even in our attitude to what goes on from day to day. We give a glance at the headlines; and then turn to the centre of the paper for the explanation. The great figures of journalism now are commentators, not reporters. And the historian, too, is expected to give us 'the low-down'. Macaulay does not; he gives us drama, sometimes unreal drama. He had lived too long in the political world. When he came to write of the past he was still present as a participant. He felt again the excitement of the great debates; knew afresh the importance of the great decisions. Everything he wrote tingled with life; but the life was artificial. The member of Parliament has to believe that the destiny of future generations depends upon his vote; the historian acknowledges this belief but knows that it is not true. The politician performs upon the stage; the historian looks behind the scenery. Macaulay often forgot that the scenery was not real even when he had painted it himself.

This is why Macaulay never got inside his characters. For him they were simply actors on the political stage. He did not attempt to read their minds. He ignored religion. This is extraordinary when you reflect that the great struggle of the seventeenth century was even more a struggle between Anglicanism and Dissent and between Protestantism and Roman Catholicism than it was between king and parliament. It never crossed Macaulay's mind that any honest man could be a Roman Catholic; therefore James II and his supporters were stupid and wicked. Nor did he inquire into the social and economic background of his characters—except to remark that the Tories were ignorant. You would not be aware from his *History* that the great Whigs were great landowners; yet it surely makes a considerable difference to a man when he owns thousands of acres. Certainly he tried to show how people lived as well as how they acted. But for him as for his great-nephew, G. M. Trevelyan, social history is 'history with the politics left out'— agreeable anecdotes, not the essential foundation which gives shape to everything else. It is an odd view that the way you make your money or the size of your family does not matter politically, and equally odd that a seat in parliament has no social importance. In short, what Macaulay did incomparably well was to write the political history of the governing class.

In this, as in everything else, Carlyle was Macaulay's opposite. He was the greatest master of English prose to spring from the people. This does not mean that he admired the people or got on with them. He despised the class to which he belonged and ran after Lady Ashburton as eagerly as D. H. Lawrence, his twentieth-century equivalent, cultivated Lady Ottoline Morell. Yet there was no escaping his origins. Though he called Christianity 'Hebrew Old Clothes' and railed against 'the multitudinous *canaille*', he remained a Scotch Calvinist with a stonemason for his father. His style is like nothing else in English. Carlyle acquired it by translating Goethe; and his writing is, in fact, German put into English word for word. If put back into German, it appears simple and unaffected. It sheds a quaint light on the two languages that Goethe, the most classical of German writers, should have inspired the most uncouth writer of English. Carlyle did not learn ideas from Goethe as well as style. His ideas are those of a man of the people who has suddenly become articulate—if only in Anglo-German; ideas spluttering and half-formed, ideas of revolt and rejection with nothing constructive to follow, but rooted in humanity, not in class-feeling or good taste.

Carlyle sensed the masses as no other writer has done. He expressed their outlook, against his own conscious convictions. He was shaped in the turbulent years when the masses of England straightened their backs and shook off respect, the great age of the Chartists. Carlyle had all the Chartist hatred of privilege, their contempt for 'the grouse-shooting aristocracy'. He knew what was at stake in 'the Condition-of-England question'. But when Chartism really stirred, Carlyle backed away. He should have been the greatest of Chartists. Instead he went sour. Betrayal is too common to need an explanation; but few have paid so high a penalty. Emerson once asked an anti-slavery agitator in prison: 'Friend, why art thou here?' The other answered: 'Why art thou not here?' The question rang through Carlyle's mind. Why was he not there? All his writings sprang from the goad of this question. To escape self-reproach, he had to reproach all the world. Too Calvinist to turn Roman Catholic, he set up as a self-made Jehovah, thundering out more violent commandments. Like the Hebrew prophets, he preached woe. He defended slavery and preached the worship of Force. He ran round the world looking for a Hero and found some odd ones. He called Bismarck 'a magnanimous, noble and deep-seeing Man'; and wanted Sir Garnet Wolseley to shut up the House of Commons, sword in hand. He wasted years of his life trying to make a hero out of Frederick II of Prussia—as perverse a task as was ever attempted. He anticipated every trick of the twentieth-century demagogue—prejudice against negroes and Jews, admiration of the Germans. The abolitionists were 'rabid Nigger-Philanthropists'; Heine 'a slimy and greasy Jew'. The 'hopefulest public fact' in his time was that 'noble, patient, deep, pious and solid Germany' had become Queen of the Continent instead of 'vaporing, restless and over-sensitive France'. The Victorians, themselves full of doubt, enjoyed his reproaches and imagined that his strenuous exhortations had a concealed message. Even Huxley supposed that he had learnt from Carlyle to work harder.

In reality Carlyle spent his life denouncing the things that he himself did well. He despised writers, particularly of long books; no one wrote longer. He admired toil, honest work; he did none. He never handled a spade; he was not horny-handed. He preached the virtues of a humble, obscure existence, far from towns and factory-chimneys. He won fame and wealth by writing successful books for rich industrialists. The rage in his books is rage against himself. The hero that he worshipped was his own opposite—silent, imperturbable, a man of action; and his praise of force was a protest against his own impotence—his social impotence, not the unsatisfactory sexual relations with his wife into which everyone inquires so eagerly nowadays. This conflict made Carlyle an un-happy man; but it made him a revolutionary writer. You do not read his books; you experience them, and what you experience in them is the storm of the world. He was a nihilist, a destroyer, despite his doctrine of toil and the heroic virtues. He once found a perfect subject, the French Revolution. That really was the end of a world; and Carlyle wrote of it like a man possessed. There is little narrative; a great many inaccuracies; none of that simplifying that we expect from the ordinary historian. Though he worked hard before he wrote it, he did not even keep up with the scholarship of his time; and Darwin was no doubt right when he said: 'As far as I could judge, I never met a man with a mind so ill adapted for scientific research.' No matter, the *French Revolution* is the only work in which the past is not merely narrated, but re-created. Carlyle has no gift for historical movement; he never describes how one situation developed into another. There is the lightning flash of genius, in which every detail stands out to remain vivid in the memory for ever. And, after it, new darkness, until broken by another vivid flash. The *French Revolution* is the most frightening of all works of history; and Carlyle was as frightened as any of his readers. He had meant to escape from Chartism into history; instead he found a Terror worse than before.

It needed the end of a world to find a use for Carlyle's gifts. There is nothing more impressive than the prophet who comes off; nothing more absurd than the prophet who does not. And for most of the time Carlyle did not come off. The world he lived in was not coming to an end. It was not being ruined by democracy and materialism. On the contrary, it was becoming more sensible, more tolerant, a better place to live in—and no thanks to Carlyle. He was a seer and a visionary, an iconoclast and a revolutionary. He exposed pretences, weighed everything anew. Macaulay was a man of commonplace mind, complacent, ordinary in everything except in his knowledge and his gift for writing. Yet Macaulay judged more wisely than Carlyle—had a better scale of values in the present, looked more accurately into the future. And we do not need to puzzle for an explanation. Macaulay had a talisman to guide him: his belief in liberty. He made liberty the theme of all his writing and looked forward to a time when everybody would care for it as he and his friends at Holland House did. Carlyle regarded liberty as an aristocratic fad which would be blown away when the people came into their own. Liberty is indeed the touchstone of every man's career. Do you respect the judgements of others as much as your own? Or are you so confident of our own judgement that you would trample that of everyone else under foot? Macaulay gave the answer for liberty; Carlyle for tyranny. The worse cause had the more powerful advocate. All the same, it was the worse cause.

5

METTERNICH

MEN live after their own deaths in the minds of others. Samuel Butler thought that this was the only form of immortality. For most men it is a wasting asset. Memories fade; causes change. Who now cares what Gladstone said in 1868? Occasionally the historian acts as a resurrection-man. He discovers that some forgotten figure was the real saviour of his country or maker of empire. Our nineteenth-century Prime Ministers, for instance, are being pushed aside; and their fame is being usurped by civil servants, hitherto obscure. There is another, and more lasting, way to survival. The historical figure is turned into a symbol. The man becomes a myth; and, though his real deeds are forgotten, he is mobilized in defence of some cause which might have surprised him. The founders of the great religions have all enjoyed this fate. Millions of men repeat their names, while knowing nothing of the details of their lives. The carpenter's son of Galilee blesses the grandeurs of the Papacy; and the tyranny of the Politburo is carried out in the name of a crabbed German scholar.

Metternich knew this success, even in his lifetime. His name was the symbol of resistance to the revolution—abused by the radicals, praised, though more rarely, by conservatives. His fall in 1848 was the decisive sign that 'the springtime of peoples' had begun. Soon he was being treated as the great opponent of German unity, his immortality turned to ridicule by Treitschke, only his interminable 'five metaphors' remembered. Every textbook of history rejoiced that 'the system of Metternich' had been overthrown; and the most humble politician assumed that any future settlement would improve on the work of the Congress of Vienna. The peace-making of Versailles began the disillusionment. Metternich crept back into favour as the exponent of a less idealistic diplomacy. The Balance of Power seemed a more sensible and a more effective principle than the League of Nations. But Metternich had to wait for his full restoration until the present cold war of creeds. He has re-emerged as 'the rock of order', and every renegade liberal in America discovers an admiration for this desiccated aristo-

crat. Metternich is again to fight the Jacobins, but this time with
the big battalions on his side. Nationalism is frowned on; and
Western Union is to replace 'the mouldering edifice' of the Habsburg monarchy, which Metternich lamented that he had spent his
life in propping up.

The new saint of conservatism is a long way from the Metternich of history. He was a very silly man. This is revealed even in
the flattering portrait by Lawrence. Vain and complacent, with
fatuous good looks, his first thought in a crisis was to see whether
his skin-tight breeches fitted perfectly and the Order of the Golden
Fleece was hanging rightly. Even his love-affairs—and he had
many—were calculated for their political effect. He sought influence on Napoleon through the Queen of Naples and learnt the
secrets of Russia from Countess Lieven. It must have been disturbing when he whispered political gossip in bed. He never made a
clever remark. His thoughts, like those of most conservatives,
were banal and obvious. 'Things must get worse before they get
better'; 'after war Europe needs peace'; 'everyone has his allotted
place in society'. Most men could do better than this when shaving.
As he grew older, he grew more sententious. His deafness gave
him an irresistible hold over his visitors. Bismarck wisely slept
during his discourse and so won the old man's favour. There are
those whom we would recall from the dead. Metternich is not
among them. Even Mr. Viereck and Professor Morganthau would
blench if he appeared on their doorstep, his empty sentences already
phrased.

He was good at his job, though it was not so difficult a job as is
often supposed. His job was diplomacy and, in particular, to maintain the greatness of the house of Habsburg. He was spared the
greatest difficulty of the diplomat, which is to convince his own
employer. The Emperor Francis gave Metternich a free run so
long as Austria was kept out of war; and even the Austrian generals
counted on being beaten. He liked to present himself in later life as
the symbol of resistance. In reality he had been the greatest of
appeasers. His first stroke was 'the Austrian marriage', by which
he hoped to buy off Napoleon with an Austrian arch-duchess. Far
from being the enemy of Napoleon, Metternich was the most
anxious of allied statesmen to compromise with him. He hesitated
to enter the last coalition; strove for an agreed peace; and
regretted Napoleon's downfall. He justified his policy by fear of

Russia; it was pointless, he argued, to overthrow one tyrant of Europe if another took his place. The truth is that he wanted others to do the fighting for him. Besides, he supposed that a plump arch-duchess would turn Napoleon into a harmless, almost legitimate monarch and that the man who had grown great through the Revolution would now tame it. It made the delusion no less absurd that Napoleon sometimes shared it.

Metternich did not invent the Balance of Power, nor do much to develop it. The Great Powers of Europe existed without his assistance; and his only initiative at the Congress of Vienna was to project an unnecessary war over Poland—a war which others had too much sense to fight. In international affairs, too, he offered a series of platitudes. 'All I ask is a moral understanding between the five Great Powers. I ask that they take no important step, without a previous joint understanding.' Even the United Nations would work if Metternich's request were granted. But what if the Great Powers disagreed? Metternich offered only lamentations and reproaches. He abused Canning for putting British interests first; yet was ready to wreck his conservative partnership with Russia for the sake of Austrian interests in the Balkans. In the usual way of statesmen who rule over a decaying empire, he urged others to preserve the Austrian monarchy for their own good. He invented an Austrian 'mission' and assured his foreign visitors how unwillingly he had added Lombardy to the empire in 1815. It is, of course, rare for upholders of empire ever to admit that they get advantage or profit from it. And as Metternich went from one palace to another or pocketed the rewards which other sovereigns as well as his own showered upon him, the cares of office were no doubt the only thought in his mind.

He played some diplomatic problems competently, though Palmerston, his contemporary, did better with less fuss. The two shared the credit for a peaceful outcome to the eastern crisis of 1840. But ten years earlier Metternich might have muddled the Belgian alarm into a war, if it had not been for Palmerston's firm handling. Again, Metternich put years of wasted effort into attempts at intervening in the Spanish civil wars. His most original move in Austrian policy was to concentrate her strength on Italy. Though himself a German from the Rhineland, he encouraged Austria's withdrawal from Germany. He did not assert her supremacy in the German confederation nor even grudge Prussia her private score of the Zollverein. Yet he was too much a man of Western Europe to be content with the Balkans as compensation. For him Asia began at the road eastwards from Vienna. Italy alone seemed worthy to be the Habsburg prize. And Metternich taught the doctrine—quite erroneous, as it turned out—that the Habsburg monarchy could remain great only so long as it continued to dominate in Italy. All his diplomatic combinations centred on the Italian provinces. Yet he knew both that the Italians hated Austrian rule and that France would not tolerate it indefinitely.

This double threat was in itself an attraction to him. It was always his aim 'to fight the revolution on the field of international politics'. He had no faith in principles or ideas despite his theoretical posturing. Though he claimed to be a disciple of Burke, he doubted whether historical institutions would hold against radical ideas. In any case, there were no historical institutions in Central Europe except for the Hungarian parliament; and this Metternich never managed to control. The kings and emperors were almost as new as Napoleon, who had indeed created many of them. The Habsburgs had laid their hands on the historic states of Hungary and Bohemia; and Poland, the greatest historic state of all, had been eaten up by Metternich and his two conservative partners of the Holy Alliance. If tradition was useless, concession was dangerous. Metternich never wearied of explaining that moderate liberalism inevitably opened the door to extreme radicalism—a judgement repeatedly belied by events. Indeed, he argued in a perverse way that extreme radicalism, being less concealed, was somehow less alarming, even less destructive, than moderate reform.

His only answer to either liberalism or radicalism was, in fact, repression. If people were not allowed to think for themselves, they would be satisfied with material prosperity—and even this could be neglected. Since he had no genuine conservative ideas himself, he denied that radical ideas were genuine; and solemnly maintained that discontent everywhere was the result of 'a conspiracy'. When Confalonieri, the Italian patriot, was brought as a political prisoner to Vienna, Metternich wrangled with him for hours in the hope that 'the conspiracy' would at last be revealed. His view of radicalism was exactly that of Senator McCarthy. The good conservative must look under the bed every night. One day he will find a radical lurking there. A conspiracy needs a centre; and Metternich found it in Paris, as his present admirers find it in Moscow. How much easier to forget men's political grievances and to raise the cry of foreign war. But Metternich had more sense than those who now tread in his footsteps. Though he advocated a conservative crusade against France and 'the revolution', he proposed that it should be fought by others. Austria did her duty to civilization by existing; it was for others to keep her going. He said in old age: 'Error has never approached my spirit.' And certainly he never made the error of getting into the front line if he could avoid it. In this way at least he set an example to us all.

6

CAVOUR AND GARIBALDI

It used to be the fashion to contrast the unification of Germany and of Italy. In Italy idealism; in Germany *realpolitik*. In Italy the spread of parliamentary liberalism; in Germany the triumph of the Prussian army. Bismarck appeared always in a general's tunic, ruthless, unscrupulous, a master of force and dishonesty. Cavour was the civilian statesman, relying on parliamentary speeches for his success. The failure of the German radicals was lamented; there were few to regret the failure of Mazzini or Garibaldi. They were impractical dreamers who did not understand the greatness of Cavour; and it was a good thing for Italy when they were shipped off Garibaldi to Caprera, Mazzini back to exile in London. More recently, Cavour has had a bad press. His private correspondence has at last been published (it is now almost complete); and his own words have shown him to be much more like Bismarck, much less like Gladstone, than used to be supposed. He wielded the weapons of traditional diplomacy with incomparable skill, but also with incomparable lack of principle; and Metternich turns out to have been his exemplar as well as his enemy.

Cavour did not care much about the unification of Italy, or at any rate ranked it low in his scale of values. Himself with little national feeling, preferring to speak and write in French, his deepest concern was for moderate liberalism. He wanted a free press, free trade, and a parliament based on limited suffrage, first in Piedmont and then perhaps in northern Italy. But he did not regard the unification of the whole peninsula as a noble idea or believe that it would of itself bring about a moral regeneration. He had nothing but contempt for idealists like Mazzini and could have said with Bismarck: 'The great questions of our day will not be settled by speeches and majority resolutions but by blood and iron.' What he lacked in blood and iron he made up for in deceit. The Italian question was for him a problem in European diplomacy, not a matter of national sentiment. He hardly thought about the Italian people except to fear them. His thoughts were concentrated on Napoleon III. And the later observer must confess that the unification of

Italy might well have been impossible, unless Napoleon III had been brought in to defeat Austria in 1859. After all, the victory of nationalism was not inevitable. Poland had to wait until the twentieth century, despite a much stronger national sentiment; the Ukraine waits to the present day.

We still need a history of Italian unification from the European angle. Professor Valsecchi of Milan is writing it; but so far he has only got to the early days of the Crimean war. Meanwhile, Mr. Mack Smith has given us a new version of the story at a later stage[1]—the stage of 1860, when Lombardy and central Italy had been united to Piedmont, but when the Two Sicilies and the Papal States (to say nothing of Venetia) had still to be liberated. This was the moment of greatest contrast between Cavour's reliance on diplomacy and the faith of the radicals in their own ideals. Cavour still feared the intervention of 'the Holy Alliance', still pinned his calculations to the favour of Napoleon. Garibaldi believed that the entire peninsula could be brought together by a spontaneous outburst of national enthusiasm; and he thought the prize worth any risk. He was determined to act somewhere—against Austria in Venetia, against Rome despite its French garrison, or, when Sicily rebelled, against the Bourbon kingdom of the Two Sicilies. It used to be held that Cavour secretly encouraged Garibaldi and was in alliance with him. The truth is less creditable. He pushed Garibaldi off to Sicily in order to get him out of the way and in the hope that failure would ruin the radicals once and for all. Instead, Garibaldi succeeded beyond his wildest dreams; and Cavour had to sweep up the pieces of a policy in ruins.

Mr. Mack Smith has produced a surprising book to come out of Cambridge. He acknowledges his debt to Professor Butterfield; and one would have expected praise of Cavour and condemnation of Garibaldi from a member of this neo-Machiavellian group. But not at all. With brilliant, though well-founded, perversity, Mr. Mack Smith turns things upside down. It is Garibaldi who was the realist, arriving at the right conclusions by instinct, and Cavour who was the dogmatic muddler. Mr. Mack Smith is perhaps a little unfair to Cavour. As things turned out, Italy in 1860 was able 'to do it herself', as she had mistakenly boasted she would in 1848; and Europe counted for little. But this could not have been foreseen when the Thousand sailed. Napoleon III still seemed to dominate

1. *Cavour and Garibaldi 1860. A Study in Political Conflict.* By D. Mack Smith.

Europe, his decline lay far in the future; and Cavour was not the only man to fear the might of France. Moreover he was right on one essential point, the question of Rome. Rome dominated the Italian problem; and even Garibaldi went to Sicily principally in order to reach Rome by the back door. Yet the French could be got out of Rome only by diplomacy, not by force; and for the sake of Italy Garibaldi had to fail before he reached Rome, unless the Pope had already withdrawn—and the French along with him. Moreover, Mr. Mack Smith underrates the danger that Austria, Prussia and Russia would come together in resistance to 'the revolution'. They nearly did when they met at Warsaw in October 1860; and they were prevented more by the diplomacy of Napoleon III (and hence indirectly of Cavour) than by Garibaldi's success in the south.

Still, by and large, the emphasis is put the right way. Cavour was blinded by his rigid hostility towards the radicals. He saw in them only 'the social peril', and was convinced that anarchy must follow their victory. His primary object was that Garibaldi should fail; only in the second place did he want Italy to be united. This view divided him not only from the radicals, but even from his king, Victor Emanuel, who was ready 'to become simple *monsu Savoia* and clap his hands at Mazzini's success if this sacrifice were necessary for the making of Italy'. Yet Cavour's own policy was more Utopian than that of any radical. He imagined that Italy could be brought into being solely by the moderate liberals—the most useless of all classes in a revolution. Ricasoli's ruthlessness made this policy work in central Italy; but in the south there was nothing between the aristocracy and the masses. The few middle-class lawyers there supported unification only in order to get the courts open again; they would not fight for it, and Garibaldi succeeded by rousing the masses. This was a social revolution against the land-owners—a revolution which Garibaldi exploited for the national cause. He had no social programme, despite his emotional sympathy with the peasants and despite Cavour's suspicions; and he allowed them to fall under the rule of a harsher, more rigid Pied-montese bureaucracy without ever understanding how he had betrayed them.

Cavour always suspected Garibaldi; Garibaldi never suspected Cavour. This is the central theme of the whole affair. Of course, Garibaldi disliked Cavour and resented his cession of Nice to Napoleon III; but he thought that, just as he had dropped his republicanism, Cavour would drop his hostility to the radicals for the sake of united Italy. If the radicals united Italy, this would certainly weaken Cavour and perhaps even lead to his fall; but again Garibaldi, being ready to make the greatest personal sacrifices on his side, could not understand that Cavour would not do the same. Cavour, like Bismarck, regarded himself as indispensable; when he proved unyielding on this, everyone had to give way to him in the last resort—and Italy paid the price. Garibaldi put Italy first; Cavour put himself first. Therefore Cavour was bound to win in the end, despite the great advantages which Garibaldi accumulated in Sicily and Naples.

For they were great advantages. The liberation of the Two Sicilies seems easy in retrospect; we almost fail to notice that it needed a leader of genius to accomplish it. European radicalism produced three great dictators—Kossuth in Hungary, Mazzini in Rome, Garibaldi in the Two Sicilies. Garibaldi was the least intellectual of the three, with few ideas and unable to formulate even these clearly. Yet he was easily the most successful. He evoked from the people and even from the politicians a personal devotion almost without parallel in modern history; again and again he chose the right course by instinct; and he showed himself the greatest general that Italy has ever produced. In the late summer of 1860 Sicily was a true radical paradise, radiating the hope—or perhaps the illusion—that every evil legacy of the past had been swept away. Cavour was not the serpent in this garden of Eden; Garibaldi's success had eclipsed him for the time being. The real trouble was that Garibaldi and the people of Sicily were at cross-purposes. They supposed that he had brought them freedom; he looked on Sicily only as the first halt on the road to Rome. Both alike resisted Cavour's plan for an immediate annexation of Sicily to the kingdom of Sardinia. But the Sicilians wanted permanent autonomy for their island; Garibaldi and his radical supporters wished to use Sicily as a base for further successes. Once Garibaldi had crossed to the mainland and carried all before him, he lost interest in Sicily; and it irritated him to have to return in order to settle its internal conflicts. Even in Naples, he listened impatiently to the republican arguments of Mazzini and the federalist schemes of Cataneo. The march on Rome was the only thing that interested him.

The resistance of the Neapolitan army on the Volturno gave

Cavour his chance. He was able to stop Garibaldi just in time. He acted no doubt cynically and basely, discrediting Garibaldi unjustifiably with the king and killing the idealism of the radical movement. But there was something wrong with a radicalism which could think only of further battles. The radicals had an aggressive foreign policy; they improvised casually in home affairs. Mr. Mack Smith is inclined to regret that Sicily and even Naples did not survive as autonomous radical states. Was Cavour alone to blame? After all he had only another six months to live; and the radicals had plenty of chance in the future if they could take it. They never made much of it; and Italy has been kept going (so far as it goes at all) by hard-headed officials of Cavour's stamp. Idealists make revolutions; practical men come afterwards and clear up the mess. Garibaldi was luckier than most revolutionary leaders. He remained an idealist to the end of the chapter. If Cavour had not existed, Garibaldi must either have failed or have ended by playing the part of Cavour himself. Perhaps it was Cavour who made the greatest sacrifice after all. Garibaldi returned to Caprera; Cavour remained in power.

7

PALMERSTON

AMONG the surprising careers of British Prime Ministers, none has contained more surprises than that of Lord Palmerston. For twenty years junior minister in a Tory government, he became the most successful of Whig Foreign Secretaries; though always a Conservative, he ended his life by presiding over the transition from Whiggism to Liberalism. He was the exponent of British strength, yet he was driven from office for truckling to a foreign despot; he preached the Balance of Power, yet helped to inaugurate the policy of isolation and of British withdrawal from Europe. Irresponsible and flippant, he became the first hero of the serious middle-class electorate. He reached high office solely through an irregular family connection; he retained it through skilful use of the press — the only Prime Minister to become an accomplished leader-writer.

Palmerston was not a member of one of the great Whig families or even connected with them. He was an Irish peer, moderately rich, who naturally entered politics to supplement his income. For a peer, he was an educated man. He went to Cambridge, which — even at the worst time — provided a solid grounding in mathematics; and he early absorbed the principles of political economy. Hence, he was not staggered, as Peel and Gladstone were, by the sudden impact of the Free Trade case; this had been a commonplace of his thought for thirty years. Born in 1784, he entered the House of Commons at the age of twenty-three, without either strong convictions or defined party ties; simply a young man of the fashionable world who wanted a good appointment and — rarity enough — was qualified to hold one. Having a reasonable grasp of figures and of economics, he was offered his choice among the junior financial offices;[1] he chose that of Secretary at War and

1. Spencer Perceval is said to have offered him the post of Chancellor of the Exchequer; even if he did, this was not the important office that it has subsequently become. The First Lord of the Treasury himself conducted the financial affairs of the country, and — if he sat in the House of Commons — held also the office of Chancellor. Spencer Perceval must have thought better of his proposal to Palmerston, for he adhered to the usual arrangement and was his own Chancellor. Peel in 1841 was the first to sit on the Treasury bench, as First Lord, with a Chancellor beside him; Russell, in 1846, the first to leave financial business to a Chancellor of the Exchequer.

retained it for twenty years. This was the equivalent of the present-day Financial Secretary to the War Office; a post strictly administrative and financial, without a seat in the Cabinet. Though Palmerston ran his office competently, he did not trouble much with politics and seemed to care only for life in society. Good-looking and fickle, he established himself as 'Lord Cupid', a name which tells everything. But the years of obscurity were not wasted: he served a more prolonged apprenticeship in administration than any other Prime Minister has ever done and, when he came to sit in Whig Cabinets, was distinguished from his colleagues by his ability to run an office. It was this ability, not his policy or his personality, which finally made him Prime Minister in 1855.

Though Palmerston served a Tory ministry, it would be wrong to describe him as a Tory; he was simply a 'government man'. Nor was he a Canningite until late in the day; what brought him over to the Canningites was his support for Catholic emancipation. With his gaiety of spirit and his easygoing morals, he hated tyranny and oppression wherever it occurred. After twenty years of comfortable office, he left it for the sake of the Catholics; just as, at the end of his life, he threatened to resign as Prime Minister rather than relax the struggle against the slave trade. In 1828 Palmerston, out of office, found himself associated with Melbourne and Huskisson, the Canningite remnant who had broken with Wellington and were drifting over to the Whigs. There were also personal grounds for this tie. After a good many adventures, Palmerston had settled down with Lady Cowper, Melbourne's married sister. He lived with her more or less openly; had children by her; and married her in the late eighteen-thirties after Lord Cowper's death. Melbourne was a more important man than Palmerston, more influential and better connected; when he joined the Whig Cabinet in 1830, he carried his illegitimate brother-in-law with him. Without the Melbourne connection, Palmerston would hardly have reached the Cabinet rank which started him on the path to the premiership; and Melbourne was to sustain him against the criticism of the orthodox Whigs at the end of the 'thirties. In the last resort, Palmerston owed his position as Prime Minister to the odd chance that the sister of one of his predecessors had become his mistress.

Palmerston was to make his name at the Foreign Office; but this was neither intended nor expected. Lord Grey, Prime Minister in 1830, had been Foreign Secretary in a remote era and meant to conduct foreign policy himself; all he wanted was a competent underling in the House of Commons. Lady Cowper was again of service. Princess Lieven, her closest friend, recommended Palmerston to Grey as presentable and well-mannered. For some time it was believed that Grey supplied the policy; Palmerston was held to be 'frivolous' and failed to establish his hold over the House of Commons. The peaceful solution of the Belgian question was primarily a triumph for Grey. When Melbourne became Prime Minister, Palmerston had things more his own way; and his conduct of British policy during the eastern crisis of 1839–41 was brilliant, perhaps the most perfect in the records of the Foreign Office. But it was a performance for experts. It did not make him popular with the general public; and it made him much disliked by many of the great Whigs, such as Holland and Durham. In 1841, when the Whig government declined into collapse, Palmerston was still a relatively little-known figure. His frequent evocation of Canning, whose policy he neither understood nor followed, was an implied confession that he could not stand on his own feet.

The five years between 1841 and 1846, when Peel was in office with a Conservative government, were decisive for Palmerston's future. The succession to Melbourne as Whig leader was open. Lord John Russell assumed that it would automatically be his as political representative of the greatest Whig family; and he thought he had done all that was necessary when he secured the allegiance of such Whig managers as 'Bear' Ellice. Palmerston could hardly play his family connection against Russell's, even if it had counted for anything; he therefore decided to play the British public. He built himself up deliberately as a public figure: established relations with the Press, and himself wrote leading articles in his forthright, unmistakable style. At the end of 1845, when Peel first resigned, the third Earl Grey made it a condition of his taking office under Russell that Palmerston should be excluded: the condition wrecked Russell's Cabinet-making. The episode was at once an unconscious recognition by the great Whigs that they had taken a cuckoo in the nest, and a sign that the cuckoo was now too strong to be ejected. Later, in 1846, Russell formed the last Whig government of our history; and Palmerston went undisputed to the Foreign Office.

This feeble government had a record of failure, broken only by Palmerston's dazzling display in foreign policy. His policy had its serious side and can be defended, as it were, on technical grounds; but there was a flamboyant touch as well—Palmerston was deliberately playing Russell off the centre of the stage. His triumph came in 1850 with the Don Pacifico debate, when he held his own against the greatest speakers of the age—Peel, Gladstone, and Cobden; held his own and worsted them. The triumph was not one of oratory in the conventional sense. Palmerston was always a bad speaker; full of 'hums' and 'haws', his voice trailing away before the end of the sentence, and the pause filled up by a flourish of his handkerchief. Rather it was a triumph of character. With his dyed whiskers and his red face, Palmerston exemplified British self-confidence and bounce.

Still, it needed the impact of war to finish the job for him. At the end of 1851 Russell finally got rid of Palmerston; early in 1852 the Russell government fell in its turn. Then, at the end of the year, Russell and Palmerston found themselves together again in the coalition of Whigs and Peelites, brought into being by Prince Albert and presided over by Aberdeen. Palmerston was relegated to the Home Office. He was rescued from it by the disasters of the Crimean War. Though he shared the common responsibility of the Cabinet, public opinion seized on him as the man of destiny, the man who would win the war. This was the moment of crisis in Palmerston's life and, for the historian, the most interesting point in his career. Again and again in modern history, Great Britain has drifted unprepared into war; then, after early failures, has discovered an inspired war-leader. How does public opinion make its choice? And what is it that Palmerston had in common with the elder Pitt, Lloyd George, and Winston Churchill? It was not done merely by advertisement, though all four made skilful use of publicity; it was not even done by brilliant speeches in the House of Commons or outside. It turned rather on the impression of resolution and courage laid down in the House of Commons over a period of years. During a crisis the members of parliament broke away from the conventional pattern—whether of family connection or party organization—and acted according to their patriotic duty. Curiously enough, the popular choice has always been right: on all four occasions it hit on a leader who was not only more colourful or more dramatic than his peace-time predecessor but who was also more efficient technically.[1] This is puzzling. The general public or even the members of the House of Commons could hardly deduce from Palmerston's speeches that he was an administrator of the first quality, who could challenge the Peelites on their own ground of efficient government without any of the high moral tone with which they found necessary to accompany it.

The government which Palmerston formed in 1855 was neither a party government nor a coalition; it was an association of individuals, united only to win the war. The old system of family connections was in decay; the new system of defined parties had hardly begun. The Conservatives were on the way to becoming a party in the modern sense; but they were doomed to perpetual minority so long as there was a middle-class electorate. Those acceptable as ministers were in confusion. The Peelites broke with Palmerston and disintegrated; when Russell bungled the conference at Vienna shortly afterwards, Whig solidarity also dissolved. Palmerston's personality was the only stable point in a fluid political system. It would be absurd to claim that his government was a war-cabinet of the highest order. Though it began the reform of the British military system, these reforms stopped half-way like the Crimean War itself. Opportunity had come to Palmerston too late in life: he was seventy-one when he became Prime Minister. More important, opportunity came at the wrong time: Great Britain could not be turned into a military nation only four years after the Exhibition of 1851. Still, in one way, Palmerston did better than his peers, those other great men who have saved their country. He not only won the war that he had been called on to win, he actually survived his success. The elder Pitt, Lloyd George, Churchill, were all ruined by victory. All three were ejected from office before the end of the war or shortly after it. Palmerston stayed safely in office; and, even more remarkable, won a general election a year after the war was over.

The general election of 1857 is unique in our history: the only election ever conducted as a simple plebiscite in favour of an individual. Even the 'coupon' election of 1918 claimed to be more than a plebiscite for Lloyd George; even Disraeli and Gladstone offered a clash of policies as well as of personalities. In 1857 there

1. On one occasion the public choice was flagrantly and persistently wrong. The younger Pitt, 'the pilot who weathered the storm', was not a good war leader; the nonentities who succeeded him did much better.

was no issue before the electorate except whether Palmerston should be Prime Minister; and no one could pretend that Palmerston had any policy except to be himself. Of course, we know very little about the general election of 1857 (or for that matter about any other in the nineteenth century); and it may turn out on detailed examination that the result of it was really determined by less obvious factors. Still, there was in it, at the least, a plebiscitary element: as though even the British had to be in the fashion and had caught the taste from Louis Napoleon. In the same way, Neville Chamberlain in the nineteen-thirties got as near the *Führerprinzip* as an Englishman could.

The political victory of 1857 was not the end of Palmerston's career. He had presided over, and in part caused, the end of the old political order; he was destined to inaugurate the new. His period of personal government lasted only a few months after the general election of 1857. The rather cantankerous patriotism which had sustained him against the Peelites and the pacifists turned on him when he tried, sensibly enough, to appease Louis Napoleon after the Orsino plot. Since no one could form a government with majority support, the Conservatives—as in 1852—formed a government without one; this in turn was bound to be followed, again as in 1852, by a coalition. But the government which Palmerston organized in June 1859 was a coalition of a different kind: not a coalition of groups which looked back to the past, but a coalition which anticipated the future. Had it not been for Palmerston himself—too individual, too full of personality to be fitted into a party-pattern—it would have been the first Liberal government in our history. Everything that was important in it was Liberal— finance, administrative reform, its very composition: the first government with unmistakable middle-class Free Traders as members. Palmerston would even have included Cobden, if he could have got him. It was Cobden who had scruples against tolerating the irresponsible survivor from an older world; and not the other way round. Of course, tolerance and good-nature had always been Palmerston's strong points; not virtues for which Radicals are usually distinguished.

Palmerston was too strong a character to be swamped by Liberalism even in old age. It was not so much that he resisted reforms; he himself had welcomed and often promoted the administrative reforms of the preceding thirty years. It was rather that he

C*

thought a government had other tasks than to be always reform-
ing: it should conduct a forceful foreign policy and strengthen the
national defences. Palmerston is one of the few Prime Ministers
who has literally left his mark on the face of the country: all those
odd-looking brick fortifications behind Portsmouth are his doing —
they are still useful and effective, which is more than can be said for
Gladstonian finance. But Palmerston in his last ministry was fighting, and winning, the wrong battle. For nearly a hundred years —
ever since Dunning's famous motion in 1780 — self-confident
British aristocrats had aimed to reduce the powers of the Crown
—to prevent its interference in the course of government and of
policy. Melbourne and Palmerston had had four blissful years on
the accession of Queen Victoria when the Crown seemed on the
point of becoming politically null. The process had been reversed
by Prince Albert; and when Palmerston was at the Foreign Office
between 1846 and 1851 he had to contend with ceaseless royal
interference—the more galling for being justified by every historical precedent. The years of the Crimean War had been too
serious to allow of constitutional squabbles; but these began again
in 1859. Between 1859 and 1861 the Crown fought persistently the
policy of Palmerston and of Russell, now Foreign Secretary;
intrigued, as George III had intrigued, with members of the
Cabinet behind the Prime Minister's back; dreamt of ejecting
Palmerston as the Fox-North coalition had been ejected in 1784.

Then, in 1861, the Prince Consort suddenly died. Victoria was
both unwilling and unable to carry on the contest; she became
again and remained the political nonentity that she had been before
her marriage. Palmerston had fulfilled the highest Whig ambition,
though after the death of the Whig party: the Crown had been
eliminated from politics. It turned out almost at once that the
victory was of no use at all. The Whigs had evoked public opinion
against the Crown; Palmerston had played off public opinion
against his Whig rivals. Now public opinion interfered more
effectively than the Crown had ever done. Though Palmerston had
been much harassed by the Crown when he was at the Foreign
Office, he had always got his way in the end; and this was equally
true of Palmerston and Russell in the severe disputes between
1859 and 1861. Despite the Prince Consort's Germanic enthusiasm
for Austria, they managed to back up Italian unification from start
to finish. Things were very different between 1862 and 1865.

Russell, for instance, would have liked to recognize the southern states in the American Civil War and go to war for the sake of Poland in 1863; Palmerston would have threatened war for the sake of Denmark in 1864. They were overruled by the majority of the Cabinet,[1] itself reflecting the opinion of the majority of members in the House of Commons, and they in their turn accurately voicing the opinion of the middle-class electorate. It is often said that Palmerston's foreign policy was a failure at the end of his life; it would be much truer to say that he was not allowed to have a foreign policy. Public opinion had pulled off the feat that was beyond the Prince Consort or even George III. Palmerston, the first—perhaps the only—Prime Minister to owe his success solely to public opinion, ended his life its prisoner.

Yet he was very near hitting on the method by which public opinion would be tamed. At the time of the general election of 1859, party organization meant nothing at all except perhaps among the Conservatives. Whig grandees put up money to fight a few constituencies, from a mixture of family and party motives; all the rest still depended on local initiative. By 1868 the Liberal Whips were handling a party fund, and were seeking subscriptions much more widely than at Brooks's. The transition took place when Palmerston was Prime Minister. He it must have been who decided to leave these matters to the Whips, and to keep the Prime Minister out of the financial side of the party-system; it may even have been Palmerston who first, though unwittingly, recommended men to honours in return for their contributions to the party chest. Gladstone found the system settled when he took over the leadership of the Liberal party in 1868. After all, it was the only way to run a party once the moneyed men pushed aside the members of the great families; and Palmerston no doubt acquiesced in it more easily since he had never belonged to these select Whig circles. Thus, without knowing it, he invented both the Liberal party and the modern party-system; no mean achievement for an individualist adventurer.

This is the essential point about him, the secret of his failures as of his success. He was never dependent on connection or on party, and rather disliked both; he was self-made. Men have written many books about his foreign policy; and will write more. Very little has

1. Six members of the Cabinet out of fourteen favoured going to Denmark's aid in June 1864.

been written, or ever will be, about his place in British political life; for it is an empty one. The British political system has no room for the rogue elephant. Though he may ruin others—as Palmerston ruined the Whigs, or as Lloyd George wrecked the Liberal party sixty years afterwards—he will certainly ruin himself. He will be barren as Prime Minister; he will not create. Our system is admirably suited to represent interests and to voice general ideas; it does not like independent characters, except as an eccentric adornment. In war both interests and ideas are pushed aside; hence, as an exception to the rule, the great individuals then triumph. Once peace comes, their power is ended, even if they cling to office as Palmerston managed to do. The steady men of solid principle and mind are the ones who achieve effective success; but the adventurers are more fun. Palmerston was not the spokesman of a class, though he defended the Irish landowners towards the end of his life; and he did not voice any great principle or idea. He was simply an individual of strong personality—resolute, self-confident, and with great powers of physical endurance. As Foreign Secretary he was always too independent of the Prime Minister and of the Cabinet; as Prime Minister, though he stood loyally by his colleagues, he failed to dominate the Cabinet or even to lead it.

He was not an Irish peer and an Irish landowner for nothing. He had the Irish jauntiness which always wins English hearts. He could never rein in his irrepressible high spirits; even his best speeches have here and there a touch of flippancy. He would rather make a good joke than win a debate. He was not, as is sometimes alleged, a survivor from the eighteenth century. Rather he had 'Regency' written all over him—in his clothes, his morals, even in his way of talking and his metallic laugh. Nor did he 'represent' the electorate of the Reform Bill, if this means that he resembled the middle-class voter. The men of the time delighted in Palmerston just as Churchill is now admired by millions who would never vote for him; but their serious taste was for Peel and Gladstone—these were the truly 'representative men'. Palmerston was certainly the most entertaining of Queen Victoria's Prime Ministers. Though there have been greater Prime Ministers, there has been none more genial; and, for that matter, none so good-looking.

8

JOHN BRIGHT AND THE CRIMEAN WAR[1]

JOHN BRIGHT was the greatest of all parliamentary orators. He had many political successes. Along with Richard Cobden, he conducted the campaign which led to the repeal of the Corn Laws. He did more than any other man to prevent the intervention of this country on the side of the South during the American Civil War; and he headed the reform agitation of 1867 which brought the industrial working-class within the pale of the constitution. It was Bright who made possible the Liberal party of Gladstone, Asquith, and Lloyd George; and the alliance between middle-class idealism and trade unionism, which he promoted, still lives in the present-day Labour party. Yet his noblest work, as certainly his greatest speeches, were made in a campaign which failed—a campaign which brought him much unpopularity and led finally to a mental collapse: his opposition to the Crimean War. His attitude caused him to lose his parliamentary seat at Manchester in 1857 and so severed his political connection with this city for ever. Bright blamed the merchant princes of Manchester for his defeat; and it is therefore especially fitting that we should look again at Bright's stand during the Crimean War on a foundation established to commemorate one of the greatest of these merchant princes.

I have personal reasons, too, for this gesture of atonement. At Bright's old school, where I was educated, there was an annual prize for a Bright oration; and I have heard his great speeches against the Crimean War recited a score of times in the school library which bears his name. I, in revolt as usual against my surroundings, sought only something to Bright's discredit and proposed to offer one of his speeches against the Factory Acts. But these were not included in his collected speeches; and I was not used, as I am now, to going through the columns of old Hansards. I therefore remained silent; and it is only now, thirty years later, that I come to repeat the greatest sentences ever uttered in any parliamentary assembly. I am not, however, concerned to defend Bright, much as I now admire him. I have also learnt to

1. This paper was first given as a lecture at the John Rylands Library, Manchester.

admire the diplomatic skill and judgement of 'the aged charlatan', Palmerston. Bright said of him:

> I regard him as a man who has experience, but who with experience has not gained wisdom—as a man who has age, but who, with age, has not the gravity of age, and who, now occupying the highest seat of power, has—and I say it with pain—not appeared influenced by a due sense of the responsibility that belongs to that elevated position.

I do not think that any historian who has examined the record of Palmerston's foreign policy would now endorse that judgement, though he would still be struck by Palmerston's jocular self-confidence and even occasionally by his levity. It is my intention—and I can say in all sincerity that I did not know when I started how the conclusion would work out—to examine Bright's criticism of the Crimean War in the light of later events and of the more detailed knowledge which we now possess, rather than to vindicate or condemn him.

When I began this inquiry, I was struck and indeed surprised by the material for my theme. I have some experience of public agitation on issues of foreign policy. I have sat on committees for Aid to Spain and Czechoslovakia and for Anglo-Soviet friendship; I can remember vaguely the pacifist movement of the First World War. I expected to find the same hubbub of public meetings, pamphlets, letters to the press, articles in newspapers and periodicals, which serve as the undertone for debates in Parliament. Gladstone used all these weapons in his attacks on Disraeli's eastern policy only twenty years later. Indeed, he did better than we. He used to stick his head out of the railway-carriage and address waiting crowds at every station he passed through. Here was Bright engaged in the greatest political conflict of his career; yet he used none of the means that we should think essential. He did not write a pamphlet; he did not address a single letter to the newspapers. He wrote one letter to Absalom Watkin, designed for publication and stating his case against the war, on 29 October 1854, when the war had already been raging for six months. He attended in all three public meetings, over a period of nearly two years; and all in Manchester. They were designed to explain his attitude to his constituents, not to appeal to public opinion. The first, held on 18 December 1854, was not organized by Bright, but to declare against him. Neither he nor his opponents could get a hearing. At the second, on 5 April

1855, he spoke for an hour. The third was held on 28 January 1856, after the peace preliminaries had been signed. Bright, speaking for two hours, defended his past conduct and collapsed at the end. Thus he made one public speech against the war while it was on; and this was to a limited audience.

We have therefore to look solely at Bright's speeches in the House of Commons. And here is another surprising thing. He never spoke against the war before it was declared. Let me refresh your memory with some dates. The diplomatic conflict between Russia and the Western Powers, Great Britain and France, began at Constantinople in May 1853. Russian forces occupied the mouth of the Danube in July. The allied fleets passed the Straits in October; they entered the Black Sea in December. Throughout all this time there are only two passing references to the crisis in Bright's diary, one at the end of May, one in July. In October he addressed a conference of the Peace Society, but mainly on generalities with little reference to immediate events. Early in 1854, the crisis grew graver; on 27 March war was declared. Again Bright remained silent. On 15 March he wrote a letter to Lord Aberdeen, the Prime Minister, not for publication, arguing in favour of peace. His first speech was on 31 March, four days after the declaration of war. It was a speech to clear his conscience, not to change the course of policy. 'I am unwilling to lose this opportunity . . . of clearing myself from any portion of the responsibility which attaches to those who support the policy which the Government has adopted.' At the end, he strikes the same note:

> For myself, I do not trouble myself whether my conduct in Parliament is popular or not. I care only that it shall be wise and just as regards the permanent interests of my country, and I despise from the bottom of my heart the man who speaks a word in favour of this war, or of any war which he believes might have been avoided, merely because the press and a portion of the people urge the Government to enter into it.

Bright did not speak again on the war until 22 December 1854. This speech, too, was vindication, not advocacy—vindication this time more of Cobden, who had been attacked by Lord John Russell, than of himself. And there is the same note of clearing his conscience:

> Let it not be said that I am alone in my condemnation of this war, and of this incapable and guilty Administration. And, even if I were

alone, if mine were a solitary voice, raised amid the din of arms and the clamour of a venal press, I should have the consolation I have tonight—and which I trust will be mine to the last moment of my existence—the priceless consolation that no word of mine has tended to promote the squandering of my country's treasure or the spilling of one single drop of my country's blood.

In February 1855, negotiations for peace—abortive, as it turned out—were opened at Vienna. On 22 February, Bright made a short speech, appealing for an immediate armistice if the negotiations showed promise of success. Though this speech contains his most celebrated oratorical passage—the Angel of Death has been abroad throughout the land—it had a practical aim; and for once Bright addressed both Palmerston and Lord John Russell in conciliatory, friendly terms. Finally, when the negotiations at Vienna had failed, Bright spoke again on 7 June. He argued that the proposed peace-terms would have been satisfactory and that there was no purpose in continuing the war. But this time he did not merely protest or clear his conscience. He appealed to the House to revolt against Palmerston's government and against the bellicose press:

> If every man in this House, who doubts the policy that is being pur-
> sued, would boldly say so in this House and out of it, it would not be in
> the power of the press to mislead the people as it has done for the last
> twelve months. . . . We are the depositaries of the power and the
> guardians of the interests of a great nation and of an ancient monarchy.
> Why should we not fully measure our responsibility? Why should we
> not disregard the small-minded ambition that struggles for place? and
> why should we not, by a faithful, just, and earnest policy, restore, as I
> believe we may, tranquillity to Europe and prosperity to the country so
> dear to us?

Thus Bright spoke in all only four times on the war in a period of nearly two years. Only his first speech and his letter to Absalom Watkin stated his case against the war at length. Indeed we may say that his reputation as an opponent of the war was gained as much by silent and sustained disapproval as by his speeches. Before I discuss his criticism of the war, I should like to turn aside for a moment to consider why Bright was relatively so inactive—so much more silent, for example, than at the time of the American Civil War a few years later. In part, he felt it hopeless to contend against the war-fever of the press. Cobden felt this even more strongly. He said in 1862:

I was so convinced of the utter uselessness of raising one's voice in opposition to war when it has once begun, that I made up my mind that so long as I was in political life, should a war again break out between England and a great Power, I would never open my mouth upon the subject from the time the first gun was fired until the peace was made.

This is a surprising tribute to the power of the press, the more surprising when one reflects that the total newspaper-reading public in England did not at that time number 100,000. Perhaps this is itself the explanation. In 1854 Bright sat for a middle-class constituency and thought only of his middle-class voters. His only public speech was an explanation to his constituents, not a general appeal. After 1858, when he sat for Birmingham, he addressed himself to working-class opinion, regardless either of the middle-class voters or the middle-class press. Indeed, it was the Crimean War which helped to set Bright on the democratic path. To adapt George III's phrase to William Pitt, it taught him to look elsewhere than the House of Commons, or even the electorate, for the will of the people.

Of course, this was not new to Bright. He was always more of a man of the people than Cobden. Cobden lived in Sussex, a failure as a business-man. Bright never moved from Rochdale, next door to his mill. Their paths diverged after the repeal of the Corn Laws. Free Trade had always been an international cause for Cobden — witness his triumphal tour of Europe in 1846; and he went on to preach international arbitration and disarmament. Bright had been interested in the practical issue of cheap bread; and he turned from Free Trade to Parliamentary Reform—a course of which Cobden disapproved. This led Bright largely to ignore foreign affairs. It is no accident that Cobden spoke in the great Don Pacifico debate in 1850 and Bright did not—it was not his subject.

The early Radicals thought in terms of criticizing the established government, not of superseding it. Witness again Cobden's remark that he could have had a great career in the United States, but that it was useless for him to harbour ambition in aristocratic England. Bright and Cobden assumed that England was fated to endure aristocratic misrule for many years—Cobden supposed at least during his lifetime. But Bright gradually moved to the more constructive position that aristocratic rule could be ended and democracy take its place. His last Crimean War speech contains a first statement of this new attitude. Yet, even now, it was the promise of a political leader of the right views from within the closed circle which gave him greater hope. This leader was Gladstone, after his resignation from Palmerston's government at the beginning of 1855. Here was the first hint of the alliance between Gladstone and Bright which triumphed in 1868—an alliance in which Gladstone was the statesman and Bright the agitator.

Bright therefore learnt his way slowly in foreign affairs, beginning with a few radical prejudices and gradually examining the practical issues. Observe: I do not say Quaker prejudices. Though Bright spoke often—as anyone would—of the horrors and bloodshed of war, he never used pacifist arguments against it. Indeed, he was not a pacifist. He supported the forcible suppression of the Indian mutiny; and he urged the North to continue the American Civil War to decisive victory, when even Cobden favoured compromise. Bright doubted, I think, the relevance of Quakerism to public life. Dr. Trevelyan remarks casually that Bright never spoke in Meeting, but draws no moral from it. Perhaps only someone of Quaker stock and upbringing can appreciate its significance. The Society of Friends was still 'quietist', concerned with the inner light, not with social duty; and, in addition, there was a distinction between 'ministers' and other members of the Society which has now almost disappeared. I do not say that Bright ever ceased to regard himself as a full member of the Society; but he thought that, by entering politics, he had made himself the humblest of members and, conversely, he kept Quakerism out of his politics. Or rather, though he kept out Quaker principles, he used Quaker methods. His speeches, for all their oratory, rely on fact and argument as much as on emotional appeal. As Bright said in answer to Palmerston: 'I am not afraid of discussing the war with the noble Lord on his own principles. I understand the Blue Books as well as he' —a claim that was fully justified.

Though Bright did not condemn war from pacificism, he certainly condemned it on grounds of economy. His Crimean War speeches all speak of the disturbance to trade and the increase of taxes. He has often been blamed for this. Tennyson wrote at the time of

> The broad-brimmed hawker of holy things,
> Whose ear is cramm'd with his cotton, and rings
> Even in dreams to the chink of his pence.

I should add, in fairness to Tennyson, that there is much other internal evidence in *Maud* to suggest that the hero, or narrator, of it was mad. Sir Llewellyn Woodward, who refers to 'the prosy and, at times, repellent religiosity of his letters and diaries', discredits Bright with the comic quotation: 'Our carpet trade grievously injured by war raising the price of tow.' Sir Llewellyn Woodward, I suspect, had heard that Bright was in the cotton trade and did not appreciate that John Bright and Bros. manufactured carpets, as they still do. What therefore more natural than that he should make a business note in his private diary? Bright showed during the American Civil War that he could rise above arguments, addressed to his economic interests or those of Lancashire. The story of Bright's commercialism, which brings together not only Tennyson and Sir Llewellyn Woodward but such strange companions as Palmerston and Karl Marx, springs largely—as Bright himself said—from the inability to answer his more serious arguments.

In any case, it is well to bear in mind the composition of the House of Commons, in which Bright delivered his speeches. Neither of the two great parties—the Conservatives under Disraeli nor the Whigs led, if that is not too dignified a term, by Lord John Russell—had a majority. The balance was held by the Peelites—the remnant of those Conservatives who had followed Peel over Free Trade in 1846—and the radicals. These last two had much in common so far as economic doctrine was concerned, despite their difference of social background. The government of Lord Aberdeen, which began the Crimean War, was a coalition of Peelites and Whigs, with one radical member, Molesworth, and possessing radical support. Palmerston's government, which took its place in 1855, was Whig and radical, the Peelites in uneasy and discredited neutrality. To whom then was Bright to appeal, if he was to achieve a practical effect at all? Not to the Conservatives; for, though they claimed to oppose Palmerston, Bright had an incurable distrust of Disraeli. Remember his reply when Disraeli said to him after the 'Angel of Death' speech: 'I would give all I ever had to have made that speech you made just now.' 'Well, you might have made it if you had been honest.' He could not appeal to the Whigs. He regarded Russell and Palmerston as the principal authors of the war and directed his main arguments against the Whig doctrine of the Balance of Power. Besides, the Whigs had a long record of frivolity and incapacity in regard to finance.

Hence, his practical object was to persuade the Peelites and radicals to take advantage of their balancing position. They could bring the Whigs to heel if they wished to do so. His economic arguments were designed for the Peelites, as were his recollections of Peel himself. 'I recollect when Sir Robert Peel addressed the House on a dispute which threatened hostilities with the United States—I recollect the gravity of his countenance, the solemnity of his tone, his whole demeanour showing that he felt in his soul the responsibility that rested on him.' This appeal certainly had its effect on Gladstone, particularly after his resignation from office in February 1855. But Bright had to appeal especially to the radicals and Free Trade liberals—his former allies who had now abandoned their principles of economy for the sake of fighting a war of liberation against Russia. This is an essential point, one lost sight of in later years, when the Eastern Question came to be regarded as bound up with the route to India. The route to India had nothing to do with the Crimean War. The Danube, not the Suez Canal, was the only waterway involved. The Crimean War was fought much more against Russia than in favour of Turkey. And it was fought not only in the name of the Balance of Power. Russia was regarded as the tyrant of Europe, the main prop of 'the Holy Alliance'; and English radicals thought that they were now getting their own back for the Russian intervention which had helped to defeat the revolutions of 1848. The veteran radical, Joseph Hume, who had moved a reduction in the army estimates every year since 1823, voted for the estimates in 1854. There could be no more striking evidence of the radical conversion.

The radical crusading spirit against Russia could be illustrated in a thousand ways. I will limit myself to one quotation from a correspondent of Cobden's:

> This, then, is my creed. I look upon Russia as the personification of Despotism—the apostle of Legimitacy. In the present state of Poland and Hungary we see her work. . . . Such a power can be curbed only by war, and must be so curbed sooner or later, if Europe is to remain free. . . . If we believe that God wills the liberty and happiness of mankind, how can we doubt that we are doing God's work in fighting for liberty against aggression?

Perhaps I should add that this is a genuine quotation from a letter of November 1855, and is not taken from yesterday's newspaper. Bright's principal arguments were directed against this radical enthusiasm. Why was he not affected by it? It was, I think, a lesson learnt from Cobden. Cobden had always preached non-intervention in European affairs. What is more, he had always looked with a friendly eye on Russian expansion. In a pamphlet which he wrote as early as 1836, he asked: 'Can any one doubt that, if the Government of St. Petersburg were transferred to the shores of the Bosphorus, a splendid and substantial European city would, in less than twenty years, spring up in the place of those huts which now constitute the capital of Turkey?' In this pamphlet Cobden even challenged the radical predilection for Poland. Russian rule, he wrote, 'has been followed by an increase in the amount of peace, wealth, liberty, civilization and happiness, enjoyed by the great mass of the people. . . . The Polish people, though far from prosperous, have enjoyed many benefits by their change of government.'

Bright had not always shared Cobden's view. As a young man, he wrote a poem in favour of Poland—a very bad poem—which he once quoted with startling effect in a parliamentary speech. But he came in time to accept Cobden's belief that Free Trade would civilize every country, including Russia, and that political freedom would follow of itself. He wrote to Cobden in 1851, at the time of Kossuth's visit to England:

> I shall go against any notion of *fighting* for Hungary or any other country. . . . By perfecting our own institutions, by promoting the intelligence, morality and health of our own country, and by treating all other nations in a just and generous and courteous manner, we shall do more for humanity than by commissioning Palmerston to regenerate Hungary by fleets in the Black Sea and the Baltic.

He struck the same note in April 1854: 'they confound the blowing up of ships and the slaughter of thousands with the cause of freedom, as if there were any connection in matters wholly apart'. This was a clear doctrine of non-intervention, applicable to all wars of intervention anywhere at any time—applicable, for instance, as much to Italy as to the Balkans. But, in regard to the Crimean War, Bright did not really take a purely neutral attitude. Not only did he think that nothing good could be achieved by a Russian victory over Turkey. He dismissed all claims that the Ottoman Empire had reformed, or was capable of reform; and he referred to 'the natural solution'—'which is, that the Mahometan power in Europe should eventually succumb to the growing power of the Christian population of the Turkish territories'. Observe that he does not refer to the national conflict between the Balkan peoples and their Ottoman rulers; and indeed he seems to have been unaware at this time that Turkey-in-Europe was inhabited by peoples of different, even conflicting, nationalities. He anticipated the establishment in Constantinople of 'a Christian state'. The Christian population would 'grow more rapidly in numbers, in industry, in wealth, in intelligence, and in political power'. Why did Bright believe this? He knew no more about Turkey than anyone else. No independent reporters had visited Turkey; and Bright took his information on conditions there from the Blue Books. His faith in the Balkan Christians rested solely on dogma — above all, on the dogma that they were more capable of absorbing the lessons of Free Trade. The dogma was well-founded. All the same, there is a striking contrast with the discussions on the Eastern Question later in the century—discussions which were based on reliable first-hand information and on awareness of the national issue.

Bright claimed to approach the Crimean War with detachment; in reality he came to it with his mind made up. First he was against the war; then he discovered the arguments to justify his opposition. But this is perhaps to anticipate what should be a conclusion. Let me turn to the arguments which he used. It will, I think, be convenient to put them into two categories, though Bright did not make this logical distinction: arguments against any war over the Eastern Question—perhaps even against any war at all—and arguments against this particular war, based on the Blue Books which recounted the diplomatic events of 1853. Incidentally, here is a practical reason why Bright only spoke so late in the day. The first Blue Book was published on 17 March 1854. Bright spoke against the war a fortnight later. He could not have made his case earlier. This speech gives Bright's main arguments against the war; and I shall analyse it in detail.

He begins, quite rightly, with the French demands of 1852 in favour of the Latin Church at Jerusalem. Then, he says, Russia 'required (and this I understand to be the real ground of the quarrel) that Turkey should define by treaty, or convention, or by a simple note, or memorandum, what was conceded, and what were the rights of Russia'. Turkey, he insists, was decaying; and Russia was bound to 'interfere, or have a strong interest, in the internal policy of the Ottoman Empire'. This Russian interference was, of

course, the mission of Prince Menshikov to Constantinople. Here
Bright makes his first substantial point. On 5 May 1853, according
to him, Lord Stratford de Redcliffe, British ambassador at Constantinople, insisted that the Turks should refuse the Russian
demands. 'He urged upon the Turkish Government the necessity
of resistance to any of the demands of Russia, promising the armed
assistance of England, whatever consequences might ensue.' He
makes the same point in the letter to Absalom Watkin. 'But for the
English Minister at Constantinople and the Cabinet at home the
dispute would have settled itself, and the last note of Prince
Menshikoff would have been accepted. . . . Lord Stratford de Redcliffe held private interviews with the Sultan, insisted on his rejection of all terms of accommodation with Russia, and promised him
the armed assistance of England if war should arise.'

Here then is the start of Bright's case. The Turks wanted to sign
the Menshikov note; the French Government did not object; 'it
was through the interference of Lord Stratford de Redcliffe—acting, I presume, in accordance with instructions from our Cabinet,
and promising the intervention of the fleets—that the rejection of
that note was secured'. On the basis of Bright's argument Stratford
de Redcliffe has been branded with responsibility for the war from
that day to this. But does our later knowledge confirm the accusa-
tion? I am afraid it does not. Firstly, there was never a secret
interview of 5 May; and Bright himself subsequently dropped the
story. Far from encouraging the Turks to resist, Stratford advised
them to meet the Russian demands fully over the Holy Places; he
took a different line only when Menshikov demanded the recognition of a Russian protectorate over all Orthodox Christians in the
Ottoman Empire. The Turks would have resisted this claim with
or without Stratford's advice—which was, in any case, directed to
compromise, not rejection; and even now he gave them no promise
at all of British support. Moreover, Russia's demands were not as
innocent as Bright made out. Menshikov wanted to make Russia
supreme at Constantinople—'to end the infernal dictatorship of
this Redcliffe' and to put that of Russia in its place. The Russian
claims were based on an interpretation of the treaty of Kutchuk
Kainardji which the Russian experts themselves knew to be false;
and in the following year the Tsar Nicholas I admitted that he had
not realized what he was doing. 'His conduct in 1853', he said,
'would have been different but for the error into which he had been

led.' The Russians were, in fact, demanding a protectorate over Turkey; and the Turks were bound to refuse, if they were to keep their independence at all. Of course, Great Britain could have washed her hands of Turkish independence; but this was not Bright's case at this stage. He claimed that the Russian demands were harmless. Stratford judged better.

At all events, Menshikov failed. Russia broke off relations with Turkey and, in July, occupied the Danubian principalities. Bright called this 'impolitic and immoral' in his letter to Absalom Watkin; he did not condemn it in his parliamentary speeches. The other Powers—England, France, Austria, and Prussia—then drew up in August 'the Vienna note' which they offered as a settlement of the quarrel. It was accepted by the Russians in, says Bright, 'the most frank and unreserved manner'. The Turks had not been shown the Note beforehand. When it reached them, they saw at once the interpretation that Russia would place on it and refused it. This certainly reflected sadly on the diplomatic gifts of the negotiators at Vienna. But surely the question is—were the Turks right in their suspicions? Nesselrode, the Russian Chancellor, proved that they were. Early in September, he issued an interpretation of the Vienna Note, claiming that it gave to Russia the full protectorate over the Orthodox Christians allegedly stipulated in the treaty of Kutchuk Kainardji. What does Bright say to this? Merely, 'I very much doubt whether Count Nesselrode placed any meaning upon the Note which it did not fairly warrant, and it is impossible to say whether he really differed at all from the actual intentions of the four Ambassadors at Vienna'. Again, 'this circular could make no real difference in the note itself'. Now this was being more Russian than the Russians. In October the tsar met Francis Joseph, Emperor of Austria, at Olomouc—the place which was then called Olmütz. He confessed that Nesselrode had made a 'forced interpretation' and now offered to withdraw it. In other words, the Russians had tried to cheat, and the Turks had caught them out; but no one would deduce this from Bright's speech.

The meeting at Olomouc offered the one serious chance of avoiding war. Nicholas I was alarmed and in a conciliatory mood; he withdrew, for the time being, the demands that he had previously made. The British Government rejected his offer; they insisted that the Russian troops should be withdrawn from the principalities; and, when Turkey declared war independently a couple of weeks later, they allowed themselves to be dragged into war on her side. Bright had a strong case here. He would have said to the Turks: 'If you persist in taking your own course, we cannot be involved in the difficulties to which it may give rise, but must leave you to take the consequences of your own acts.' But he weakens this case irremediably when he says a few sentences previously: 'It is impossible fairly to doubt the sincerity of the desire for peace manifested by the Emperor of Russia.' This is just what it was possible to doubt from the record of the previous months. Desire for peace perhaps; but equally a desire to get his own way at Constantinople even at the risk of war. Bright failed to allow for the suspicions which Russian policy had caused and for the Russian aggressiveness which the hesitation and muddle of British policy encouraged. Indeed, the war would have been avoided if Great Britain had followed the resolute line advocated by Palmerston and Russell — whom Bright blamed for the war. The responsibility for the war lay with the pacific Lord Aberdeen, whom Bright admired; and Aberdeen later admitted it himself. Like King David, he refused to rebuild a church on his estates. 'But the word of the Lord came to me, saying, Thou hast shed blood abundantly and hast made great war: thou shalt not build an house unto my name.'

So much for Bright's criticism of the diplomatic background to the Crimean War. But his criticism did not stop at diplomatic detail; indeed, this was not much more than a *tour de force* designed to show that he could meet ministers on their own ground. In reality, Bright did not accept this ground; he rejected the basic assumptions of British diplomacy. The major part of his speech of 31 March 1854 shows this. He turns from the Vienna Note and the Olomouc meeting to challenge the doctrine of the Balance of Power.

He has great fun quoting the opinions of the great Whigs — Burke, Fox, and Lord Holland — against any idea of supporting Turkey; opinions that must have much embarrassed Lord John Russell, the last of the great Whigs, yet an enthusiastic supporter of the Crimean War. Bright continues: 'If this phrase of the "balance of power" is to be always an argument for war, the pretence for war will never be wanting, and peace can never be secure.' 'This whole notion of the "balance of power" is a mischievous delusion which has come down to us from past times; we ought to drive it from our minds, and to consider the solemn question of peace or war on more clear, more definite, and on far higher principles than any that are involved in the phrase the "balance of power".' This last sentence seems to promise that Bright will at any rate hint at an alternative foreign policy; but he does not do so. He merely goes on analysing the excuses for the Crimean War and demolishing them.

The integrity and independence of the Ottoman Empire? But Turkey cannot be independent with three foreign armies on her soil. If the government had wanted to preserve the independence of Turkey, they would have advised the Turks to accept either Menshikov's conditions or the Vienna Note. 'I will not insult you by asking whether, under such circumstances, that "integrity and independence" would not have been a thousand times more secure than it is at this hour?' This was exactly the argument—if you will forgive a contemporary allusion—with which Lord Halifax justified the desertion of Czechoslovakia in 1938: 'I have always felt that to fight a war for one, two, or three years to protect or re-create something that you knew you could not directly protect, and probably could never re-create, did not make sense.'

Next, what about curbing Russian aggression? Bright answers that it cannot be done. 'Russia will be always there—always powerful, always watchful, and actuated by the same motives of ambition, either of influence or of territory, which are supposed to have moved her in past times.' 'It is a delusion to suppose that you can dismember Russia—that you can blot her from the map of Europe—that you can take guarantees from her, as some seem to imagine, as easily as you take bail from an offender, who would otherwise go to prison for three months. England and France cannot do this with a stroke of the pen, and the sword will equally fail if the attempt be made.'

Finally, 'how are the interests of England involved in this question? . . . It is not a question of sympathy with any other State. . . . It is not my duty to make this country the knight-errant of the human race, and to take upon herself the protection of the thousand millions of human beings who have been permitted by the Creator of all things to people this planet.' On the other hand, taxes have gone up, trade is injured, thousands of men are being killed. 'My doctrine would have been non-intervention in this case. The danger of the Russian power was a phantom; the necessity of permanently upholding the Mahometan rule in Europe is an absurdity. . . . The evils of non-intervention were remote and vague, and could neither be weighed nor described in any accurate terms. The good we can judge something of already, by estimating the cost of a contrary policy.' (These two sentences are from the letter to Absalom Watkin, but they fit in with the argument of Bright's speech.) Finally, Bright moves on to assert the general merits of non-intervention for this country 'where her interests were not directly and obviously assailed'. If we had adopted non-intervention for the last seventy years:

> This country might have been a garden, every dwelling might have been of marble, and every person who treads its soil might have been sufficiently educated. We should indeed have had less of military glory. We might have had neither Trafalgar nor Waterloo; but we should have set the high example of a Christian nation, free in its institutions, courteous and just in its conduct towards all foreign States, and resting its policy on the unchangeable foundations of Christian morality.

Every orator must be forgiven something in his peroration.

The speech of 31 March 1854, which I have analysed at length, gives Bright's considered case against the Crimean War. The two speeches of 22 December 1854 and of 23 February 1855, do not add anything to that case. The one, as I said earlier, was a defence of Cobden; the second urged an armistice during the negotiations at Vienna. We can leave them aside when considering Bright's views. If we were considering his oratory, it would be a different matter; for they contain his most moving and also —a characteristic sometimes forgotten—his most humorous passages. The speech of 7 June 1855, however, raises some new points. In it Bright discusses not the causes of the war, but how it should end. I must turn aside to explain the diplomatic background. In the autumn of 1854 Austria—not herself a combatant, but wooed by the western allies —drafted 'Four Points' as reasonable terms of peace. These Four Points were accepted by England and France in the hope of drawing Austria into the war; then they were accepted by Russia in the better hope of keeping her out. The four Powers met in conference at Vienna in March and April 1855 in order to define the Four Points more closely and to turn them into practical terms. There was no difficulty about three of them. Russia was to give up her protectorate of the Danubian principalities; the freedom of navigation of the Danube was to be secured; and the Christian populations of the Ottoman Empire were to be put under a general European guarantee, instead of under that of Russia. Incidentally,

these three Points were already an answer to the assertion that war
accomplishes nothing. Russia would never have agreed to them
without the Crimean War. I don't venture to determine whether
they were worth a war; but that is a different question.

The dispute at Vienna came over Point III. This provided that
the Straits Convention of 1841 should be revised 'in the interests
of the Balance of Power'. In other words, Turkey was to be given
some sort of security against Russia's naval preponderance in the
Black Sea. Lord John Russell, the English representative, and
Drouyn de Lhuys, the French representative, went to Vienna with
instructions that they could agree to one of two things: either the
Russian fleet in the Black Sea should be limited, or the Black Sea
should be neutralized altogether. Gorchakov, the Russian delegate at Vienna, refused to accept either. Buol, Austrian Foreign
Minister, then came forward with another proposal: equipoise. The
Russians could keep their existing fleet; but, if they increased it,
the British and French could send ships into the Black Sea to
balance the increase. Neither Russell nor Drouyn was authorized to
agree to this scheme; but Drouyn was afraid of missing any chance
of peace, and Russell was afraid of getting out of step with Drouyn.
Both therefore accepted 'equipoise'. But when they returned home,
Napoleon III rejected the compromise; and the British government followed suit. The peace conference was abandoned; and the
war was renewed. This was a bad, muddled piece of diplomacy. It
is hardly surprising that Bright saw his chance and took it.

There is much the same pattern as in the earlier speech of 31
March 1854. He begins by meeting ministers on their own
ground and attacking their incompetence; gradually, he shifts his
emphasis and moves over to more general principles. He asks what
the war is about. It is not a war for Poland or for Hungary or for
Italy. It is solely a war—and here he quotes ministers themselves—
for the security of Turkey. Very well then, we want to reduce
Russian preponderance. 'How is that preponderance to cease?'
Bright looks first at the idea of neutralizing the Black Sea and dis-
misses it with vehemence. 'I conceive that was so monstrous a proposition, in the present condition of Europe, that I am surprised
it should have been entertained for a moment by any sensible man.'
He says much the same of limiting the Russian fleet. 'If any diplomatist from this country, under the same circumstances as Russia
was placed in, had consented to terms such as the noble Lord had

endeavoured to force upon Russia—I say, that if he entered the door of this House, he would be met by one universal shout of execration, and, as a public man, would be ruined for ever.' Bright has an alternative: the Straits should be opened to everybody:

> Our fleets would visit the Black Sea in the course of the season, and the Russian Black Sea fleet, if it chose, would visit the Mediterranean. There would be no sort of pretence for wrangling about the Straits; and the balance of power—if I may use the term—between the fleets of Russia, France and England would be probably the best guarantee that could be offered for the security of Constantinople and Turkey, so far as they are in danger of aggression either from the Black Sea or the Mediterranean.

This is a surprising proposal. I say nothing of the fact that Russia would have rejected it emphatically, whatever Gorchakov might hint at Vienna. But Bright, in his eagerness to discredit imposing any terms on Russia—terms that certainly could only be imposed after her defeat—is reduced in practice to the crudest *realpolitik*. He says in effect: no treaty stipulations are of any value; the only effective course is to maintain a balance of power, a balance of actual force, by keeping a large fleet in the eastern Mediterranean. If Palmerston had said this, what an outcry Bright would have made; what assertions of Russian good faith; what cries, and justified cries, about the weight of taxes to maintain such a fleet. It has often been said that non-intervention and splendid isolation are luxuries dependent on naval supremacy; but Bright never came so near admitting it as in this passage. His judgement of fact, however, was not correct. Six months after he made this speech the Russians accepted the neutralization of the Black Sea, which he had dismissed as a monstrous proposition. It is true that they denounced it again fifteen years later, when the diplomatic structure of Europe had changed fundamentally. Nevertheless Bright underrated what a Power will agree to when it has been defeated.

The rest of Bright's speech moves away from these diplomatic questions. He points to the folly of saying that Austria must be preserved and yet trying to draw her into a war that would exhaust her; he warns against the danger of relying on France as an ally; he denounces the idea of defending the liberties of Europe:

> What a notion a man must have of the duties of the . . . people living in these islands if he thinks . . . that the sacred treasure of the bravery,

resolution, and unfaltering courage of the people of England is to be squandered in a contest . . . for the preservation of the independence of Germany, and of the integrity, civilization, and something else, of all Europe!

He quotes the things that Palmerston and Russell said against each other in the past. But his greatest emphasis is on the burden of taxation and the crippling effect which this will have in our competition with the United States.

Hon. Members may think this is nothing. They say it is a 'low' view of the case. But these things are the foundation of your national greatness, and of your national duration; and you may be following visionary phantoms in all parts of the world while your own country is becoming rotten within, and calamities may be in store for the monarchy and the nation of which now, it appears, you take no heed.

It may seem a little unfair to end the survey of Bright's speeches on this note; but it is the note on which he himself chose to end and, in the parliamentary circumstances of 1855, perhaps rightly. What are we to say, after this examination, of Bright's attitude towards the Crimean War? We are bound, I am sure, to admire the courage with which Bright expressed his views and still more the brilliance of his performance. If I had merely read to you one of his speeches, instead of trying to analyse them, you would certainly have been swept away and have been convinced, without further argument, that the Crimean War was all that Bright said —unnecessary, unjust, in short a crime. But do we feel the same if we escape from their spell? I have suggested, during the course of this lecture, that Bright was not always sound when he came to the details of diplomacy. It is difficult, when criticizing the government of your own country, not to skate over the faults of other governments; and Bright did not escape this danger. He was harsher towards Stratford de Redcliffe than to Prince Menshikov; professed more faith in the statements of Nesselrode than in those of Palmerston; gave the Russian, but not the British government the benefit of the doubt. There was certainly much muddle and confusion in the diplomacy of the Crimean War; but, to judge from Bright's speeches, you would imagine that it was all on the British side. This one-sidedness is almost bound to happen in parliamentary speeches. You may achieve some effect by attacking your own government; you will achieve nothing by attacking foreign statesmen. In exactly the same way, Charles James Fox was often more charitable towards Bonaparte than towards William Pitt; and pacifists of the First World War, such as E. D. Morel, had more sympathy for German than for British imperialism.

One looks in vain in Bright's speeches for any satisfactory explanation of the causes of the Crimean War. He seems to suggest that it was due solely to newspaper agitation and to the irresponsibility of Palmerston and Russell. 'The country has been, I am afraid, the sport of their ancient rivalry; and I should be very sorry if it should be the victim of the policy which they have so long advocated.' Cobden was more cautious. He held that Russia, too, was 'much in the wrong'; and therefore kept quiet, washing his hands, as it were, of both sides. Bright often implied that Russian expansion against Turkey was an unexceptionable, even a praiseworthy process. Not always. He said in his first speech: 'If I were a Russian, speaking in a Russian Parliament, I should denounce any aggression upon Turkey, as I now blame the policy of our own Government; and I greatly fear I should find myself in a minority, as I now find myself in a minority on this question.' But is not this justice a little more than even-handed? Does it not imply that to attack Turkey and to defend her are equally reprehensible and provocative? If Russian aggression, though deplorable, is inevitable, then is not resistance to this aggression equally inevitable? Or do we make allowances only one way? In the next eastern crisis of 1876–8 Gladstone took a clearer and more consistent line. He held that the destruction of the Turkish Empire in Europe was eminently desirable; and therefore he wished Russia to succeed, preferably in association with England. Though he opposed the actual course of British policy, he offered a positive alternative. Bright's attitude was one of aloof neutrality.

He was not clear about this himself. In a speech to the Peace Society, which he made on 13 October 1853 — before the Crimean War broke out — he attacked the idea of war 'for the miserable, decrepit, moribund Government which is now enthroned, but which cannot long last, in the city of Constantinople'. Surely the logical conclusion from this should have been to co-operate in the Concert of Europe, as Gladstone later advocated. But Bright always denied that he favoured the Russian cause; and in a later speech on foreign policy, which he made on 29 October 1858, preached high-minded isolation. This country should have 'adequate and scientific means of defence'.

But I shall repudiate and denounce the expenditure of every shilling, the engagement of every man, the employment of every ship which has no object but intermeddling in the affairs of other countries.

He refused to admit that an active foreign policy could ever be justified. 'This foreign policy, this regard for "the liberties of Europe", this care at one time for "the Protestant interest", this excessive love for the "balance of power", is neither more nor less than a gigantic system of out-door relief for the aristocracy of Great Britain.' All foreign policy was unnecessary. Instead 'we have the unchangeable and eternal principles of the moral law to guide us, and only so far as we walk by that guidance can we be permanently a great nation, or our people a happy people'.

When Bright said this, he had left Manchester and was already the representative of Birmingham. This was symbolic. Though he seemed discredited while the Crimean War was on, he triumphed afterwards. By 1858 he was back in the House of Commons; and his version of the Crimean War was already being accepted. English people usually think their wars a mistake, when they are over; and they thought this of the Crimean War sooner than usual. As a matter of fact, it achieved its purpose rather better than most wars. Russia's control of the Danube mouth, which was the largest issue in the war, was recovered only in 1945; and Turkey, whose demise has been so often foretold, possesses Constantinople and the Straits to this day. I do not venture to say whether these achievements are desirable. Bright, however, said that they were impossible. Most Englishmen soon came to agree with him. It is Bright's version of the Crimean War which has triumphed in popular opinion and in the history books. Bright had more success. Once it was agreed that the Crimean War had been a mistake, it was easy to draw the further conclusion that all wars were a mistake. The moral law which Bright invoked turned out to be the doctrine of the man who passed by on the other side. It is no accident that Bright, at the end of his life, had Joseph Chamberlain as his colleague in the representation of Birmingham. There was a continuity of ideas from Bright to Joseph Chamberlain; and from Joseph Chamberlain to Neville. The Munich settlement of 1938 was implicit in Bright's opposition to the Crimean War. I am not sure whether this condemns Bright's attitude or justifies Munich.

9

DIZZY

'I AM their leader; I must follow them.' This, we suppose, is the essence of leadership in a democratic community. The members of a party, or the rank-and-file of a trade union, express their wishes; and it is the duty of the leader to translate these wishes, prejudices, or ambitions into action. We interpret the past in the same spirit. History is no longer the record of the achievements of extraordinary men. Our historians accumulate the biographical details of a thousand forgotten figures; and the great men, if brought in at all, merely provide decorative symbols for the prevailing outlook. Napoleon becomes a shorthand-sign for the profiteers of the French Revolution; Hitler for the German capitalists or for the German middle classes who have lost their savings; even that erratic genius Winston Churchill is made to appear somehow as 'old England'. Prime Ministers were once little less than gods, shaping the destinies of the country by their individual genius. Now they are lay-figures, their sole function to wear the appropriate period clothes. The two Pitts represent aggressive commercial imperialism; Palmerston a declining Whig aristocracy; Gladstone the Free Trade manufacturers. Lloyd George speaks for those who made money out of the First World War, and Baldwin for those who lost it.

Of course, there is some truth in this way of looking at things. A public man who cared only for outworn causes would no more command a following than a writer who used classical Latin in an age of vernacular literature would sell his books. Yet reality has a perverse way of going against the pattern that it ought to follow. The leader strays wildly from the class that he is supposed to symbolize and bears little resemblance to a composite picture of his followers. The millions of members of the Labour party, if superimposed one upon another, would never turn into a portrait of Ramsay MacDonald—or even of Clement Attlee. The shrewd operator of symbols could never divine that 'the gentlemen of England' were led by one who was unmistakably the son of a Lancashire mill-owner, or the Radical Nonconformists by a High

Churchman of classical education, whose devotion to the traditional institutions of the country was dwarfed only by his absorp-
tion in the writings of the Early Fathers. Indeed, the greatest
failures as leaders are those who best reflect their followers.
Charles James Fox had Brooks's written all over him; Lord John
Russell really belonged to a great Revolution family; and Neville
Chamberlain had in fact been 'a good Lord Mayor of Birmingham
in an off-year'.

Great political leaders are much more than symbols. They are
individuals, capturing a cause for their own purpose and giving it
an unexpected twist. This is tiresome for the historian, but—to
adapt Trotsky's phrase—he who wants a quiet mind should
choose some other study than that of history. Systems, patterns,
faiths are an attempt to impose an artificial simplification on the
infinite variety of the past. The historian remains sceptical of them
all, and he can derive only malicious amusement from the efforts of
present-day politicians to enlist their great predecessors in contemporary disputes. What would Oliver Cromwell have said about
the nationalization of steel? He would have been even more tongue-
tied than was usually the case with him. Benjamin Disraeli would
hardly have expressed himself on Tradition and Change as the
nine Conservatives did who evoked his shade at Oxford.[1] Indeed,
he would not have chosen such a fatuous, banal subject. But, once
landed with it, he would have said something provocative, though
perhaps wrongheaded. The Oxford lectures specialize in the
balanced platitude—the conservatism which Disraeli defined as
'Tory men and Whig measures'. Highest award must go, of
course, to Mr. R. A. Butler, who described class privileges as
'*the richness of developed differences*'. But the others qualify, too.
Mr. T. E. Utley, concealing the poverty of his thought by the
incoherence of his style; Professor Hugh Sellon, ending his survey
of foreign policy with the question, 'Are the old principles still a
sufficient guide in the new world in which we live?' and answering
plaintively, 'I do not know'; Mr. Angus Maude voicing his confidence in 'the instincts of our people'—every lecture is excessively
pleasurable, and only 3d. each into the bargain.

Disraeli deserves to be lectured about. He was the oddest great
man in our public life by a long chalk. Nothing connected him with
the Tory party of the early nineteenth century— nothing, that is,

1. *Tradition and Change*. Nine Oxford Lectures. Conservative Central Office.

except his calculation that its leadership would be easier to attain than that of the Whigs. He owned no land; he was not English in blood; he was lucky to be even a nominal member of the Anglican Church. In temperament he was even less conservative than in origin. He had a flighty mind, which drifted from smart triviality to adolescent day-dreaming and back again. He held nothing sacred except perhaps some Hebrew phrases vaguely remembered. He despised the members of the aristocracy even more than he disliked the poor. He did not even enjoy power when he achieved it. It was not merely that, in his own phrase, 'it came too late'. Power was too practical an affair to interest him. He relished the trappings of power, not the reality—the drama of great debates, the high-sounding titles, his name echoing through history. Yet in appearance he was least conservative of all. Thick black ringlets, fancy waistcoats, powder and scent were not the marks of a gentleman or even of a politician; and his affected voice—half-drawl, half-lisp—completed the foreign impression. Disraeli increased the obstacles in his path for the pleasure of overcoming them.

He was first and last a great actor, watching his own performance and that of others with ironic detachment. He cared for causes only as a means of combat. Having ousted Peel from the leadership of the Conservative party by defending the Corn Laws, he cheerfully proposed the next year that Protection should be dropped; and he did nothing to aid agriculture when the great depression hit it at the end of the eighteen-seventies. He attacked Palmerston's irresponsible support of Turkey during the Crimean War; yet repeated this support even more irresponsibly twenty years later. He foresaw the independence of the wretched colonies —'a millstone round our necks'—and welcomed this dissolution of the British Empire; a few years later he claimed a great stroke by making Queen Victoria Empress of India—the biggest piece of tushery even in his career. *Sybil* is supposed to contain a profound social analysis. In fact, it says no more than that the rich are very rich and the poor very poor—by no means a new discovery. His own social policy, when he came to power, turned out to be nothing more startling than municipal wash-houses. He took one step of real importance when he placed the trade unions above the law; but this was a matter of electoral calculation, not of social justice. His only genuine emotion in politics sprang from personal dislike—of Peel in his early career, of Gladstone even more strongly towards the end. What these two men had in common was a readiness to put their convictions above their ambition—the worst of offences in Disraeli's eyes.

In his novels Disraeli invented an interpretation of political history which is sometimes still taken seriously, and was repeated in the twentieth century by our only anti-Semitic writer, Hilaire Belloc. This was the myth of the Venetian oligarchy which was supposed to have taken the Crown prisoner at the time of the Glorious Revolution and from which the Crown should rescue itself by an alliance with the people. This myth had no glimmer of truth. Though eighteenth-century England had indeed a rich and powerful aristocracy, the Crown was always the head of the executive and the ministers were its servants. The Whigs certainly talked of 'forcing the closet', but they never succeeded in doing so effectively until after the great Reform Bill, and then only for a decade. The Crown was still of great weight in politics at the time of the Crimean War. By a wild irony, it was Disraeli himself who finally excluded the Crown from politics and turned it into a decorative figurehead. When he introduced household suffrage in 1867 in order to dish the Whigs, he made mass-parties inevitable, and these could not be swayed, as the old aristocratic politicians had been, by personal loyalty to the Crown. Disraeli disguised this, perhaps even to himself, by the flattery which he gave to Queen Victoria, as to many other distinguished ladies; but this was play-acting, not politics.

The two-party system does not figure much in Disraeli's writings, but it was the real basis of his political life and his legacy to posterity. The Whigs had had a theory of party conflict; but they regarded this as a conflict between the party of the Crown and the party of the people, by which, of course, they meant themselves. Even when Peel recognized after the Reform Act that the Crown could not sustain a party of its own and therefore built up the Conservative party, he did not acknowledge any loyalty, as leader, to his own followers, and said firmly in 1846: 'I am not under any obligation to any man or to any body of men.' This was his unforgivable sin in Disraeli's eyes. Disraeli hounded Peel out of the party leadership and seized the vacant place. He was the first politician to put loyalty to party above loyalty to country; and his example has been universally admired, though not always followed. Disraeli, and Disraeli alone, riveted on our political life the conception that politics consist entirely in two parties fighting for office. These two parties were to represent not programmes but interests. What interests Disraeli did not much mind. Sometimes he talked of the Conservative party as 'the landed interest'; sometimes he appealed to all who had 'a stake in the country'; in practice his party was an alliance between the City and the mob. None of this mattered. The important thing was the struggle for power—a tradition which the Conservative party has faithfully observed to this day. It is true also to Disraeli's tradition in not knowing what to do with power when it has got it. To catch the other side bathing and make off with their clothes is still its only resource.

One can understand how Disraeli achieved the leadership of the party by offering the prospect of unremitting combat. The field always prefers a huntsman who halloos them on. But Disraeli knew better tricks. His novels, his speeches, his casual remarks, all held out the promise of a mystery which he never revealed, which was not, in fact, there to reveal. He, not Napoleon III, was the true Sphinx without a secret. Or, rather, his secret was the absence of moral earnestness. A rarefied mountain-air becomes intolerable in time, and the holiday-maker is glad to escape to Monte Carlo. So it was with the Victorians. No age has been more high-minded; and the strain often became unendurable. Gladstone was the Victorian conscience; Disraeli the release from it.

10

THE USE OF MONARCHY

BENTHAM asked of every law, custom and institution: 'What's the use of it?' Harold Nicolson's life of George V is an attempt to answer this question for British monarchy in the twentieth century.[1] He shows what part George V played in the democratic constitution; and he justifies that part with insidious persistence. At the end it is difficult not to feel both that George V was a very good King and that this is a very good life of him.

Such feelings need scrutiny; after the chorus of praise, a little criticism, or even fault-finding, will do no harm. Mr. Nicolson writes with all his accustomed charm and ability. He is grave without being pompous; and he does not pretend that George V played more than a minor part, though occasionally a decisive one, in determining the course of events. He has worked conscientiously through the royal archives; and includes enough original material to satisfy the historian without tiring the general reader. He strikes the right balance, very difficult to achieve in royal biography, between the personal life of his subject and general history.

But his detachment lessens as he comes to events within his own experience. For instance, he looks at the economic crisis of 1931 with the eyes of a contemporary who has learnt nothing, though he may have forgotten a certain amount. It passes belief that in 1952, after the experience of the New Deal and years of Keynesian economics, anyone can still regard deflation and a cut in unemployment benefit as the right answer to a slump. The members of the Labour Government may have been at sixes and sevens; but at least they recognized the wrong course, though they were vague about the right one. The National Government were obdurate in wrong-doing and wasted the most precious decade of the century.

It would be tolerable if Mr. Nicolson treated all politics and politicians with amiable frivolity; but his blind eye is turned in only one direction. George Lansbury, perhaps the best Socialist of the century, is described as 'a man of quick emotions and a slow

1. *King George V. His Life and Reign.* By Harold Nicolson.

sense of reality'. The speeches of Sir John Simon during the General Strike, on the other hand, were 'brilliantly constructive' — so constructive indeed that the Tory Government had to change the law in order to catch up with their interpretation of it. Mr. Nicolson concludes his account of the General Strike: 'the tragedy was felt to be a common tragedy. . . . Every section of the community felt sorry for the other sections, as well as for themselves.' By an odd oversight, the wealthier classes did not carry this sorrow so far as to give the miners a living wage.

This may seem remote from the position of George V; in reality it shows the sympathy between the biographer and his subject. Mr. Nicolson, too, belongs to the Establishment, though his sophistication almost enables him to conceal it. There was nothing sophisticated about George V. He was simple, direct, an outdoor man without intellectual interests. Mr. Nicolson rubs in his Philistinism in matters of taste; and perhaps there was no time in our history when the Court counted for so little in the world of literature and art. On the other hand, no King tried harder to do his duty.

Before 1910 the Sovereign often took these duties lightly. Victoria would bury herself at Balmoral for months at a time, as George IV had at Brighton. Edward VII gave to politics only the hours he could spare from a garish Society. George V made constitutional monarchy a whole-time occupation. He was always available to his Ministers; constantly visiting factories, hospitals and mills; opening new buildings, receiving civic greetings. He visited India, and, if he had had his way, would have visited each of his Dominions. He saw, with startling perception, that the Crown had become essentially a symbol; and he showed how this symbol could be personified in a very ordinary man with very ordinary tastes. He was conscientious; he was decent; he was straight. These are high virtues.

His strictly political activities showed the same virtues; and with their help he gave the political position of the Crown a new and simpler definition. Victoria had often intrigued against her Prime Minister with other Cabinet Ministers or even with his political opponents. George V gave each of his Prime Ministers unstinted support. Though he sometimes discussed questions with the leaders of the Opposition, the Prime Minister always knew and approved; and the object of these conversations was to make the Opposition more moderate and conciliatory. In 1913 many distinguished men urged George V to dismiss Asquith and force a general election, in order to prevent Home Rule. In 1923 many distinguished men urged him not to appoint Ramsay MacDonald. The King disregarded these suggestions, almost without argument. He took the simple direct course.

In the bitterness of 1931 many people in the Labour movement complained that George V had abused his constitutional position and had himself manufactured the National Government. The charge was baseless. The Labour Government resigned of its own accord. The leaders of the Liberal and Conservative parties, who together had a majority, advised the King to appoint Ramsay MacDonald as head of a National Government; and he took their advice. He was often urged to insist on a dissolution of Parliament or to refuse one as an independent act of the prerogative. Again, he took a simple direct line; he regarded it as the exclusive right of the Prime Minister of the day to advise on this as on everything else.

Indeed, the reign of George V reduced the independent actions of the King to one: he appoints the Prime Minister according to his own judgement. Once the Prime Minister accepts office, the King follows his advice on everything until he resigns. George V arrived at this position by instinct, and did not openly admit it in argument; it was a wise position all the same. If King George's straightforwardness had been realized at once, it would have been unnecessary for Asquith in November 1910 to demand a secret promise that the King would create enough peers to override the House of Lords if the Liberals won the second general election. The King's own 'fair play' could have been relied on.

'Fair play' was the keynote of all his actions. But is fair play enough? After appointing the first Labour Government, he wrote to his mother: 'They have different ideas to ours as they are all Socialists, but they ought to be given a chance and ought to be treated fairly.' No doubt George V was extremely patient and sympathetic with his Labour Ministers, but this was easier the less Socialist they were.

The duties of a constitutional King, according to a hard-worn phrase, are 'to advise, to encourage, and to warn'. When George V received his first Labour Ministers, he said to them, 'The immediate future of my people is in your hands, gentlemen. They depend

upon your prudence and sagacity.' These were good words to have
addressed to a Conservative administration; prudence and sagacity are the best that can be expected of it. They are not the right
virtues for a government of the Left. Initiative, energy, creative
daring—these are the qualities which even a minority Labour
government should have shown. If not, why go to the trouble of
having a Labour party at all? Why not leave it to the Conservatives?

It is the inevitable function of a constitutional monarchy to act
as a brake and therefore to slow down the process of political
and economic reform. This is held to be a desirable result. Is
it? Would it not be better to have the change over and done
with? There would surely have been advantages, not only for the
Labour party, in settling the nationalization of steel in 1948
instead of letting the industry drag on in uncertainty to the present
day.

Or take some incidents of now purely historical interest. In
1911 the influence of the King and of all moderate opinion persuaded the House of Lords to accept the Parliament Act at the last
minute and so saved the House with its existing composition.
Would it not have been better from every point of view to create
the five hundred new peers that were designed? Mr. Ensor, no
radical witness, says of Asquith's list: 'they were a very strong
body, and in proved character, intellect, business, and public
activity certainly outweighed the then existing House of Lords, if
a score of leaders in the latter were deducted'. As to Home Rule
itself, it is difficult to measure the advantages to both Ireland and
the Commonwealth if it had become law without the delays of the
Parliament Act.

There is something to be said for conservatism (though I can
never recollect what); there is much to be said for radical change;
the defects of gradual reform are greater than is commonly supposed—and it is gradual reform which the British constitution
and monarchy inevitably promote.

Still, fair play in all things. Though George V did his best to
steer his Labour Ministers away from Socialism, he also tried to
moderate extremism on the other side. His standards of decency
were often higher than those of his Ministers. He disliked the
campaign against aliens and conscientious objectors during the
First World War; he objected to the violence of the *British Gazette*

D*

(edited by Winston Churchill) during the General Strike; he protested against the Black-and-Tans and against the forcible feeding
of suffragettes. With General Smuts's assistance, he made a notable
appeal for conciliation in Ireland, when he opened the first parliament in Belfast. He even complained against some of Lloyd
George's nominations for honour. He complained in vain.

This is where fair play breaks down. If a government of the
Left had nominated an unbeliever or a divorcee, they would at
once have withdrawn the name on the King's objection. A Right
government did not scruple to insist on these financial scoundrels,
even though it offended opinion in more than one Dominion. The
explanation is simple. The Right always regards itself as 'the
loyal party'; therefore it does not need to take any notice of
the King's objections. Even when Carson set up a seditious and
rebellious organization in 1912, its members pledged themselves
'as loyal subjects of his Gracious Majesty King George V'.

With the best will in the world (and George V had it), a King
who sees only wealthy and titled people weighs with two weights
and judges with two measures. On 27 July 1912, Bonar Law, leader
of the Conservative party, said: 'I can imagine no length
of resistance to which Ulster will go, which I shall not be
ready to support.' Within two months, Bonar Law was a guest of
the King at Balmoral. Suppose (an impossibility indeed) that
Ramsay MacDonald had said in April 1926: 'I can imagine no
length of resistance to which the miners will go, which I shall not
be ready to support.' Would he have been the King's guest before
the end of June? If at all, it would have been in prison, not at
Balmoral.

George V was franker than his latter-day admirers: 'they have
different ideas to ours as they are all Socialists'. The function of
constitutional monarchy is to conserve, to put the brake on. When
Tories are in power, the brake is not needed, and the King can
wish them success without reservation. The best he can hope for
from a Socialist government is that their bark will be worse than
their bite—and it usually is. We may reverse George V's judgement and say of the British royal house: 'they have different ideas
to ours as none of them is Socialist'. Since more than half the
electors of this country now vote Socialist, this is perhaps a mis-
fortune.

George V, much against his personal taste, ensured that if the people of this country wanted a social revolution they could have it without a political upheaval. Still, a Labour government should bear in mind that when a sovereign exercises his right 'to advise, to encourage, and to warn', his admonitions, however sincere, will not be directed to the victory of Socialism. He has different ideas to ours, and we have different ideas to his.

11

ECONOMIC IMPERIALISM

IDEAS live longer than men; and the writer who can attach his name to an idea is safe for immortality. Darwin will live as long as Evolution; Marx be forgotten only when there are no class-struggles. In the same way, no survey of the international history of the twentieth century can be complete without the name of J. A. Hobson. He it was who found an economic motive for Imperialism. Lenin took over Hobson's explanation, which thus became the basis for Communist foreign policy to the present day. Non-Marxists were equally convinced; and contemporary history has been written largely in the light of Hobson's discovery. This discovery was an off-shoot from his general doctrine of under-consumption. The capitalists cannot spend their share of the national production. Saving makes their predicament worse. They demand openings for investment outside their saturated national market; and they find these openings in the undeveloped parts of the world. This is Imperialism. In Hobson's words, 'the modern foreign policy of Great Britain has been primarily a struggle for profitable markets of investment'—and what applied to Great Britain was equally true of France or Germany. Brailsford put it a few years later in a sharper way:

> Working men may proceed to slay each other in order to decide whether it shall be French or German financiers who shall export the surplus capital (saved from their own wages bill) destined to subdue and exploit the peasants of Morocco.

This idea is now so embedded in our thought that we cannot imagine a time when it did not exist. Yet the earlier Radical opponents of Imperialism knew nothing of it. They supposed that Imperialism sprang from a primitive greed for territory or a lust for conquest. The more sophisticated held that it was designed to provide jobs for the younger sons of the governing classes (a theory which James Mill invented and himself practised and which Hobson did not discard). Marx had no theory of Imperialism. In classical Marxist theory, the state exists solely to oppress the working classes—to silence their grievances, destroy their trade

unions, and force them ever nearer to the point of absolute star-
vation. Marx jeered at the 'night-watchman' theory of the state;
but the only difference in his conception was that it stayed awake in
the day-time. Hobson added a true Marxian refinement. Marx had
demonstrated that the capitalist, however benevolent personally,
was condemned by economic law to rob the worker at the point of
production. Similarly Hobson showed that the capitalist, however
pacific, must seek foreign investment and therefore be driven into
imperialist rivalry with the capitalists of other states. Previously
Marxists had condemned capitalism as being pacific, and particularly for preventing the great war of liberation against Russia.
Now all wars became 'capitalistic', and war the inevitable outcome
of the capitalist system. It is not surprising that, when the First
World War had broken out, Lenin seized on Hobson's 'bourgeois-
pacifist' theory and made it the cornerstone of his neo-Marxism.
Like most prophets, he boasted of his foresight only when his
visions had become facts.

Hobson wrote his book immediately after the partition of
Africa, and when the experiences of the Boer War were fresh in
everyone's mind. For him, Imperialism was mainly the acquisition
of tropical lands; and what he foresaw next was the partition, or
perhaps the joint exploitation, of China. In the spring of 1914
Brailsford applied similar doctrines to a wider field. *The War of
Steel and Gold* (1914) is a more brilliant book than Hobson's,
written with a more trenchant pen and with a deeper knowledge of
international affairs. Though less remembered now, it had prob-
bably a stronger influence on its own generation; and American
historians between the wars, in particular, could hardly have got
on without it. Our own thought is still unconsciously shaped by it.
Brailsford speaks more of our condition. The aggressive, self-
confident Imperialism of the Boer War seems remote to us; the
competition of great armaments is ever-present in our lives.

Both writers wrote with Radical passion. The first sensation in
re-reading them is to cry out: 'Would that we had such writers
nowadays!' Take Hobson's peroration:

> Imperialism is a depraved choice of national life, imposed by self-
> seeking interests which appeal to the lusts of quantitative acquisition
> and of forceful domination surviving in a nation from early centuries of
> animal struggle for existence. . . . It is the besetting sin of all successful
> States, and its penalty is unalterable in the order of nature.

Or Brailsford's:

> Let a people once perceive for what purposes its patriotism is prostituted, and its resources misused, and the end is already in sight. When that illumination comes to the masses of the three Western Powers, the fears which fill their barracks and stoke their furnaces will have lost the power to drive. A clear-sighted generation will scan the horizon and find no enemy. It will drop its armour, and walk the world's highways safe.

These are heavyweights of political combat. The intellectual diet of the mid-twentieth century cannot nourish such stamina. But we must stay the flood of our admiration with some doubting questions. Was the Hobsonian-Leninist analysis of international capitalism a true picture either then or now? Has the struggle for overseas investments ever been the mainspring of international politics?

The export of capital was certainly a striking feature of British economic life in the fifty years before 1914. But its greatest periods were before and after the time of ostensible Imperialism. What is more, there was little correspondence between the areas of capitalist investment and political annexation. Hobson cheats on this, and Lenin after him. They show, in one table, that there has been a great increase in British investments overseas; in another that there has been a great increase in the territory of the British Empire. Therefore, they say, the one caused the other. But did it? Might not both have been independent products of British confidence and strength? If openings for investment were the motive of British Imperialism, we should surely find evidence for this in the speeches of British imperialists, or, if not in their public statements, at any rate in their private letters and opinions. We don't. They talked, no doubt quite mistakenly, about securing new markets and, even more mistakenly, about new openings for emigration; they regarded investment as a casual instrument. Their measuring-stick was Power, not Profit. When they disputed over tropical African territory or scrambled for railway concessions in China, their aim was to strengthen their respective empires, not to benefit the financiers of the City. Hobson showed that Imperialism did not pay the nation. With longer experience, we can even say that it does not pay the investors. But the proof, even if convincing, would not have deterred the advocates of Imperialism. They were thinking in different terms.

The economic analysis breaks down in almost every case which has been examined in detail. Morocco has often been treated as a classical case of finance-imperialism, by Brailsford himself and in more detail by E. D. Morel. In fact, the French financiers were forced to invest in Morocco, much against their will, in order to prepare the way for French political control. They knew they would lose their money; and they did. But Morocco became a French protectorate. Again, Brailsford made much play with the British investments in Egypt, which Cromer had promoted. But Cromer promoted these investments in order to strengthen British political control, and not the other way round. The British held on to Egypt for the sake of their empire; they did not hold their empire for the sake of Egypt. Even the Boer War was not purely a war for financial gain. British policy in South Africa would have been exactly the same if there had been no gold-mines. The only difference is that, without the profits from the dynamite-monopoly, the Boers would have been unable to put up much resistance. Rhodes was a great scoundrel in Radical eyes, and quite rightly. But not for the reasons that they supposed. Rhodes wanted wealth for the power that it brought, not for its own sake. Hence he understood the realities of politics better than they did.

Those who explained Imperialism in terms of economics were rationalists themselves; and therefore sought a rational explanation for the behaviour of others. If capitalists and politicians were as rational as Hobson and Brailsford, this is how they would behave. And of course a minority did. They took their profits; agreed with their enemy in the way; and died quietly in their beds. But they did not set the pattern of events. It is disturbing that, while Hobson and Brailsford were so penetrating about the present, they were wrong about the future. Hobson ignored Europe altogether—rightly, since he was discussing colonial affairs. He expected the international capitalists to join in the exploitation of China and even to recruit Chinese armies with which to hold down the workers of Europe. Brailsford looked at Europe only to reject it. He wrote—this in March 1914: 'the dangers which forced our ancestors into European coalitions and Continental wars have gone never to return'. And again, 'it is as certain as anything in politics can be, that the frontiers of our modern national states are finally drawn. My own belief is that there will be no more wars among the six Great Powers.' Even if there were a war, 'it is hard to believe that . . . German Socialists would show any ardour in shooting down French workmen. The spirit which marched through Sedan to Paris could not be revived in our generation.' It may be unfair to judge any writer in the light of what came after. Yet men with far less of Brailsford's knowledge and intellectual equipment foresaw the conflict of 1914, and even the shape that it would take. The true vision of the future was with Robert Blatchford, when he wrote his pamphlet, *Germany and England*, for the *Daily Mail*.

This is a sad confession. Hobson and Brailsford are our sort. We think like them, judge like them, admire their style and their moral values. We should be ashamed to write like Blatchford, though he was in fact the greatest popular journalist since Cobbett. Yet he was right; and they were wrong. Their virtues were their undoing. They expected reason to triumph. He knew that men love Power above all else. This, not Imperialism, is the besetting sin. Lenin knew it also. Hence, though a rationalist by origin, he turned himself into a wielder of power. Thanks to him, there is nothing to choose between Rhodes and a Soviet commissar. Nothing except this: the capitalist may be sometimes corrupted and softened by his wealth; the Soviet dictators have nothing to wear them down. If the evils which Hobson and Brailsford discovered in capitalism had been in fact the greatest of public vices, we should now be living in an easier world. It is the high-minded and inspired, the missionaries not the capitalists, who cause most of the trouble. Worst of all are the men of Power who are missionaries as well.

12

THE RISE AND FALL OF DIPLOMATIC HISTORY

HISTORIANS have been writing diplomatic history for a long time, indeed ever since they penetrated into the archives of state. Ranke spent his happiest and most profitable years examining the papers of the republic of Venice. Sorel wrote a masterpiece, *Europe and the French Revolution*, which bears in its title the evidence that it is in part diplomatic history. Vandal reached the same supreme level in his study of *Napoleon and Alexander I*. These themes were relatively remote from the date when the books were published. Moreover, the evidence from the diplomatic papers was subordinated to a general narrative. Political ideas and the personalities of statesmen counted for more than 'what one clerk said to another clerk'. The novelty some forty years ago was twofold. Historians set out to write the history of international relations purely from foreign office archives. More important, they claimed to be able to write about contemporary events with as much detachment as they had written about more distant periods. Their claim may have been justified. But it would be foolish to pretend that their sudden interest in contemporary history was detached and 'scientific'. It was a political interest, forced upon them by events and in particular by the event of the First World War. The twentieth century would have shown less concern with diplomatic history if the Bismarckian peace had endured. The diplomatic history of our time has always been a study of war origins, by no means to its advantage.

Historians seek to be detached, dispassionate, impartial. In fact no historian starts out with his mind a blank, to be gradually filled by the evidence. Is it conceivable, for example, that any document would have induced Macaulay to confess that the Glorious Revolution had been after all a great mistake? Or even conceivable that Ranke might have come to regret the rise of Prussia as a Great Power? The historians of the early twentieth century had lived through the First World War; and nearly all of them lamented it. Their reaction took different forms. German, and to some extent French, historians were anxious to prove that their Governments had been right. British and American historians were anxious to prove that their Governments had been wrong. Soviet historians were a class apart. They were delighted to distribute the blame among all 'imperialist' Governments, the old Russian Government perhaps most of all. But even they trimmed their sails to political convenience.

Diplomatic history was pushed to the front both by the way that the First World War started and by the way that it ended. The European crisis of July 1914 was peculiarly an affair of diplomacy. Few maintained then, and fewer would maintain now, that the outbreak of war was deliberately foreseen and planned by any Power or even by any general staff. Lloyd George expressed the general opinion: 'We muddled into war.' The outcome had been determined by what diplomatists said, or failed to say, to each other. Moreover, what they said seemed to have been shaped by the existing diplomatic structure—the Triple Alliance, the Franco-Russian alliance, or the vaguer commitments of Great Britain to France. Every Great Power sought to justify itself by publishing a selection of its diplomatic papers; and the very inadequacy of some of these suggested that the truth would emerge from a fuller, franker publication. The peace settlement reinforced the demand for impartial inquiry. The treaty of Versailles followed on the defeat of Germany; but its moral justification was that Germany had been solely 'responsible' for the outbreak of war, either deliberately or from negligence. No doubt the statesmen at Paris would have made much the same arrangements even if they had been convinced that all the Great Powers were equally at fault; but they would have had a harder time with their consciences, and still more with those of others.

It is not surprising therefore that German historians took up the struggle against 'the lie of war-guilt'. They did not need to prove that Germany had always been right; it was enough for them to show that she had not always been wrong. The first republican Government employed Kautsky to make a very full publication of the German records on the events immediately preceding the outbreak of war. This did not serve the German purpose. For it seemed to show that, whatever the faults of others, the German Government was very much to blame. The German historians therefore

shifted their ground back from July 1914 to the diplomacy of the
preceding years and ultimately even to the epoch of Bismarck.
Within less than a decade after the peace treaty Thimme published
fifty-four volumes of diplomatic documents running from 1871 to
June 1914. It was not the first publication of the kind. The French
were doing it for the origins of the Franco-Prussian War. But the
French proceeded slowly—they finished their task only in 1930;
the events with which they were concerned were already distant
and somewhat parochial. The German publication eclipsed the
French series in size and excitement. Historians all over the world,
and not only in Germany, took their version of events from it.
Even today an historian will catch himself following its pattern
even when he resolves not to do so; and the 'received idea' of the
world before 1914 still rests on *Die Grosse Politik*, though this
origin is forgotten.

Die Grosse Politik was the first and most grandiose publication
of documents on the origins of the First World War. There is
another reason for its success. The interpretation underlying it cor-
responded to that which British and American historians had
already formed in their minds. It is perhaps a special Anglo-Saxon
characteristic to see the virtue in the other side of the case, and
even to start out with a prejudice against one's own Government.
The official case had been challenged in England from the beginning. The Union of Democratic Control had been founded in
September 1914; and its central doctrine was that 'secret diplomacy' caused the war. E. D. Morel, who inspired and led it, had
already exposed secret diplomacy in Morocco; his *Truth about
the War* soon followed, with the clear implication that earlier ver-
sions had been lies. Some of the diplomatic historians in England,
such as Lowes Dickinson and Dr. G. P. Gooch, were members of
the U.D.C.; none escaped its influence. The Englishmen who wrote
on contemporary history were as much cut from E. D. Morel's
cloak as the Russian novelists were from Gogol's. This spirit
soon spread to the United States. There was the same desire for
fair play; the same readiness to distrust the national Government;
and American historians had always been more closely linked to
German scholarship. Apart from this, the American people as a
whole shook off sooner the passions of the war years and came to
distrust an outlook associated with the spirit of Versailles.

American historians were following a national trend; British historians were helping to make it.

The years between the peace settlement and Hitler's victory were great days for the 'pure' diplomatic historian. Men wanted to understand the contemporary world; and historians assured them that they could do so if all diplomatic secrets were 'revealed'. The British documents were published from 1898 to 1914; the French plodded laboriously on (as they are still doing) with a publication of documents from 1871 to 1914. The Italians asserted themselves as a Great Power by refusing to publish anything. More recently they have turned round and made the same assertion by proposing to publish everything from 1861 to 1943. Even the Russians abandoned their traditional secrecy and began to publish on a grand scale; then, repenting their frankness, abandoned the enterprise and tried to suppress what they had revealed already. If the diplomatic archives really contain the key to history, then the door was decisively unlocked. Yet the result was curiously disappointing. For the most part the spate of documents confirmed what men thought already. The Germans and the former members of the U.D.C. demonstrated that Germany had not caused the war; Soviet historians continued to blame capitalist imperialism; and the cynical were still convinced that all statesmen lurched in a fog from one blunder to the next. What was wrong? Why had the golden key jammed in the lock? Perhaps the revelations had not been complete enough. Some discovered defects in the *Grosse Politik*; and these existed, though dwarfed by its great merits. The British Government confirmed half-formed suspicions by imposing a hocus-pocus of secrecy on the so-called 'Cabinet papers'; and some future generation of historians will be disappointed to find what trivialities these contain.

The doubts about diplomatic history went deeper. It was not merely that we had missed some revelation or were being denied some material. We were asking the wrong questions, using the wrong method. We must turn from the Foreign Offices to the more profound forces which shape the destinies of men. Even Professor Renouvin, the leading French diplomatic historian of the day, has done this recently, though with some backsliding. There was from the start an undercurrent of opinion which tried to give diplomacy an economic interpretation—an opinion partly Marxist, but also stemming from English radicals such as J. A. Hobson.

Markets and raw materials, not alliances, had caused the war. This
view, though also held by some members of the U.D.C., took
longer to become respectable. Teachers of history put the works of
Dr. Gooch or Professor S. B. Fay on the top of their table and
consulted Brailsford's *War of Steel and Gold* under the desk. The
economic interpretation did not win the field until the days of the
Left Book Club; and even then it was not much applied in detail.
Historians setting out to describe an 'imperialist' conflict, lost
their balance in the flood of diplomatic documents. Some of them
even reached the conclusion, perhaps correctly, that conflicts such
as Morocco or the Bagdad railway had more to do with power
and less with profits than they had originally supposed. Certainly it
is difficult to point to any really successful work of scholarship
applying this economic interpretation, even by a Russian. There is,
of course, always the excuse that, whereas Foreign Office secrets
have been revealed, those of the counting-house and the company
promoter have not; and the unknown is always a safe source to
look to for further enlightenment.

There have been other and wider forms of retreat from 'pure'
diplomatic history. It is fitting that historians in what is called the
age of the masses should abandon the archives for the study of
public opinion—a study, however, more easily preached than
practised. How can we take a Gallup poll among the dead? The
study of public opinion has changed only too often into a study of
newspapers—a subject also of great interest but one attended
with more difficulties than the unworldly historian supposes. Do
newspapers voice public opinion or make it? Do they lead or
follow? Often neither. They obey the directive of a government
agent; dance to the whims of a proprietor; or, more rarely, express
the policy of a great editor. Most frequently of all, they put in
enough news and articles to fill the space. Little of this was recognized by the earnest scholars, usually American, who pursued the
trail of public opinion. How surprised Frank Harris would have
been, for instance, to learn that he had supplied the evidence for
British hostility to Germany by a single leader in the *Saturday
Review*. Some outstanding work has indeed been done in this field.
Eckart Kehr wrote an amazingly brilliant book years ago on the
building of the German navy and party politics—so brilliant indeed as almost to make one forget that the German admirals must

have had something to do with it. More recently Professor Chabod has dissected with infinite subtlety what the Italians thought of foreign affairs in the year 1870. The intellectual achievement could hardly be bettered. But our shelves will groan if every nation is to require 600 pages for each year of its public thoughts.

Historians have run too eagerly after some subjects, and passed others by. It is curious that a generation which experienced two world wars should still neglect the papers of the service departments. No muckraking Radical has penetrated their secrets; even respectable historians have only been allowed a selective glance. The generals and admirals have defended the secrets of their enemies as zealously as they defend their own. The records of the German Admiralty have been reposing in London since 1945, inviolate from any prying eye. The Americans have not done much better with the records of the German General Staff which they carried off to Washington. We know what Hitler planned to do in war; how far was the German Army equipped to carry out his intentions? The answer would be not without interest. Solidarity, worthy of a trade union, ensures that we shall not learn the answer.

Wars are the eclipse of diplomacy, and therefore of diplomatic history. This, no doubt, explains why there are few books on the diplomacy of the First World War and why the archives for this period are still rigorously sealed, even though the documents of the inter-war period are being published. More specifically we continue to live in a war atmosphere in the immediate present— first the Second World War against Germany, then the more insidious 'cold war', which seems equally impervious to diplomacy. The arguments and manœuvres of diplomatists have become little more than an entertainment, imperfectly cloaking the 'out-door relief' for members of the ruling class which John Bright regarded as the object of all foreign policy. What goes on at Lake Success is of little moment; therefore, we think, diplomacy never mattered, and the diplomatic historian is wasting his time as well as ours.

This depreciation of diplomacy started even before the Second World War. The dictators, Hitler and Mussolini, refused to play according to the accepted rules. What was the sense of negotiating, still less of making agreements with them? And therefore, even more, what sense is there in writing about these barren negotiations and meaningless pacts? The 'pure' diplomatic historian has been perhaps too readily discouraged. It was the outbreak of the

Second World War, not the first, which led Sir Lewis Namier to write a masterpiece—largely from diplomatic documents of the most formal, dreary kind. Foreign policy of a sort will go on so long as there are sovereign States, even though its instrument may be an atomic test instead of a dispatch. Diplomatic historians may have to learn new tricks and to lament their vanished 'purity'. Certainly the records of Foreign Offices no longer arouse much curiosity. Once it was believed that they contained as much explosive matter as Pandora's box. Now it appears that the patron saint of the archives is Joanna Southcott.

13

THE CONFERENCE AT ALGEÇIRAS

THE conference of Algeçiras was a decisive moment in European diplomacy. With uncanny foreboding, it anticipated the course of policy which the Great Powers would follow even when diplomacy gave place to war. It was the first great demonstration of the Triple Entente; it was the first demonstration, too, that Italy was drifting away from the Triple Alliance and that the United States were drifting into sympathy with the *Entente Cordiale*. The conference was more than a demonstration of alliances and friendships; it helped to create them. When the delegates went to Algeçiras, relationships between the Powers still seemed fluid; when the conference ended, a pattern of European affairs was laid down which lasted until the peace of Brest-Litovsk and the armistices of November 1918.

It is now possible to study in detail every episode of this decisive diplomatic engagement. The German[1] and British[2] documents have long been in print, though the British documents are a rather slight selection and miss a few points. A selection from the Russian documents was published in *Berliner Monatshefte* for April 1931; and American policy can be followed in the life of Henry White,[3] the principal American delegate. The French documents[4] complete the picture. No doubt there is a little to be learnt from the Italian and Austro-Hungarian archives; but Italian policy can be followed from the British and French documents, and Austro-Hungarian from the German. Already we have the most complete case-history of an international conference, which should be studied in detail by every diplomatic historian and by every intending diplomat. The French volume contains, as well, the journal kept by Révoil, the principal French delegate, from 12 January to 9 April. This journal comes from his private papers. It would be interesting to know for what purpose he kept it. Though very precise, it is also extremely discreet; it is, for the most part, a

1. *Die Grosse Politik der Eüropäischen Cabinette.* Vol. XXI.
2. *British Documents on the Origins of the War.* Vol. III.
3. *Henry White.* By Allan Nevins.
4. *Documents diplomatiques français 1871–1914,* 2ᵉ Serie (1901–11), Tome IX. 1ʳᵉ partie (16 janvier–1 mars 1906); 2ᵉ partie (2 mars–7 avril 1906). Paris, 1946.

summary of his official telegrams. Perhaps Révoil was one of those men who can think clearly only when they summarize their thoughts and acts on paper. There is no indication that the journal served any official purpose. There is no copy in the archives of the Quai d'Orsay and presumably it was not shown to the Foreign Minister. Was it perhaps kept for the benefit of André Tardieu? Tardieu's remarkable book, *La Conférence d'Algéçiras*, the first great essay in contemporary history, is accurate almost in every detail. Once or twice he is a day wrong in his dates; but he has far more information than could have been learnt in the ordinary way, and often he seems to be quoting Révoil. On the other hand, there is no evidence in the documents or the journal that Révoil and Tardieu actually collaborated during the conference; and on at least one occasion (the article in *Le Temps* on 20 March) Tardieu seems to have acted on his own—to Révoil's annoyance. Probably this problem will never be solved unless there is material in Tardieu's private papers.

When the delegates met at Algeçiras on 16 January 1906, they had no idea that their actions would shape international relations for years to come. It had been many years since a conference of such importance had been held; and both sides had forgotten the lesson of the Congress of Berlin: that great international gatherings succeed only when the broad decisions have been made beforehand. Révoil had been told to secure the general mandate of the Moorish police for France;[1] Radowitz, the German delegate, had been instructed to resist a general mandate.[2] Both had been told not to allow their country to be isolated; but little had been done to build up support. Révoil had a plan by which, at the right moment, the Russian delegate would put forward the French proposals as his own; but this plan was never operated—it would have turned all the German hostility on to Russia. The British were so ill prepared by the French that Nicolson did not at first realize the importance of the police question and as late as 21 January wrote to Grey: 'My own opinion is that if I were French I would be quite ready to surrender the police duties to anyone for a limited period provided I had predominant control over the Bank.'[3] The Germans, on their side, had communicated their

1. Rouvier to Révoil, 12 January 1906. D.D.F. VIII, No. 395.
2. Bülow to Radowitz, 3 January 1906. G.P. XXI, No. 6922.
3. Nicolson to Grey, 21 January 1906. B.D. III, No. 251.

general intentions to their allies[1] and had received a vague promise of support from Vienna. The German ambassador in Rome
gave repeated warnings that Italy was not to be relied upon;[2] but
these warnings were disregarded in Berlin, and in any case the
Germans thought they had a trump-card in the United States, which
would be brought on to the German side by the blessed word
'Internationalization'. This reliance on the United States was perhaps the fundamental blunder of German policy at Algeçiras. The
Germans overlooked the fact that the Americans, in so far as they
were indifferent, would not estrange France for the sake of something that did not matter to them; and in so far as they were
concerned (either with Morocco or with the relations of the Great
Powers) they would prefer the side of the Anglo-French entente.
The only method by which the Germans might have persuaded
Roosevelt to play an active part (as he had done between Russia
and Japan) would have been to threaten war with France; and this
threat, though it might have made Roosevelt act, would not have
made him act on the German side.

The tactical question at the conference was simple, and it never
changed. Whichever side submitted a plan for the police would
expose itself to attack; therefore the side which held out longest
without proposing anything would win. Patience, and strong
nerves, would decide the issue. The Germans, who had begun the
Moroccan conflict solely as a question of prestige, asked only to get
out without disgrace; the French were determined to control the
police, since this would give them victory both in Morocco and in
'la grande politique'. This concrete objective gave France a great
advantage. The French knew what they wanted; the Germans
only what they did not want. Still, the nerves of both sides were
severely tested before the Germans finally gave way.

After the formal opening on 16 January, the deadlock showed
itself at once. Révoil waited for the Germans to approach him.
He was warned both by the Italians and by White, the American
delegate, that Germany would not agree to a general mandate for
France; but Nicolson, despite secret doubts, encouraged him to be
firm, and on 19 January Révoil noted: 'Sir Arthur and I have
complete faith in each other.'[3] A false alarm followed. The French

1. Bülow to Monts, telegram, 22 December 1905. G.P. XXI, No. 6912.
2. E. G. Monts to Bülow, 2 January 1906. G.P. XXI, No. 6921; 6 January 1906.
G.P. XXI, No. 6928.   3. *Journal*, VIII, 19 January 1906.

Senator d'Estournelles de Constant visited Berlin in an effort at unofficial mediation. All he got from Bülow was the suggestion that the question of the police should be postponed: 'Wait some years, three years, perhaps two, then we'll see. Appearances will be saved.' Estournelles de Constant summed up his impression to Rouvier, the French Premier: 'They don't want war, but also they don't want peace. The truth is they don't know what they want.'[1] By some misunderstanding, it was at first supposed that Bülow had proposed direct discussions between Paris and Berlin.[2] Jules Cambon at once sent urgent advice from Madrid against such a course;[3] and inquiry at Berlin showed that Bülow had not in fact proposed it. The episode served only as an illustration of the control exercised over Rouvier by his ambassadors. On 23 January Revoil noted: 'We are in agreement that a waiting attitude is still necessary.'[4] Meanwhile the first German approach to Roosevelt,[5] made on 20 January, had miscarried. The Americans did not like the idea of partitioning Morocco even for police purposes;[6] on the other hand they would not support French claims — in fact they were determined not to be pushed into the position of arbitrators,[7] yet unless someone would arbitrate there was no purpose in an international conference.

The British did not yet understand that they had lost their freedom of action in the Moroccan question; they still supposed that they could mediate between France and Germany. On 24 January Nicolson described the deadlock at Algeçiras;[8] this led Grey to urge private talks on France and Germany. Bülow replied that he had no objection 'to the intervention of any third Power';[9] the French rejected the approach—since the Germans had appealed to the conference, they must abide by the appeal.[10] As a matter of fact Radowitz had already approached Révoil for a private

1. Estournelles de Constant to Rouvier, 21 January 1906. D.D.F., No. 22.

2. Bihourd to Rouvier, telegram, 21 January; Rouvier to Bihourd, telegram, 21 January; Bihourd to Rouvier, telegram, 22 January 1906. D.D.F. IX, Nos. 27, 28, 32.

3. Jules Cambon to Rouvier, telegram, 22 January 1906. D.D.F. IX, No. 33.

4. Révoil, *Journal*, XII, 23 January 1906.

5. Bülow to Sternburg, telegram, 20 January 1906. G.P. XXI, No. 6956.

6. Sternburg to Bülow, telegram, 23 January 1906. G.P. XXI, No. 6958.

7. Jusserand to Rouvier, telegram, 23 January 1906. D.D.F. IX, No. 41.

8. Nicolson to Grey, telegram, 24 January 1906. B.D. III, No. 254.

9. Lascelles to Grey, telegram, 25 January 1906. B.D. III, No. 255.

10. Rouvier to Paul Cambon and others, telegram, 26 January 1906. D.D.F., No. 60. This British approach to France, and its rejection, is not recorded in B.D.; a curious omission.

discussion on 24 January. Radowitz, though rather in disgrace since the fall of Bismarck, was an experienced diplomatist and no doubt wished to score a personal success. The meeting between Radowitz and Révoil on 25 January proved barren: Révoil would reveal nothing, and Radowitz had nothing to reveal.[1] The Germans were, in fact, still waiting for American support; and they did not lose hope even when the Americans again rejected the German advances on 29 January.[2]

On 27 January Rouvier showed the first sign of giving way. He telegraphed to Révoil that, if no agreement could be reached, 'Perhaps it would be wise to find out whether we could not get it accepted that the *question*, and not merely the *mandate for a general organisation*, should be formally *put off* for agreement later';[3] this would have given the Germans all they asked. This proposal by Rouvier was strongly opposed by his diplomatic associates. On 27 January Paul Cambon urged from London a policy of delay with the German Government: 'It must be drawn into making proposals to us one after another without our putting up counter-proposals. . . . So when the Russian proposal is brought out and we support it after a brief hesitation, it will look as though we were making a sacrifice.'[4] From Rome Barrère telegraphed against any weakening.[5] Révoil ignored Rouvier's telegram; or rather answered indirectly, by showing that Russia, Italy and the United States were becoming increasingly sympathetic to the French case.[6] Finally, on 31 January, Rouvier himself warned Révoil against any private concessions to the Germans. Since this telegram was drafted and signed by Georges Louis, it may well represent a victory of the professional diplomats over Rouvier—a last display of the pressure exercised on him after the fall of Delcassé.[7] Certainly Rouvier's telegram of 27 January was a sign of retreat on the French side.

1. Radowitz to Foreign Office, telegram, 25 January 1906. G.P. XXI, No. 6964; Révoil to Rouvier, telegram, 26 January 1906. D.D.F. IX, No. 56; *Journal*, XIV. This meeting is one of the few occasions when Tardieu is wrong in his dates. He gives Radowitz's approach as 25 January and the conversation as 26 January. Tardieu, *La Conférence d'Algéçiras*, p. 139.

2. Bülow to Sternburg, telegram, 27 January; Sternburg to Bülow, telegram, 29 January 1906. G.P. XXI, Nos. 6968, 6971.

3. Rouvier to Révoil, telegram, 27 January 1906. D.D.F. IX, No. 74.

4. Paul Cambon to Rouvier, 27 January 1906. D.D.F. No. 76.

5. Barrère to Rouvier, telegram, 30 January 1906. D.D.F. IX, No. 93.

6. Révoil to Rouvier, telegram, 30 January 1906. D.D.F. IX, No. 92.

7. Rouvier to Révoil, telegram, 31 January 1906. D.D.F. IX, No. 100.

On 31 January Grey and Paul Cambon discussed the question of British aid to France in case of German aggression. This conversation, which defined Anglo-French relations at least until the sharper crisis of 1911, is already well known from the British documents. It had, however, little immediate importance for the course of diplomacy at Algeçiras. Rouvier's outlook was determined by a conviction that British help would be of little use to France; and any hope which he received from Cambon's report must have been more than offset by a gloomy account of Russia's military situation which came in at about the same time.[1]

February had now been reached without any break in the deadlock. Rouvier had weakened for a moment, but had been checked by his associates. Radowitz was the next to try his hand at compromise. On 3 February he had another interview with Révoil and hinted at German willingness to place the police in the hands of France and Spain, if only some cover could be found—such as an inspector from another Power or an assertion of the sovereignty of the Sultan—which would keep up a pretence of international authority.[2] While Radowitz was discussing with Révoil, Tattenbach, the second German delegate, met Nicolson and made a crude attempt to detach him from the French side. This attempt offended Nicolson deeply, the more so as Tattenbach's reminder that Nicolson had previously been violently anti-French ('My present warm support of the French differed considerably from the attitude which I had assumed a few years ago at Tangier') was a shot that went home.[3] Révoil surmised that Tattenbach's approach to Nicolson had been designed in order to prove to his superiors in Berlin the hopelessness of their intransigent policy and the necessity of compromise.[4] There is no means of checking this surmise, since the editors of the *Grosse Politik* suppress all mention of Tattenbach's manœuvre; this is their usual method when a clumsy German move does not succeed.

Certainly Radowitz made no secret of his desire to accept the

1. Moulin to Étienne, Minister of War, 27 January 1906. D.D.F. IX, No. 77.

2. Révoil to Rouvier, telegram, 4 February 1906. D.D.F. IX, No. 117; *Journal*, XXIII, 3 February. Radowitz to Foreign Office, 3 February 1906. G.P. XXI, No. 6980. Radowitz's report is unreliable, since he was anxious to be conciliatory without revealing his initiative to Berlin.

3. Nicolson to Grey, telegram, 4 February 1906. B.D. III, No. 267. Révoil to Rouvier, telegram, 4 February; Bertie to Rouvier (enclosing British correspondence), 15 February 1906. D.D.F. IX, Nos. 118, 203.

4. Révoil to Rouvier, telegram, 4 February 1906. D.D.F. IX, No. 120.

compromise at which he had hinted on 3 February. The Russians had held back so long as there was a danger of open conflict between Germany and France. Now that Germany seemed in retreat, they wished to get the advantage of having acted as mediators and on 7 February appealed to the Germans to be conciliatory.[1] The Russians had counted without Holstein at the German Foreign Office. On 6 February Radowitz appealed to the Foreign Office to accept the French terms.[2] Holstein, however, was convinced that neither the Kaiser nor Bülow would give way.[3] A reply was therefore sent to Radowitz on 8 February, rejecting the French proposal and instructing him to work with the American and Austro-Hungarian delegates in order to defeat French ambitions.[4] Radowitz was now in an embarrassing position. He could not tell his government how much he had offered to concede; neither did he wish to confess in Algeçiras that his government had overruled him. He therefore resorted to the manœuvre of a 'leak' to the press; and on 10 February the German telegraph agency Wolff released a misleading account of the private discussions which had been taking place. This is another piece of German diplomacy which is passed over by the editors of the *Grosse Politik*.

Holstein not only assumed that the Kaiser and Bülow would stand firm; he also hoped that Rouvier might give way, as he had done the previous June. Radolin was therefore instructed to see him and to renew the vague offers of Franco-German friendship which had played their part at the time of the fall of Delcassé. But Rouvier had learnt a bitter lesson from the negotiations of July and September 1905; though still anxious to compromise, he was determined not to be drawn into direct discussions and therefore rejected Radolin's advance on 13 February.[5] But, on the same day, he telegraphed to Révoil, agreeing to an international control over the Franco-Spanish police;[6] Rouvier was, in fact, once more in retreat. On 13 February, too, Radowitz tried again. At a meeting with Révoil, he suggested abandoning the idea of an international

1. Bompard to Rouvier, telegram, 7 February 1906. D.D.F. IX, No. 140. Spring-Rice to Grey, 7 February; telegram, 8 February 1906. B.D. III, Nos. 272, 273.

2. Radowitz to Foreign Office, telegrams, 5 February; 6 February 1906. G.P. XXI, Nos. 6984, 6985.

3. Holstein to Radolin, telegram, 10 February 1906. G.P. XXI, No. 6994.

4. Bülow to Radowitz, 7 February (sent 8 February) 1906. G.P. XXI, No. 6987.

5. Note du Département, 13 February 1906. D.D.F. IX, No. 176. Radolin to Foreign Office, telegram, 13 February 1906. G.P. XXI, No. 7001.

6. Rouvier to Révoil, telegram, 13 February 1906. D.D.F. IX, No. 172.

mandate for the police and instead entrusting the organization of the police to the Sultan. Révoil thought that this would be an acceptable compromise, if the Sultan were instructed that he could only appoint Frenchmen and Spaniards.[1] German honour would be satisfied; and Franco-Spanish interests in Morocco would be satisfied at the same time. Révoil therefore drafted a compromise on these lines and gave it to Radowitz on 16 February.[2] He had little hope of a successful outcome, or so he told Nicolson; no doubt he exaggerated his depression in order to hold Nicolson's sympathy. Nicolson tried to cheer him by saying that, if the conference failed, 'it might be possible for direct negotiations to lead to a more satisfactory result'. Révoil replied: 'Every point in a direct agreement would be directed against Great Britain and inspired by a desire to disturb or overthrow the existing Anglo-French understanding.'[3] Nicolson needed no convincing of this; Révoil's remarks were rather directed to Grey, who was beginning to grow anxious at the prolonged deadlock.

The compromise proposed by Révoil—that the Sultan should be allowed to appoint the police so long as he appointed only French and Spanish—was approved by both Austria-Hungary and the United States, the two countries on whom Holstein had been counting.[4] In fact, Goluchowski, Austrian Foreign Minister, had made the same suggestion independently just before it had been put forward by Révoil.[5] Both Austria-Hungary and the United States asked nothing of the conference except to be out of it without offending either side. Also, the Austrians knew, from their experiences in Macedonia, the impossibility of an international police. All this was ignored by the Germans. Révoil's suggestion was at once rejected by Berlin;[6] and this rejection was repeated sharply to Vienna,[7] and in a more conciliatory tone to Washington.[8] Deadlock was once more complete. It was now 19 February. A

1. Révoil to Rouvier, telegram, 13 February 1906. D.D.F. IX, No. 174. Radowitz to Foreign Office, telegram, 13 February 1906. G.P. XXI, No. 7004.
2. Révoil to Rouvier, telegram, 15 February 1906. D.D.F. IX, No. 193.
3. Nicolson to Grey, 15 February 1906. B.D. III, No. 287.
4. Austrian approval: Radowitz to Foreign Office, telegram, 17 February 1906. G.P. XXI, No. 7022. American approval: Sternburg to Foreign Office, 19 February 1906. G.P. XXI, No. 7019.
5. Wedel to Foreign Office, telegram, 14 February 1906. G.P. XXI, No. 7007.
6. Bülow to Radowitz, telegram, 18 February 1906. G.P. XXI, No. 7013.
7. Memorandum by Kriege, 16 February 1906. G.P. XXI, No. 7009.
8. Bülow to Sternburg, telegram, 21 February 1906. G.P. XXI, No. 7020.

month had passed since the opening of the conference. Nothing had been achieved. Apart from Radowitz in his exposed position, German nerve seemed unshaken. The entente position was the reverse. Nicolson and Révoil had kept their courage; Rouvier, and to a lesser extent, Grey, found it difficult to stand the strain. As for the Russians, the approach of the crisis at Algeçiras made their position increasingly embarrassing. They dared not offend France for the sake of the loan which was so urgent to them; they dared not offend Germany for even more obvious reasons.

After the deadlock of 19 February, Russian appeals to Germany for a compromise became desperate. Lamsdorff urged compromise on the German ambassador; and Witte—the great advocate of a 'Continental league'—was enlisted by Bompard[1] to write a letter appealing to William II.[2] Bompard also appealed directly to the Tsar and got from him the promise of 'his entire personal support',[3] but not a promise to write to William II. The Russian appeals to Germany were unavailing; Bülow refused to leave the police to France and Spain. Grey had much the same experience. On 19 February he did his best to shake Metternich, the German ambassador, with the argument that Anglo-German relations would be much better if the Moroccan question was out of the way.[4] The conversation achieved nothing; and Grey was now convinced that Germany would not yield. The only solution seemed to him to attempt to bribe Germany with the offer of a Moorish port. He recognized that the French might feel that they were being deserted; but he hoped they would realize that 'in a war with Germany our liabilities would be much less than theirs'. He added, as an afterthought, that if there had to be a conflict with Germany it would be better to wait until Russia had recovered and an Anglo-Russian entente made.[5] It was this argument of a Triple Entente, revising the question of Moroco in favour of France, which Grey used to Cambon on 22 February: 'Once France, England and Russia were on good terms, they could reopen the question of the police in Morocco. . . . Therefore we must play for time.'[6]

1. Bompard to Rouvier, telegram, 20 February 1906. D.D.F. IX, No. 231.
2. *Grosse Politik*, XXI, Nos. 7027–30.
3. Bompard to Rouvier, telegram, 22 February 1906. D.D.F. IX, No. 263; Bompard to Rouvier, 24 February 1906. D.D.F. IX, No. 292.
4. Grey to Lascelles, 19 February 1906. B.D. III, No. 296.
5. Grey, memorandum, 20 February 1906. B.D. III, No. 299.
6. Paul Cambon to Rouvier, telegram, 23 February 1906. D.D.F. IX, No. 274.

Pressure to compromise was also brought on Rouvier from another quarter. French policy (and Rouvier's position in particular) had been weakened from the beginning by the unofficial French 'experts' on Germany who had thrust themselves forward in the belief that they knew the Germans and would bring them to a reasonable settlement. In every case, these 'mediators' had strengthened German confidence. Courcel, former ambassador at Berlin and London, was the last of them. He took advantage of a visit to Berlin to see William II, Bülow and Holstein. All three gave him friendly words; on the question at issue they remained unshakable. Bülow told him frankly: 'What matters to us is, as they say, to save our faces', and held out the prospect that after four or five years (not two or three as he told Estournelles de Constant) France would be free to act in Morocco. At present Germany would allow the French to control the police in *one* Moorish port; all the rest must be organized on an international basis, even including German officers. Courcel of course tried to emphasize that he had no official position; all the same he did not conceal his agreement with the German proposals and even said that he would support them, when the occasion arose, in the Senate. It is not surprising that the Germans thought the French on the point of giving way; and themselves became more confident. Bülow, indeed, was so confident that he counted on the Italians, as well as on Austria-Hungary and the United States. He told Courcel: 'I know the Italians. . . . Italy will not desert us.'[1]

Rouvier, summarizing Courcel's report, concluded on 24 February: 'He has brought back from his conversations in Berlin the very clear impression that Germany will not accept an arrangement on terms favourable to us.'[2] Rouvier therefore prepared to retreat. Late in the evening of 23 February, he telegraphed to Révoil that there was no hope of agreement on the basis of the present French plan and that he was being urged even from London to compromise. 'It may be then that we shall have to think of new solutions.'[3] This telegram was the nearest point to victory ever reached by the Germans.

For, just as Rouvier began to weaken, the Austrians began to

1. Courcel to Rouvier, 24 February 1906. D.D.F. IX, No. 291. Memoranda by Holstein, 22 February 1906. G.P. XXI, Nos. 7034, 7035.

2. Rouvier to Révoil, Jules Cambon, Paul Cambon, telegram, 24 February 1906. D.D.F. IX, No. 276.

3. Rouvier to Révoil, telegram, 23 February 1906. D.D.F. IX, No. 272.

E

weaken also. On 23 February Francis Joseph himself warned
the German ambassador that German policy was driving Russia
into the arms of England and France;[1] and on 21 February
Goluchowski had made it clear to the French ambassador that he,
too, disapproved of German policy.[2] The best the Austrians could
do to save the situation was to propose that the conference should
adjourn without making any decisions. The Austrian suggestion
was the signal for the professional French diplomats to go into
action. Here, at last, was a proposal (of a negative kind) from the
side of the Central Powers; France, by defeating it, could show
Germany's isolation. On 24 February both Paul Cambon and
Jules Cambon telegraphed to Rouvier, urging that France should
not allow the conference to separate without a vote having been
taken on the question of the police;[3] and Paul Cambon sent a
further telegram denouncing the plan which Courcel had brought
back from Berlin: 'The suggestion about the police is the least
acceptable of any that have been made to us.'[4] Jules Cambon sent a
similar attack on Courcel's plan the following day.[5] Révoil dismissed Courcel's plan with equal firmness: 'The proposals that
M. de Courcel regards as offering the basis for agreement are
absolutely contrary to the principles which we have defended up
till now and which we cannot give up.'[6]

In face of this firm attitude, Rouvier—as on previous occasions—
recovered his nerve and allowed the professionals to have their
way. Révoil was asked if he could obtain a vote 'which would provide us with a certain moral strength'; and on 27 February Courcel
told the German ambassador sadly that Rouvier 'much against his
inner conviction was being dragged along by shortsighted hostile
forces which were growing stronger every day'.[7] Révoil now had
a free hand. Policy had been decided; and the problem was now
technical—how to mobilize the strongest voting strength. Révoil
at first thought it would be impossible to devise a formula for which
the 'neutrals' would vote; and abstention would not be effective.

1. Memorandum by Bülow, 24 February 1906. G.P. XXI, No. 7039.
2. Reverseaux to Rouvier, telegram, 21 February 1906. D.D.F. IX, No. 252.
3. Paul Cambon to Rouvier, telegram, 24 February; Jules Cambon to Rouvier,
telegram, 24 February 1906. D.D.F. IX, Nos. 279, 281.
4. Paul Cambon to Rouvier, telegram, 24 February 1906. D.D.F. IX, No. 284.
5. Jules Cambon to Rouvier, telegram, 25 February 1906. D.D.F. IX, No. 299.
6. Révoil to Rouvier, telegram, 24 February 1906. D.D.F. IX, No. 289.
7. Radolin to Foreign Office, 27 February 1906. G.P. XXI, No. 7047.

White, the American delegate, was especially insistent that he could not vote on a question of general principle, however much he agreed with the French case; and the Italians were almost as difficult. It is not clear how, as a result of a week's thought, it was decided that the vote should be forced, not on any actual proposal, but simply on a motion that the question of the police should be considered. Révoil at first planned that the Russians should force a decision by submitting the scheme for the police which they had held in reserve since the opening of the conference; but on 27 February the Russians grew timid—'The Russian delegation does not want to get the blame for producing the storm.'[1] Révoil gives no further indication how the vote of 3 March was prepared. It may be that Nicolson, as his biographer implies,[2] made up his own mind to force a decision and acted without warning his colleague. His tactic certainly succeeded. When on 3 March he proposed that the question of the police should be taken at their next meeting, all voted for his motion, except the delegates of Germany, Austria-Hungary, and Morocco. Bülow commented on the meeting: 'Wenig erfreulich!'[3]

The vote of 3 March at last shook the confidence of Berlin. They could no longer suppose that they were supported by all the neutral powers. Holstein had nothing to propose except a new intrigue with Rouvier through Courcel; and this threadbare expedient was actually tried out. Rouvier rejected the approach firmly. Perhaps he had at last learnt from experience; more probably, as he was on the point of leaving office, he wished to retire with a clean record behind him.[4] The only effect, at any rate, of this manoeuvre was to convince the French that the Germans were losing their nerve. Jules Cambon telegraphed: 'Confidence is beginning to be shaken at Berlin and we have only to stand fast.'[5] The episode would hardly be worth remark, except that it proved to be the last diplomatic act of Holstein. The German delegates at Algeçiras understood the position better. They realized that it was they who must give way. On 5 March Tattenbach devised a new

1. *Journal*, XLVII, 27 February 1906.   2. Harold Nicolson, *Lord Carnock*, p. 189.
3. Radowitz to Foreign Office, telegram, 3 March 1906. G.P. XXI, No. 7051.
4. Holstein to Radolin, telegram, 4 March; Radolin to Foreign Office, telegrams, 5 March, 6 March 1906. G.P. XXI, Nos. 7055, 7059, 7067. Rouvier to Révoil, telegram, 5 March; Rouvier, circular telegram, 7 March 1906. D.D.F. IX, Nos. 358, 375.
5. Jules Cambon to Rouvier, telegram, 7 March 1906. D.D.F., No. 382.

proposal on the police virtually conceding all the French wishes, except that there should be a neutral inspector, who should also be in command at Casablanca.[1] This proposal was accepted by Bülow, and the Austrians were asked to put it forward as mediators; a neutral commander at one port was to be a *sine qua non*.[2]

This proposal was an adroit move; and its reception showed that, if the Germans had been more conciliatory from the beginning, the results of the conference might well have been very different. In practice, the new proposal gave the French the footing in Morocco that they wanted; in theory, it preserved the principle of internationalization and so saved the face of the Germans. Sentiment at Algeçiras swung round to the German side. The delegates were, above all, anxious not to commit themselves if it could be avoided; and the German offer seemed to be designed to save them. They waited impatiently for the French to compromise in their turn. The French could not explain that, quite apart from their objections to the principle, Casablanca was the port on which they proposed to base their penetration of Morocco; they had therefore to give the appearance of harsh obstinacy. It was serious enough that the Russian delegate should welcome the German move; it was even more serious that Nicolson regarded it as a genuine compromise. From 8 March to 14 March Nicolson persistently urged Révoil to give way on the question of Casablanca.[3] Grey in London was even more emphatic. On 8 March he told Cambon that the proposal 'represented a real concession on the part of Germany' and quoted Nicolson's opinion in its favour;[4] Cambon's report does its best to weaken the force of Grey's remarks and even implies that Grey was persuaded to co-operate in resistance.[5] Cambon, no doubt, hoped to encourage Rouvier to take a firm line, as he had done with his somewhat selective reporting the previous June. On 12 March Grey repeated his arguments more strongly than before: 'Casablanca is of no importance.' This time Cambon recorded Grey's remarks with reasonable fairness.[6]

1. Radowitz to Foreign Office, telegram, 5 March 1906. G.P. XXI, No. 7060.
2. Bülow to Wedel, telegram, 6 March; Bülow, memorandum, 7 March 1906. G.P. XXI, Nos. 7065, 7069.
3. Nicolson to Grey, telegram, 9 March; telegram, 14 March 1906. B.D. III, Nos. 332, 349. Révoil, *Journal*, LVI, 8 March; LVIII, 10 March 1906.
4. Grey to Bertie, telegram, 9 March 1906. B.D. III, No. 333.
5. Paul Cambon to Rouvier, 9 March 1906. D.D.F. IX, No. 414.
6. Grey to Nicolson, telegram, 12 March 1906. B.D. III, No. 344. Paul Cambon to Rouvier, telegram, 12 March 1906. D.D.F. IX, No. 429.

The general feeling at Algeçiras, and above all the attitude of Nicolson, caused Révoil to retreat. On 10 March Nicolson sounded Radowitz on the possibility of compromise and came away convinced that the Germans would insist on neutral control of Casablanca.[1] Révoil then suggested that a neutral officer might be acceptable if he was instead allotted Tangier (which the French had never hoped to control).[2] On 12 March Radowitz, in conversation with Nicolson, rejected this proposal.[3] On 13 March Révoil therefore decided to give way and recommended the French Government to agree to Swiss control of Casablanca with certain safeguards. 'We must choose between breaking off and agreeing to entrusting the Casablanca police to a neutral Power. After careful reflection, I think that we must not break off.'[4] Once more the Germans, though they did not know it, were in sight of victory. Once more victory escaped them at the last moment.

The German setback had two causes. In the first place the Germans overplayed their hand. On 11 March Radowitz telegraphed: 'It is said to me by all my colleagues, including the English, that after our attitude in the full session they would regard the French insistence on the points described as definitely unacceptable by us as no longer justifiable and that they have told Révoil so.'[5] In view of Nicolson's opinion, expressed to Révoil and to Grey, Radowitz's report was well-founded, though unwise. No doubt, after so many failures, he wished to boast of a success. On 13 March Metternich repeated Radowitz's remark to Grey; and Grey re-replied: 'I did not think that Sir A. Nicolson had said the French ought to accept the Austrian proposal unconditionally.'[6] Grey also telegraphed to Nicolson: 'I replied that you could not have said that France ought to accept the Austrian proposal unconditionally.'[7] Nicolson was now anxious to cover himself with Révoil. He therefore told him of the conversation between Grey and Metternich

1. Nicolson to Grey, telegram, 11 March; 11 March 1906. B.D. III, No. 339.

2. Révoil to Rouvier, telegram, 11 March 1906. D.D.F. IX, No. 422.

3. Révoil, *Journal*, LX, 12 March 1906. Nicolson to Grey, telegram, 13 March 1906. B.D. III, No. 345. Radowitz seems to have rejected the offer of Tangier without referring to Berlin.

4. Révoil to Rouvier, telegram, 13 March 1906. D.D.F. IX, No. 437.

5. Radowitz to Foreign Office, telegram, 11 March 1906. G.P. XXI, No. 7089.

6. Grey to Lascelles, 13 March 1906. B.D. III, No. 348. Metternich does not record Grey's denial. Metternich to Foreign Office, telegram, 13 March 1906. G.P. XXI, No. 7100.

7. Grey to Nicolson, telegram, 14 March 1906. B.D. III, No. 351.

and repeated Grey's sentence in a more emphatic form: 'It is impossible that Sir Arthur has come out for the Austrian proposal.'[1] Révoil, transmitting the story to Paris, made it more emphatic still: 'What you tell me is impossible.'[2] The French Government was thus led to believe that Grey had given Metternich the lie direct; and Nicolson, to cover his indiscretion, had henceforth to appear as a violent opponent of the German plan for Casablanca.

The second cause of Germany's failure was the change of government in France, which was accompanied by a journalistic manœuvre conducted by Tardieu and perhaps assisted by Bertie, the British ambassador. On 7 March Rouvier's government fell on a domestic issue; a new government, with Bourgeois as Foreign Minister, was not formed until 13 March. The new ministers had heard the rumours of Nicolson's endorsement of the Casablanca plan and came into office convinced that England was about to desert them. But on 13 March *le Temps* published the instructions which, it claimed, Rouvier had confirmed to Révoil before leaving office. As a matter of fact, Rouvier had merely telegraphed to Revoil on 8 March: 'The debate which took place in the Chamber yesterday did not touch on anything concerning foreign policy and therefore your instructions remain unchanged';[3] and the article in *le Temps* was a concoction summarizing Rouvier's previous instructions, though not in diplomatic language. Bourgeois denied, no doubt correctly, that Rouvier was responsible for the 'leak'.[4] Révoil, however, was probably less innocent, to judge from the complacent way in which he refers to the publication 'of the last instructions that I received'.[5] Probably the manœuvre was arranged between Révoil and Tardieu to stiffen the new government.

The *Temps* article was, however, unexpectedly effective with the British Government. Bertie telegraphed extracts from it to Grey; and his telegram must have been in emphatic form,[6] for it convinced Grey that the French would not yield over Casablanca. He

1. Révoil, *Journal*, LXII, 14 March 1906.

2. Révoil to Bourgeois, telegram, 15 March 1906. D.D.F. IX, No. 450. It is in this form that the phrase appears in Tardieu, p. 329.

3. Rouvier to Révoil, telegram, 8 March 1906. D.D.F. IX, No. 388.

4. Bourgeois, circular, 15 March 1906. D.D.F. IX, No. 452.

5. Révoil to Bourgeois, telegram, 15 March 1906. D.D.F. IX, No. 450.

6. Unfortunately Bertie's telegram is not printed in B.D. It is referred to in Bertie o Grey, 17 March 1906. Grey, *Twenty-five Years*, I, 105–10.

therefore withdrew his earlier promptings of compromise and instructed Bertie to promise British support to the French.[1] Bertie
made the most of these instructions. On 14 March he saw
Georges Louis, the *directeur politique*; on 15 March he sent a message to Bourgeois through Crozier, French Minister at Copen-
hagen, and saw Bourgeois, Étienne, Minister of War, and
Clémenceau, Minister of the Interior; on 16 March he saw
Étienne, Clémenceau, and Bourgeois again. The French ministers
had meant to complain that Great Britain was not supporting
them; instead they were met with 'spontaneous' offers of support
from Bertie and with strong urging not to give way. Of course
Bertie, in his reports to Grey, made out that the French ministers
had taken the initiative; but reading between the lines and judging
from his conduct on other occasions (such as the Haldane mission
in 1912), it is reasonable to assume that he made his own contribution to policy. He exaggerated the doubts of the French ministers to Grey; he exaggerated Grey's firmness to the French
ministers.[2] The manœuvre succeeded. On 13 March Grey had still
wanted the French to give way, and Révoil had made up his mind
to do so. Three days later the British were committed to supporting a firm French line—though much against their will;[3] and the
French ministers would not compromise for fear of British disapproval.

Rouvier's fall had not affected German plans. Tardieu is wrong
when he argues that the Germans had been prepared to give way
on 7 March and renewed their obstinacy on 11 March because of
the change of government in France;[4] it is the one major error in
his narrative. The Germans remained resolute about Casablanca
until 12 March. On that day Bülow lost his nerve and took over
the conduct of affairs from Holstein; German policy became in-
gratiating and conciliatory, instead of being obstinate and harsh.
This policy might have produced a response from Rouvier, who in
his heart had always desired a compromise; Bourgeois, reinforced

1. Grey to Bertie, telegram, 14 March 1906. B.D. III, No. 350.
2. Bertie to Grey, telegrams, 15 March; telegram, 16 March; 17 March 1906.
B.D. III, Nos. 355, 356, 358. Grey, *Twenty-five Years*, pp. 105–10. Bourgeois to
Révoil, telegram, 14 March; to Paul Cambon, telegram, 15 March 1906. D.D.F. IX,
Nos. 440, 448.
3. Grey to Bertie, 15 March; Hardinge to Nicolson, 15 March 1906. B.D. III,
Nos. 353, 354.
4. Tardieu, pp. 313–15.

by Bertie, reacted quite differently. On 15 March he rejected
the Casablanca proposal in a conversation with the Austrian
ambassador;[1] and he repeated this rejection in another conversation on 17 March.[2] The Austrians were weary of the battle; they
urged Bülow to be content with a neutral inspector who would not
command at Casablanca.[3] Bülow was weary too; his only concern
was to be finished with the question of Morocco, and he accepted
the Austrian advice. By 19 March France had won. The police of
Morocco would be controlled by France and Spain alone.

During this time Russia and America had been left aside. When
it looked as though France would give way, Bülow had urged
Lamsdorff to join in urging conciliation on France.[4] This put
Lamsdorff in a difficult position. If France gave way, he wanted to
have the credit for it; if France remained obstinate, he did not want
to be blamed for having taken the German side. On 14 March he
sounded Bompard as to the intentions of the new government and
hinted that the Germans expected it to be more conciliatory than
the previous one; Lamsdorff seems also to have revealed his suspicion that the new government might revert to Rouvier's old
plan of buying Germany off in Morocco by offering French parti-
cipation in the Bagdad railway.[5] When Bourgeois rejected the
Austrian compromise, it was necessary for Lamsdorff to show
that he, too, had never been out of step; and on 19 March he
telegraphed to the Russian ambassador at Berlin, supporting the
French position. This was enough in itself to annoy the Germans;
but Nelidov, Russian ambassador at Paris, made matters worse. In
his anxiety to prove that Russia had never wavered, he showed a
copy of Lamsdorff's telegram to Tardieu; and the message
appeared in *le Temps*, two hours before it was shown to Bourgeois
and a day before it was delivered to the German Foreign Office.[6]
Russia paid the penalty for this, when Germany refused to parti-
cipate in the great Russian loan.

The United States provided a curious, almost absurd, epilogue.
Roosevelt had refused to express an opinion when his action could
still have been of some use to the Germans; he acted now when it

1. Bourgeois, circular, 15 March 1906. D.D.F. IX, No. 452.
2. Bourgeois to Révoil, telegram, 17 March 1906. D.D.F. IX, No. 466.
3. Bülow to Radowitz, telegram, 19 March 1906. G.P. XXI, No. 7117.
4. Bülow, Directive, 12 March 1906. G.P. XXI, No. 7091.
5. Bompard to Bourgeois, telegram, 14 March 1906. D.D.F. IX, No. 442.
6. Bourgeois to Bompard, telegram, 26 March 1906. D.D.F. IX, No. 557.

was too late. Without warning he turned violently against the Austrian scheme. He discovered in it an implicit partition of Morocco and even suspected that Casablanca was being set aside as Germany's share. He proposed instead a joint Franco-Spanish police in all the ports. This plan was unwelcome to all parties. It offended the French by barring the way against partition;[1] it offended the Spanish by putting them under French supervision; it offended the British by putting French police in Mediterranean ports[2]—it had been one of the principal objects of the Entente agreement to prevent this. It even offended the Germans; for it called upon them to begin the diplomatic struggle all over again. Had Roosevelt's proposal been made at the opening of the conference, Germany and the United States might have worked together and secured the backing of the wavering Powers, Austria-Hungary and Italy, perhaps even of Russia. Now it was too late. The Germans stood aside and allowed the French to argue Roosevelt out of his tardy inspiration. Jusserand, the French ambassador, insisted to the Quai d'Orsay that he could get Roosevelt to withdraw more easily if he were not supported by his British colleague —an odd ending to this story of Anglo-French co-operation.[3]

Agreement was reached on 23 March; the Franco-Spanish plan for the police was formally accepted on 27 March, and the final act of the conference was signed on 7 April. It remained to settle French relations with her friends. Both Jules Cambon[4] and Paul Cambon[5] would have liked to surrender Tangier to Spain; this would both please the Spaniards and burden them with the difficulties with England which were bound to be the lot of whoever controlled Tangier. Révoil and his departmental colleagues refused to be moved by these arguments of *la haute politique*; and Tangier was to remain in dispute, or at any rate in suspense, forty years after the conference of Algeçiras. Paul Cambon also urged that France should reward the British for their support by co-operating with them in the question of the Bagdad railway. Though the Quai d'Orsay was ready to assist in reconciling England and Russia, it

1. Révoil to Bourgeois, telegram, 21 March 1906. D.D.F. IX, No. 502.
2. Grey to Bunsen, 21 March; to Durand, telegram, 22 March 1906. B.D. III, Nos. 372, 374.
3. Jusserand to Bourgeois, telegram, 23 March; 2 April 1906. D.D.F. IX, Nos. 528, 598.
4. Jules Cambon to Bourgeois, telegram, 27 March 1906. D.D.F. IX, No. 563.
5. Paul Cambon to Bourgeois, 29 March 1906. D.D.F. IX, No. 577.

E*

shrank from becoming involved in an Anglo-German conflict: 'Immediately after the conflict over Morocco, France has something better to do than to renew in the Near East the struggle begun so unsuccessfully at Tangier by the Emperor William.'[1]

After the conference a report on the effects of Algeçiras on the relations of the Great Powers was drawn up by de Billy, secretary of the French delegation; it is the last document in the present volume. The Triple Alliance, de Billy wrote, was changing its character. Formed to restrain an aggressive France, it had acted to restrain an aggressive Germany. Austria-Hungary had asserted her independence of Germany and had acted as a mediator instead of as an ally; Italy had resisted German pressure. 'Formerly co-operating with England and Spain to prevent any French activity in Morocco, Italy has now agreed with England to keep Germany out of the western Mediterranean.' The Triple Alliance was based on jealousy between Italy and Austria-Hungary; it should be the object of French diplomacy to reconcile them. As to Russia, the conference had shown that Germany was the principal danger to the peace of Europe and, since Russia needed peace, this had destroyed the plans for a Russo-German reconciliation. Algeçiras had also brought England and Russia together; and Nicolson had used the conference to prepare for his *ambassade* at St. Petersburg. According to de Billy, England had hesitated between a policy of war against Germany and a policy of European alliances which would render Germany harmless without war; Algeçiras had convinced her of the possibility of the second course. Spain had been shown that she could attain her aims in Morocco in co-operation with England and France; but she would listen to German temptations if there was ever division between them. The United States had emerged from isolation; she had discovered that she had no quarrel with England and France, but that Germany threatened her future prosperity. 'The Washington government dislikes the brutal and realistic policy of the Berlin government and answers it by a policy equally realistic, but pacific, because peace and time are working for the United States and against Germany.'

Thus de Billy, revealing no doubt the judgement of French diplomatists, saw in the conference of Algeçiras more than a French success over Germany. He believed that the conference had brought into being a coalition of pacific Powers which would resist

1. Paul Cambon to Bourgeois, 7 April 1906. D.D.F. IX, No. 625.

any Power 'seeking to overturn the Balance of Power for its own advantage'. This coalition was indeed to become a reality in the First World War. At Algeçiras most of the Powers had been concerned only to discharge their obligations without too much embarrassment. None of them, except the two principals, worried about the Balance of Power; and the French succeeded largely by creating the impression that nothing beyond the policing of Morocco was at stake. All the same it had been touch-and-go. On more than one occasion, the chance of a few hours could have altered the entire pattern of negotiations; and then 'the inevitable course of history' would, no doubt, have proceeded in quite a different direction.

14

HOLSTEIN: THE MYSTERY MAN

THE First World War has always been a happy hunting-ground for theories of the 'Hidden Hand'—men of mystery behind the scenes who manœuvred human destiny. Even before 1914, many English radicals held that Sir Edward Grey was the prisoner, perhaps unwitting but certainly helpless, of the Foreign Office. The Foreign Office was not condemned alone. The Quai d'Orsay and, still more, the Wilhelmstrasse fell under the same verdict. The Wilhelmstrasse had a special feature. All its members were wicked, but one was more wicked than others. Friedrich von Holstein—the spectre, the evil genius of the Wilhelmstrasse, the man with hyena eyes, blackmailer and psychopath, the perfect man of mystery.

Holstein died in 1909, five years before the outbreak of war. He had retired from the Foreign Office in 1906. He could hardly, therefore, be blamed for the war itself. What he got was the blame for the decline in Germany's position: she was the decisive factor in Europe when Bismarck left office in 1890—'the tongue in the balance', he called her. By 1906 she had become isolated and 'encircled', no ally except the moribund Habsburg monarchy, war soon to be forced on her, and defeat following. And Holstein had done it. He manœuvred himself into the dominant position in the foreign ministry; planted his creatures out in the leading embassies; and then ruined everything by his insane suspicions. His first act as adviser in 1890, when Bismarck went, was to stop the renewal of the Reinsurance treaty with Russia and so force her into the arms of France. Then he followed a policy of irritating pin-pricks towards England, trying to blackmail her into a formal alliance; but when the British statesmen came along with an offer in 1901, he answered with, according to the title of one book about him, 'Holstein's Great No'. So there we are: the Anglo-French entente as well as the Franco-Russian alliance was all his doing.

His evil influence was not shown only in affairs of grand policy; he was also a corrupter of individuals. Sitting at the centre of his spider's web in Berlin, corresponding privately with ambassadors and spying on them, he taught them to be servile—as though

Germans needed any teaching in that—uncritical, unreliable. He got hold of scandalous secrets about Princess Bülow, the Chancellor's wife, or, according to another account, about Bülow himself, and he used these secrets to blackmail the Chancellor, not only keeping himself in office but dictating policy to suit his whims. Even when he was got rid of, he released scandal against Prince Eulenberg, the Kaiser's closest friend. The scandals ruined Eulenberg and discredited William II into the bargain. Certainly a fine record of destruction. The papers from the German foreign ministry did not show much of this when they were published in the nineteen-twenties. Holstein appeared as a hard-working official, very competent technically, perhaps rather inclined to see the weak points in any policy rather than its advantages, but not malignant or destructive. Still, the legend survived. It was known that Holstein had carried off most of his private papers; and these hung like a dark cloud over the record, scholars rubbing their hands and saying: 'Wait until they are published. Then we shall see something!'

I have no doubt about the importance of Holstein's career. The years between 1890 and 1906 were vital in the history of Germany, years of decision at their most intense. 1906, I am tempted to think, is the real beginning of contemporary history so far as Europe is concerned; certainly it began the era of the German wars, an era perhaps now closed. The real question of interest in regard to Holstein is not whether he blackmailed people, but how far he contributed to the changes in Germany's position. On the personal side the first volume of his papers, which has just been published,[1] is disappointing. There may be more excitement in the later volumes which will contain his private letters.

This one turns out to be very much a damp squib. It contains his so-called 'memoirs', partly scraps of recollections, from his early years, some amusing anecdotes about Bismarck, spiteful and less amusing remarks about his colleagues; and partly reflections on policy put down after his retirement—German relations with the principal Great Powers, the influence of William II, and so on. There is nothing new here, certainly nothing sensational. Holstein had always been an assiduous worker. Thrown out of his job, he was bored, restless, perhaps resentful; and he obviously meant to write a vindication of his career, much as Bismarck had

1. *The Holstein Memoirs*. Cambridge University Press.

done in similar circumstances fifteen years before. But, like most professional diplomatists, like Bismarck himself, he could not manage a sustained narrative. It is all a rigmarole, just like all the other memoirs by professional diplomatists since the world—their world—began: gossip; personal trivialities; the same grievance or episode repeated again and again. You end by being sorry for Holstein. He obviously had not much idea of what was going on in the world beyond his official desk. But then it has always puzzled me why people should expect members of a foreign office, German or other, to understand what is going on in the world. They are a monastic order—cut off from their own country by always having to deal with foreigners and foreign questions, and yet cut off from the foreigners by belonging to their own country. They have to translate hard, often unpleasant, facts into artificial, fine-spun formulas; and they often mistake the formulas for the reality. It is a profession that both attracts neurotics and produces them. They have their uses so long as we remember this, so long as we accept them as advisers and experts, never as the men who determine policy.

Holstein perhaps stepped over the line here, though I am not sure about this. If you look at the advice he gave, it does not seem to me markedly more suspect, pathological, destructive—whatever you like—than the advice given by similar diplomatic officers in other countries: by Eyre Crowe, for example, his contemporary in the British Foreign Office. In fact, I think Eyre Crowe was even quicker on the draw in spotting traps and frauds in every seemingly innocent German proposal than Holstein was with English ones—perhaps justifiably, of course. To make a case against Holstein you need something more than his advice, however pathological; you have to get him on the charge of deciding and directing policy, without being officially responsible for it. And there is something in it—though Holstein was not by any means the only one. He did sometimes go behind the back of the Chancellor, particularly in the days of Bülow; he certainly tried to keep affairs away from William II, who was theoretically the supreme authority. But for the most part he stuck to advice; and if his superiors usually swallowed his advice, it was because they were not capable of anything better on their own.

Bülow, for instance, the man whom the liberals wanted as the saviour of Germany as late as 1917, though a brilliant orator in his way, had to have every word written out for him beforehand; even his celebrated impromptu replies to interruptions had to be rehearsed. There was no guiding hand in Germany, no one truly responsible, between 1890 and the outbreak of the First World War (nor, for that matter, after it). But the blame, if you want to put it at someone's door, does not rest with Holstein. It was Bismarck who had destroyed every independent, outstanding figure in politics except himself; or perhaps there never were any. It certainly must have been nerve-racking to work under William II; and I have little doubt that Holstein would have liked to turn the Kaiser into a harmless constitutional monarch, but I do not think he did much more than grumble. And I cannot get up much interest in the other personal affairs that Holstein was supposed to be involved in.

The real interest of Holstein's career, it seems to me, is of quite a different kind: not the mystery, the shady stories, the melodrama, but the policy he advised and perhaps conducted. There certainly was a great change in Germany's European position between 1890, when Bismarck was overthrown, and 1906, when Holstein left office. Her relations with Russia and with England were certainly less intimate. But was this change really owing to personal whims and misunderstandings on one side or the other? Did Holstein help to wreck the Reinsurance treaty simply because it was associated with Bismarck and he wanted to prevent the Bismarck family returning to office? Did England and Germany drift apart in 1895, as Holstein suggests in one of the present essays, simply because Lord Salisbury failed to keep an appointment with William II one summer morning at Cowes? Or, to take the biggest point of all, was the alliance of England and Germany, which was constantly proposed by British statesmen, especially Joseph Chamberlain, between 1898 and 1901, prevented simply by Holstein's unbalanced suspicions? I do not believe a word of it. Look at the Anglo-German alliance which British and German liberals so lamented when the story became known. What the British wanted was an ally against Russia in the Far East. They would provide a navy; and the ally would provide the men. Very nice for the British. But from the German point of view it was an insane proposition—to use that favourite word again—to commit themselves to a large-scale war, a war of life and death, for the sake of British investments in Shanghai and the Yangtse Valley.

The key to Holstein's policy is simple. His attitude, like Bismarck's before him, was purely European. Though he knew the outside world unusually well—spoke perfect English and lived for some years in the United States and in South America—he had no sympathy whatever with what contemporaries called 'World Policy'. Most Germans, indeed most people all over Europe, thought that European conflicts were finished and Europe was settled for good. The future conflicts were going to be for world markets. Holstein would have agreed with Bismarck when he said to a colonial enthusiast: 'Here is Russia, and here is France. That is my map of Africa.' Bismarck had kept German ambitions under control. Holstein could not. But he claimed quite rightly to have opposed every step of Germany's world policy which estranged the two World Powers, England and Russia. Perhaps 'opposed' is too strong. Holstein was not in a position of power where he could oppose anything. But he did not have anything to do with these steps, and he warned against them. He did not favour the Bagdad railway, which helped to estrange Russia. He was in no way responsible for the Kruger telegram, which challenged the British in South Africa. And he did what he could against the plans for a great German navy. Of course, his opposition was futile; and even more futile was his line with British statesmen and journalists that, since he disliked Germany's world policy, they should not resent it—even though it was happening. He was a brake that failed to work, a melancholy position, as he himself came to recognize.

He wanted solely to rely on the German Army and to give Germany security in Europe by means of 'the free hand'. This really was not very different from Bismarck's policy, though he used rather different ways of doing it. I do not believe that he ever intended for a moment to make a binding alliance with either England or Russia, whatever his talk of making them bid higher. He held—quite rightly from Germany's point of view—that she had everything to gain by letting England and Russia quarrel and remaining uncommitted in the middle. As European policy this was foolproof. What wrecked it was the German insistence on having a world policy as well: to be a great imperial Power in the Far East, in Africa, and on the seas. For this annoyed England and Russia, and pushed them together. Alliance between Russia and the Western Powers is the worst of situations for Germany, just as estrangement between them is the best.

There was, and is, only one way out for Germany. If she is going to challenge the world Powers, she must become not *a* European but *the* European power. She must start with the whole continent under her control. Hitler held this doctrine; so, I think, do the present German advocates of European unification. Holstein arrived at it also, towards the end of his life. Since he could not prevent world policy, he would make it possible. In 1905 he launched the first Moroccan crisis with France with the deliberate object of turning her into a German satellite—perhaps by threats, if not by war. Again, in 1909, he pushed Bülow into standing 100 per cent. behind Austria-Hungary in the Bosnian crisis, with the object of making Mitteleuropa at any rate a solid military block. His policy did not come off. But it was the only way out for Germany if she wanted to be a world Power.

The moral of the story? A personal one: it is a sad life being a private adviser who cannot direct events, but that is a risk private advisers always take. A literary one: the secrets of the archives are mostly humbug. Government departments guard their records because it flatters their self-importance, not because there is anything startling to be revealed. Most of all, a political moral: when Russia and the Western Powers are on bad terms, Germany is the only gainer. Holstein could play his tricks at the beginning of the century; the present rulers of Germany do much the same now. Very nice for the Germans no doubt, but I have never been able to understand why we or the Russians should get any pleasure from it.

15

THE SECOND INTERNATIONAL

THE nineteenth century travelled hopefully. We have arrived. Everyone is prosperous, secure: television sets and second-hand cars firmly embedded as a cost-of-living. The will of the people prevails at every general election—a will no doubt accurately expressed in a precise balance between two equally ineffective parties. Keynesian principles guard us against every economic ill; and now the hydrogen bomb, it is said, guards us against war. We are in the earthly Paradise. The only price we have paid is to cease to believe in it. Progress has been the great casualty of our age. There is no longer a MacDonald to hold out the prospect of 'up and up and up and on and on and on'. There would be no audience even if a new MacDonald appeared. To recapture the belief in Progress we must return to the twenty-five years before the First World War, years in which European civilization reached its zenith. These years were exactly spanned by the Second International, the subject of the third volume in G. D. H. Cole's *History of Socialist Thought*.[1] Its thousand pages present a theme now remote and unsympathetic—futile debates, empty phrases, barren and impotent leaders. Yet there was in it deep tragedy—the tragedy of disappointed Hope and the greater tragedy of Hope Fulfilled.

In Cole's earlier volumes there were few Socialists but much thinking. In the present volume there is a great Socialist movement and virtually no thought. Take away Rosa Luxemburg, and everyone—reformist or revolutionary, Fabian or Bolshevik—scrabbled over phrases, while throwing his real energy into winning votes or enlisting members. All were convinced that the victory of Socialism was inevitable and that it would be achieved in a democratic way. The German revisionists and English Fabians indeed held that the victory would be imperceptible: there would be no precise moment at which capitalism ended and Socialism began. The orthodox continued to believe in 'the revolution'. There

1. *The Second International*. Vol. III of *A History of Socialist Thought*. By G. D. H. Cole. Macmillan. 2 vols.

would be at some point a jerk, a change of gear, when the Socialist commonwealth could be acclaimed. But for them, too, the revolution was simply part of an inevitable process; in democratic countries it would be little more than the appearance of a Socialist majority in Parliament. Even in countries not yet democratic — Germany in particular — the revolution would be political, not economic: the Social Democrats would insist on a change in the constitution once they got a majority, and thereafter Socialism would flow inevitably on. Kautsky, the high priest of Marxism, postulated in *The Way to Power* that the secret of success lay in doing nothing: the longer the Social Democrats sat tight and allowed their supporters to accumulate, the greater and more irresistible would be their triumph when it came.

The greatest handicap of the Social Democrats was their adherence to the Marxist scriptures. Their adherence was selective. They suppressed or ignored Marx's advocacy of violent revolution; and therefore clung the more obstinately to his economic analysis. This was not surprising. Marx saw more deeply than any previous observer; but he drew from the Lancashire textile industry generalizations of world-wide application. The capitalists would grow fewer and richer; the workers poorer and more numerous. In the end there would be nothing in between. Hence the working-class party would inevitably become 'the democracy' by the mere passage of time. The prophecy worked satisfactorily until just before the First World War. Then the German Social Democrats realized that their rate of increase was grinding to a stop, as that of the British Labour Party has now done. The insoluble dilemma was approaching: do we abandon Socialism or Democracy? The Bolsheviks, never having enjoyed Democracy, were to choose Socialism; others, doubtful in any case about Socialism, preferred to wait for the majority that never came.

This was not the only gap in Marx's teaching. He had always promised to provide the equation demonstrating the collapse of capitalism; but he never found it and for this reason left the second volume of *Capital* unfinished. He had nothing to say about the peasants except that they must be destroyed. Later Socialists have improved on this only by proposing (as Lenin did) that the peasants should be gulled until the moment for their destruction arrived. Again Marx had no answer to the national question except that it did not exist: 'The workers have no country.' The German leaders of the Second International interpreted this to mean that, since they had achieved their national freedom, the other peoples of Central Europe should be delighted to become Germans also. When this bargain failed to attract, the 'Austro-Marxists' of Vienna invented the legend of the Habsburg Monarchy as a great Free Trade area, an International in miniature; and their example has been loyally followed by Socialist enthusiasts for the British Commonwealth in our own day. The Second International was a combine of master-nations, secure in their own rights and be-wildered by the claims of others. Even more striking, the International was a purely European affair with a solitary Japanese representing nobody. The few Socialist parties outside Europe were the work of immigrants and usually faded away with the second generation. Professor Cole includes a chapter on China for the sake of Sun Yat Sen. It is modelled on Johnson's chapter on snakes in Iceland: there was no Socialism in China. In this the International reflected the universal assumption of the time. Europe was civilization; therefore no Socialist movement could flourish outside it.

The Second International carried belief in Progress to its highest point. Progress was both the inspiration of Social Democracy and its ruin. Marx shared with Samuel Smiles the belief that if men pursued their material betterment persistently enough Utopia would arrive. The only difference was that Marx preached this doctrine to the working class instead of to the entrepreneurs. But the principle was the same: demand higher wages, shorter hours, and International Socialism will be here in no time. The Social Democrats discovered to their confusion that the workers, having secured high wages and shorter hours, now demanded wages still higher and hours still shorter and that Socialism was further off than ever. This outcome affected the Social Democrats themselves. Once the German Social Democrats had built up a gigantic party-machine for class war, they shrank from using it for this or any other purpose. The party bosses came to regard themselves as the purpose of the party machine long before the Russian Communists made the same discovery. Ebert, Viktor Adler, or Arthur Henderson might well have said: 'We are all Stalinists nowadays.'

The same law operated between nations. The peoples of Europe had once been oppressed. By the end of the nineteenth century they were living on the plunder of the rest of the world as they still do. The more hard-headed Social Democrats proposed that the workers should enter into a junior partnership with their own capitalists for the exploitation of others—a line taken by some German Social Democrats during the First World War and by Ernest Bevin in England after the second. Most Socialists shrank from the cynicism, but they were not altogether at a loss. The Fabians, in particular, were delighted to demonstrate that the exploited peoples were being plundered for their own good. They differed from their rulers only in holding that the Powers should not run into conflict as to which should shoulder the greatest share of 'the white man's burden'. The international 'consortium' was a happy invention before the First World War; the international 'mandate' an even happier after it. The Second International held fast to its high principle: fair shares, at any rate for the Big Brothers.

Imperialism landed the Social Democrats in the problem of war, much to their surprise. Marx had given them no warning. He had blamed capitalism for being too pacific, not too warlike. The capitalists of Cobden's day had refused to fight the great war of liberation against Russia which Marx passionately advocated. Even now the Social Democrats went on dreaming that the magnates of finance would pull off a great merger at the last moment. Still they tried to discharge their responsibility. The Second International discussed the problem of war again and again. It laid down a simple truth: the workers could prevent war if they wished to do so. But suppose they did not wish to prevent war, what then? Viktor Adler gave the answer in 1914 when he supported Austria-Hungary's attack on Serbia the moment that the crowds in the streets of Vienna demonstrated in its favour. It is often said that the World War ruined International Socialism. A more careful reading of the record shows that it was the other way round. The Second International was already torn wide apart before the crisis of 1914. If it had possessed the unity and strength even of ten years before, the outbreak of war would have been impossible. Success ruined the Social Democrats. They thought that it was essential to be on the winning side; for, by definition, Progress means simply the side that wins. Things are much easier now that Progress has come to an end. Who cares about Success? Right is still Right though the heavens fall. And, by the way, the ones who stuck to their hopeless principles got Success as an unlooked-for bonus. Lenin achieved

16

THE OUTBREAK OF THE FIRST WORLD WAR

ON 4 August 1914, this country declared war on Germany. The European war had already started. Austria-Hungary declared war on Serbia on 28 July. Germany declared war on Russia on 1 August, and on France on 3 August. The Austrians, late as usual, declared war on Russia only on 6 August; Great Britain and France answered by declaring war on Austria-Hungary on 12 August. This delay was significant. Though the Austrians had wanted a war against Serbia, a general European war was not part of their plan, and their empire became its principal victim. Their little Balkan war was swamped in a struggle of the European Great Powers; and there began a general upheaval in Europe which destroyed its stable civilization—an upheaval which has lasted to the present day. The First World War caused vast destruction and the slaughter of more human beings than anything since the barbarian invasions. But its moral impact—the thing which made it difficult for men to think rationally about it—was that it came after a longer period of peace than any known in the recorded history of Europe.

Great Britain had not been involved in a general war since the battle of Waterloo in 1815. The last war between two European Powers had been the war between France and Germany which ended in 1871. There had been colonial wars; and there had been Balkan wars—the last in 1912 and 1913. But these had all been a long way from what was regarded as civilized Europe. Men went on talking about war; there were diplomatic crises; and every Great Power had vast armaments by the standards of the time. The British Navy had never been so powerful; and every Continental country had millions of men trained to enter the field. All the same, the reality of war was remote from men's minds. Everyone assumed that the system, or lack of it, would go on working, as it had worked for so long. There would be alarms and even mobilizations; but somehow peace would come out of it. War, in the phrase of the time, was unthinkable.

So, when war came everyone demanded an explanation; and the search for this has been going on ever since. Special institutes were set up for the study of war-origins; periodicals devoted solely to it were published. Every Great Power published thousands of diplomatic documents. A full bibliography, if one were ever made, of war-origins would run into thousands of volumes. We know what happened between 28 June and 4 August 1914 in more detail than we know of any other five weeks in history. Indeed, if we cannot understand these events and agree about them, we shall never understand or agree about anything. The problem was not merely historical. It went on being of burning political importance. The victorious allies insisted on Germany's war-guilt. The Germans challenged this; and the evidence which they produced shook many scholars, particularly in England and America. Germany, it was felt, had been harshly treated, hastily condemned; and these feelings made many people sympathize with German grievances even when they were voiced by Adolf Hitler. In fact the controversies over the origins of the First World War helped to bring about the second.

These controversies centred at first on the events which followed the murder of Archduke Franz Ferdinand of Austria at Sarajevo on 28 June. Soon men went much further back. The Germans blamed the Franco-Russian alliance which had been concluded in 1894; the French blamed the policy of Bismarck, although he left office in 1890. Others blamed things in general—the structure of alliances or the armaments of the Great Powers. Some blamed more specifically the armament manufacturers. Lenin and other Marxists after him blamed capitalist imperialism. Psychologists blamed the pugnacity of human nature. The worst of such general theories is that they will explain almost anything. The very things that are blamed for the war of 1914—secret diplomacy, the Balance of Power, the great Continental armies—also gave Europe a period of unparalleled peace; and now we are often inclined to think that, if only we could get back to them, we should have peace again. If we are going to probe far back into history, it is no good asking, 'What factors caused the outbreak of war?' The question is rather, 'Why did the factors that had long preserved the peace of Europe fail to do so in 1914?' Perhaps then we should conclude that diplomacy was not secret enough; that the balance did not balance properly; that the expenditure on armaments was too small.

I would point to one factor which has not perhaps been sufficiently explored. Men's minds seem to have been on edge in the last two or three years before the war in a way they had not been before, as though they had become unconsciously weary of peace and security. You can see it in things remote from international politics—in the artistic movement called Futurism, in the militant suffragettes of this country, in the working-class trend towards Syndicalism. Men wanted violence for its own sake; they welcomed war as a relief from materialism. European civilization was, in fact, breaking down even before war destroyed it. All the same, we have tended to look too much for the deeper causes of war and neglected its immediate outbreak. Despite these deeper causes, individual men took the decisions and sent the declarations of war. You may say that they should not bear all the responsibility, but they had some. If two or three men had acted differently, war would not have occurred at that particular moment. And we have a new guide. A famous Italian publisher, Luigi Albertini, when Mussolini excluded him from politics, turned to the study of war-origins. For nearly twenty years he studied the documents and interviewed the surviving statesmen. Two massive volumes of his work have been translated into English; with a third to come. It is unlikely that we shall ever know more of the political and diplomatic events which preceded the war of 1914. We might learn something more from the military records, particularly in Germany and Austria-Hungary, but not, I think, much.

Let me take the events as we know them. The starting-point was the assassination of Archduke Franz Ferdinand at Sarajevo. Why was he there at all? As a gesture of defiance against Serb nationalism; as a demonstration that Bosnia, though inhabited by Serbs and Croats, was going to remain part of the Austrian empire. That explains, too, why Princip and his friends set out to assassinate the Archduke. They were Bosnian Serbs who wanted their national freedom; and far from being encouraged by Serbia, still less acting under Serb orders, their activities were most unwelcome to the Serb Government. Serbia was just recovering from the Balkan wars of the previous year; she had not absorbed her new lands; and war with Austria-Hungary was the very last thing that the Serb Government wanted. No one has ever managed to show that the Serb Government had any connection with the plot, though they may have had some vague knowledge. Indeed it was easy to guess that an Austrian Archduke would be shot at if he visited Sarajevo on 28 June, Serbia's national day. One Serb knew all about it—

Colonel Dimitrevic, or Apis, as he was called, the head of a secret national society. But though he approved the plans, he did not initiate them, or give much serious help. The plot was the work of six young high-minded national idealists. Two of them are still alive. One is a professor at Belgrade University; the other curator of the museum at Sarajevo.

The plans of such young men are not very skilful. In fact all six of them missed their mark. Princip, the strongest character among them, was standing disconsolately on the pavement about to go home when an open car, with Franz Ferdinand in it, stopped right in front of him. The driver had taken a wrong turning and was now about to back. Princip stepped on to the running-board, killed Franz Ferdinand with one shot and, mistakenly, the Arch-duke's wife with the other—he had hoped to kill the governor of Bosnia. This was the crime of Sarajevo. The Austrian Government were not much concerned to punish it. They wanted to punish a different crime—the crime that Serbia committed by existing as a free national state. The Austrians wanted to prove that they were still a Great Power and somehow to destroy Serbia. They decided to go to war with Serbia, whatever her excuses and apologies. This was the first decision which brought about the world war. The man who made it was Count Berchtold, a frivolous aristocrat, but the Foreign Minister of Austria-Hungary.

He needed the approval of his German ally; and on 5 July he got it. William II, the German Emperor, agreed over the lunch table: Austria-Hungary, he said, must act against Serbia, even at the risk of war with Russia. Bethmann Hollweg, the Chancellor, turned up during the afternoon: and he approved also. There was no formal council, no weighty consideration of the issues. Of course the Germans were bluffing. They thought that Russia would let Serbia be destroyed. But, if not, they were ready for war. The German army was at the height of its strength; the French army was being reorganized; the Russian army would not be properly equipped until 1917. The German line was: if there is to be war, better now than later. William II often talked violently, though he usually repented soon afterwards. The new factor was that Bethmann also supported a policy leading to war. Hence this worthy, pacific man must bear more responsibility than any other individual for what followed. He alone could have stopped the war; and instead he let it happen.

After 5 July, nothing followed for nearly three weeks. The Austrians prepared an ultimatum to Serbia in their usual dilatory way. The other Powers were helpless; they could do nothing until the Austrian demands were known. All sorts of wild guesses have been made about French and Russian activities. But there is not a scrap of evidence that Russia promised to support Serbia or that France promised to support Russia. In fact Serbia agreed to nearly all the Austrian demands. It was no use. The Austrians broke off relations and on 28 July declared war. They did this deliberately, to make a peaceful outcome impossible. Now Russia had to do something. The Russians had no aggressive plans in Europe. In fact they had no interest in Europe except to be left alone. But they could not allow the Balkans, and so Constantinople and the Straits, to fall under the control of the Central Powers. If they did, their economic life, which in those days depended on the outer world, would be strangled — as indeed it was during the war. They tried to warn Austria-Hungary off Serbia. When that failed, they announced their mobilization, first against Austria-Hungary alone, then on 30 July a general mobilization. This was not an act of war — the Russian armies could not be ready for at least six weeks. It was a further gesture of diplomacy — a warning that Russia would not stand aside.

But it was also the last act of diplomacy. The German plans depended on getting in their blow first. If war came, whatever its cause, they must knock out France in the first six weeks and then turn with all their strength against Russia. The plan had been made by Schlieffen, who died in 1913. It made certain that any war in Europe must be a general war — it could not be localized; and it also made certain that, once Germany began to mobilize, war was inevitable. People everywhere had the habit of saying 'Mobilization means war'. This was only true of Germany; other countries had mobilized in the past without war: the British navy in 1911, the Austro-Hungarian army in October 1913. And it was true of Germany only because Schlieffen had said it must be true. In this sense a dead man had the deepest responsibility of all for the European war. On 31 July Germany began to mobilize. With this step effective diplomacy ceased. The diplomatists, and even the kings and emperors, went on trying; but there was nothing they could do. Once the German armies mobilized, war had to be brought on, not averted; and the German diplomatists had to do what they were told by the German soldiers. They were not being consciously more wicked than other diplomatists; they had been told for years that only the Schlieffen plan could save Germany, and they believed what they were told.

Russia was asked to stop mobilizing. When she refused, Germany declared war on her on 1 August. France was asked to promise to stay neutral and to surrender her principal fortresses as security. The French evaded this demand; and on 3 August the Germans declared war on them also. It is often said that the alliances caused the war; but the alliances were not observed in 1914. Germany had promised to aid Austria-Hungary if she were attacked by Russia; but in fact Germany declared war on Russia without this happening. France had promised to aid Russia if she were attacked by Germany. But in fact the French were attacked by Germany before they had made a decision of any kind. No doubt they would have decided to aid Russia; and maybe Russia would have attacked Austria-Hungary. As it was, neither of these things happened. The German rulers launched a preventive war.

As to Great Britain, the German generals never gave her a thought. She had no army on a Continental scale; and they never considered the British Navy. The German armies had to go through Belgium as part of the Schlieffen plan in order to knock out France; and it was the German invasion of Belgium which brought Great Britain into the war. People then and since said that this was not the real reason—that we were pledged to France or that we had encouraged Russia. The fact remains that, but for the invasion of Belgium, British policy would have been much more confused and hesitant, the British people certainly not united. As it was, the British action was not much more than a moral gesture. Their army contributed little: it was the French, not the British, who won the battle of the Marne.

Could the war of 1914 have been averted? You can make all kinds of conditions: if Austria-Hungary had given her peoples more national freedom; if nationalism had never been thought of; if Germany had relied more on her economic, and less on her military power. But in the circumstances of 1914, Great Britain could have kept out of war only if she had been prepared to let Germany defeat France and Russia. France could have kept out of war only if she had surrendered her independence as a Great Power. Russia could have kept out of war only if she had been willing to be strangled at the Straits. In short, they could have avoided war only by agreeing that Germany should become the dominant power of the Continent. None of these Powers decided on war. The three men who made the decisions—even if they too were the victims of circumstances—were Berchtold, Bethmann Hollweg, and the dead man Schlieffen.

17

MARX AND LENIN

UNIVERSITIES nowadays have Professors of almost everything—
Brewing at one, Race Relations at another, Town Planning at a
third. Yet there is still room for a pious benefactor. No university
has a Professor of Marxism; and the theoretical background of the
only religion which is still making converts on a grand scale remains
neglected. Mr. Plamenatz will be a strong candidate for this Chair
when it is created. It may seem unlikley that anyone should write
at this time of day a book about Marxism which is both new and
sensible; but Mr. Plamenatz has done it.[1] The existing books are
special pleading, almost without exception. They start by assum-
ing either that Marx was right or that he was wrong; and they
go on developing one or other of these assumptions at interminable length. Mr. Plamenatz has merely assumed that Marx
was a political thinker of the first rank, who should be taken seriously; and he has then examined Marxist doctrine with detached
common sense. He treats Lenin as a master of practical politics,
not as a serious thinker, and shows how Bolshevism transformed
Marxism, somewhat as Paul is said to have done with the teach-
ings of Christ.

Though this is a good book, it is not the book that Mr. Plamenatz set out to write, if his title is any guide. The first and more
important part is about Marx, not about German Marxism. But
Marx cannot be treated as a purely German thinker even in his
methods. He himself claimed to have combined German philosophy, English economics, and French politics; and this is a good
deal nearer the truth, though it would be still truer to say that he
rode three separate horses and never got them teamed together.
The only German quality in Marx was the 'dialectic' framework
which he learnt from Hegel; and, as Mr. Plamenatz shows, this
was a gigantic nuisance which Marx increasingly abandoned when
he wrote on serious questions. Marx's economics derived solely
from English writers, principally from Ricardo; and the practical
basis of them—made into a generalization of universal application

1. *German Marxism and Russian Communism.* By John Plamenatz.

—was capitalist England of the textile age. His political outlook was that of an extreme French radical; and the only political
events on which he made any valuable observations were the
French revolution of 1848 and the Paris Commune of 1871. The
English Labour party has come nearer than any other to applying
the economic part of Marx's programme; just as the French and
those who have learned from them are the only ones to have a
genuinely revolutionary proletariat.

Neither Marxist economics nor Marxist politics suited German
conditions; and the German Marxists had to adapt these doctrines
to quite different conditions, a process in which Engels himself
led the way. How they did this would make a fascinating study,
never yet attempted. It is not enough to mention Bernstein's re-
visionism or to assert that the German Social Democrats wanted a
welfare state, not social revolution. Such a study would have reinforced the argument of Mr. Plamenatz's book; for it would then
have appeared that the Germans set the example which the Russians followed. Kautsky first built up a Marxist orthodoxy devised
for German conditions; and Lenin learnt the trick from him. Both
were forcing a given theory to fit into existing conditions, instead
of deriving their theory from these conditions—a confusing, but
very usual, process. Mr. Plamenatz sees this clearly enough with
the Bolsheviks. They made a revolution, established themselves
in power, and then asked: 'how can Marxism be used to justify
what we have done?' But the Germans had done exactly the same;
and if Mr. Plamenatz had brought this out, he would then have
realized that it applied to Marx also. Marx wanted certain things;
and he therefore devised theories which proved that they would
happen. Principles and actions came before theory in Marx's case,
as in everyone else's.

Of course Mr. Plamenatz goes some way to recognizing this.
Indeed much of his book is given over to a careful logical demonstration that Marx's theories were dogmas, which could not be
justified by the facts. For instance, Marx insisted that the number
of labourers increased faster than the machines which employed
them; therefore 'the reserve army of the unemployed' would grow
ever larger. He expressed this by a mathematical formula which is
made more telling by being repeated again and again. But the
formula could be proved true only by statistics which Marx did
not possess and which indeed do not exist. As a matter of fact

scientists often proceed in this way. It is a great mistake to suppose that they generalize only from a random body of experience. More usually they first formulate a theory and then collect the evidence to prove that it is true. The great scientist is not distinguished by guessing less, but by guessing better. The process is much more difficult to apply in history. The natural scientist can make his laboratory produce the necessary evidence to justify his theory. The historian can only turn to the records; and these were never kept to answer the questions which he had in mind. Hence it has been plausibly maintained that no serious history can be attempted before about 1850, when accurate statistics begin; and even these are so faulty that some dismiss the possibility of rigorous history before the outbreak of the Second World War. All historians before then, including Marx, were literary artists — a description which most historians of the present day certainly do their best to avoid.

Marx's generalizations about history can never be shown to be either true or false. They are merely curious. It would be more rewarding to explain how he came by them and what results he expected from them. In fact what we want is a Marxist analysis of Marx. Mr. Plamenatz has a mastery of Marx's writings which would enable him to do it. Unfortunately, like most political theorists, he will not condescend to the routine task of learning history. He treats Marx in detachment without much reference to the intellectual climate of the time. He has therefore missed a discovery of the first importance, though he is constantly on the edge of it. For though Marx was the greatest of Socialist writers and the founder of modern Socialism, he was as a thinker the last flower of Individualism. He achieved Socialism simply by taking *laissez-faire* economics and rationalist psychology and standing them on their heads; but despite this inversion they remained individualist theories. Take, for instance, the class struggle, which is the central point of his doctrine. This is true only if we accept the principle — universally assumed in the middle of the nineteenth century — that every man recognizes his economic interest and pursues it. Every proletarian fights his employer and co-operates with every other proletarian; every peasant or shopkeeper knows that he belongs to a dying class and therefore joins the rising one. If rationalist individualism is true, then Socialism must follow from it. It is not true; and that is why we have not got Socialism.

In exactly the same way, Marxist economics are individualist economics. They assume the working of 'economic laws' and project them into the future. Mr. Plamenatz finds it puzzling why Marx thought that a capitalist should pursue higher profit when he had plenty already. But, given the contemporary assumption that capitalists were capitalists all the time, it must necessarily follow. If a man stopped behaving as a capitalist even for a minute of the day, economic laws would break down, as they always do in practice. Again, it seems an extraordinary thing that Marx had no theory of foreign trade; and the lack of it has handicapped Socialists from then until now. But in the era of Free Trade, no theory of foreign trade was necessary; or rather it was there already. Marx merely assumed that Socialist communities would go on trading with each other according to the best principles of the division of labour. Indeed he even assumed that Socialism would work without planning or conscious forethought; and so it would, if every man followed his own economic interest logically.

Similarly, when Marx came to politics, he shared the individualist radicalism of his time. He, too, assumed that it was highly desirable to strangle the last king with the bowels of the last priest; and he believed that inestimable benefit would follow from this. His only novelty was to show that the last capitalists (and by Marxist laws these would be few) should be strangled at the same time. Mr. Plamenatz keeps asking impatiently: 'but why should Utopia arrive merely because this curious operation has been carried out?' Marx would have answered: 'Because every serious political thinker of my time from Bentham to Mazzini says so.' Marx was superior to his contemporaries in seeing that democracy could not work without a social revolution; but, living in the age of rationalism, he could not be expected to see that it needed a psychological revolution also.

This surely explains Lenin's creation of a new Marxist theory. Mr. Plamenatz makes it clear that he was a different sort of man; but this is not an interesting discovery—all men are different, as well as being the same. The important thing is that he was a man of a different age. Marx was a rationalist, believing in Progress and anxious to discover its laws. He was satisfied when he showed that progress was going in the same direction as himself. Lenin belonged to the age of collective man and of the struggle for power. He himself once said that the only interesting question in life was

F

'who whom?' Who exploits whom? Who sentences whom to death? He was not interested in where history was going. He wanted to know how to get to the right end of a gun and stay there. This is not an attractive question for the political theorist, but it has its importance in certain societies and at certain moments. Leninism is not a political philosophy; it is a guide to political practice in the era of gangster-warfare, the sort of guide that Marx often tried to write but never succeeded. Mr. Plamenatz suggests that Lenin vulgarized Marx's theories and perverted them. But he believes this only because he prefers the age of rational individualism to that of the gangsters. Everyone can have his private tastes, but they have no place in historical study. John Stuart Mill has long been in his grave; and we have to live with the secret police, the televised politician and the hydrogen bomb. 'Who whom?' is a question that will last our time.

18

TROTSKY

ONE early morning, in October 1902, Mr. and Mrs. 'Richter' were still abed in their lodgings near King's Cross. There was a violent knocking at the door. Mrs. Richter, opening it, called out: '*The Pen* has arrived!' In this way Trotsky, 'the young eagle', burst—under his first pseudonym—into Lenin's life. The meeting was a symbol of their future. Lenin was orderly, quiet in speech and habit, hardly to be distinguished from his neighbours. Trotsky rode contemptuously over the conventions, knocking violently at doors and expecting them to open at the impact of his genius. He was at a loss when there was no door to force open. Lenin was to end as a sacred mummy, in the silence of death still dominating the lives of two hundred million people. Trotsky was to be murdered far from Europe and—what would seem worse to him—his very name has been erased from the history-books. Mention Bronstein, and men think you are referring to a chess player. The greatest writer and perhaps the greatest leader that revolution ever produced is forgotten; and the younger generation of readers will puzzle why a book has been devoted to him.

Mr. Deutscher has done a striking work of rehabilitation.[1] This is the story of Trotsky's triumph. It carries him through the victory of the revolution and the civil war to his highest moment, when he seemed the predestined successor of Lenin. A further volume will tell the story of his fall and of his unquenchable resistance until he was rubbed out by an ice-pick. Mr. Deutscher has mastered all the printed sources and has been the first to use extensively the Trotsky archives now at Harvard. Yet it may be questioned whether he is the right man for the subject. We can perhaps get over his ponderous style, suitable enough when he is pontificating on Bolshevism in the columns of the Astor press. But, like all Marxists—even the lapsed ones—he wants always to discover profound historical forces where there was only the will of men. He writes of the early Bolsheviks: 'Lenin's party had its roots deep in Russian soil'; this of some two or three thousand men, bewitched by an academic

1. *The Prophet Armed: Trotsky 1879–1921.* By Isaac Deutscher.

ideal. In 1917 'the whole dynamic of Russian history was impelling
Lenin and Trotsky, their party, and their country towards the
revolution'; when it would be truer to say that these two wrenched
'history' (whatever that may mean) violently from its course. In
the most preposterous passage of all he describes the Russian working class of 1917 (who, poor chaps, had no idea what was happening to them) as

> one of history's wonders. Small in numbers, young, inexperienced,
> uneducated, it was rich in political passion, generosity, idealism, and
> rare heroic qualities. . . . With its semi-illiterate thoughts it embraced
> the idea of the republic of the philosophers.

The reader must put up with this hocus-pocus for the sake of the
gigantic individual who overshadows it.

Trotsky himself used to claim that history was on his side.
When he came to the Congress of Soviets fresh from the conquest
of power, he called to the protesting Mensheviks: 'You have
played out your role. Go where you belong: to the dustheap of
history.' Yet no man ever chose his role in greater isolation or followed a course of more determined individualism. Trotsky carried
to its peak the era of individual greatness which had begun with the
French Revolution. His was a more powerful voice than Danton's,
self-educated, self-made, self-advised. One could say of him as of
Napoleon: 'his presence on the battlefield was worth ten divisions'.
It is ironic that Trotsky, the greatest of revolutionary Socialists,
should have owed his success to liberal enterprise and capitalist
freedom. The age of the individual was finished when men were
eclipsed by machines—and nowhere more decisively than by the
machine of the great political party. In the First World War genius
still counted. Lloyd George, Clémenceau, Trotsky, were each in
their separate ways the saviours of their countries. It is no accident
that the careers of all three ended in barren failure when the war
was over. The leaders of the Second World War needed bureau-
cracies and party organizations. Even Winston Churchill had to
become leader of the Conservative party; and only backward
countries, Yugoslavia or France, could produce heroes—a Tito or a
de Gaulle. Trotsky came just in time. Now he could never rise from
provincial obscurity.

Trotsky had no background of Marxist training or of party
experience. Mr. Deutscher writes: 'He diligently studied Marxism,

which in this its golden age gave the adept a solid mental equipment.' In reality Trotsky learnt from Marxism only that capitalism was doomed—a fact which he knew instinctively already. His own writings that have survived never dealt with economic developments; they were concerned always with poiltical strategy, owing more to Clausewitz than to Marx. He never adapted himself to the needs of practical work in a party. When he first came to London in 1902 it was as a detached individual; and he stood outside the conflict between Bolshevik and Menshevik. Though himself a revolutionary, he opposed Lenin's exclusiveness; and always hoped to close the breach between the two Socialist currents. Even after the revolution of 1905, when his actions had outstripped Bolshevik theory, he kept up a tolerant association with the Mensheviks; and the outbreak of the First World War found him more solitary than ever. He joined the Bolshevik party only in the summer of 1917, some two months before he was to carry it to supreme power. The exact date is unknown; and the possession of a party-card meant nothing to him. His position in the world did not depend on the accuracy of a filing-cabinet.

In the slovenly decay of imperial Russia Trotsky's voice could fill a continent. When the revolution of 1905 broke out, he was an unknown youth of twenty-five. At St. Petersburg, knowing nobody, representing nobody, he forced himself on to the Soviet; and before it ended he was its dominating figure. At the final meeting he even ruled out of order the police officer who had come to arrest the members: 'Please do not interfere with the speaker. If you wish to take the floor, you must give your name.' In those days words were more powerful than armies. It was the same on a more gigantic scale in 1917. The Bolsheviks did not carry Trotsky to power; he carried them. Lenin made the party resolve on insurrection, but he was still in hiding when it broke out and at first could not believe in its success. The seizure of power in October was Trotsky's work; and Lenin acknowledged this immediately afterwards, with supreme generosity, when he proposed that Trotsky be put at the head of the new revolutionary government. One may even ask—what did Lenin and the Bolsheviks do during the civil war? They held on clumsily to the reins of civil power in Moscow. It was Trotsky who created the armies; chose the officers; determined the strategy; and inspired the soldiers. Every interference by the Soviet government was a mistake; and the greatest mistake was the campaign against Poland, which Trotsky opposed. The achievement was not only one of organization. It was the impact of a fiery personality, the sparks from which flew round the world.

The man of action in Trotsky was always second to the man of words, even at the greatest moments of decision. He was never happy over a victory until he had written about it; and in later years literary triumph seemed almost to atone with him for the bitterness of defeat. Bernard Shaw said that, as a political pamphleteer, he 'surpassed Junius and Burke'; what is even more to the point, he is the only Marxist who has possessed literary genius. Time and again the force of this genius posed problems that were still unperceived by others and even pointed to solutions that were unwelcome to Trotsky himself. Immediately after the revolution of 1905, when he was still in prison, he discovered the central dilemma which a victorious Russian revolution would face and which indeed the Soviet Union still faces. How was revolutionary Russia to maintain itself in a hostile world? Backwardness made revolution easy, but survival difficult. Trotsky gave already the answer to which he adhered all his life: permanent revolution. The Russian revolution must touch off revolutions elsewhere. 'The working class of Russia will become the initiator of the liquidation of capitalism on a global scale.' It was in this belief that Trotsky led the revolution of 1917, defied the German empire at Brest-Litovsk, and composed the most ringing phrases in the foundation manifesto of the Communist International. But what if the more advanced proletariat failed to respond? It was useless to maintain for long Trotsky's earliest answer: 'luckily for mankind, this is impossible'.

The impossible is what men get from events—and often at its most unwelcome. Trotsky foresaw even in 1905 the conflict that would follow between workers and peasants, if they were ever cooped up together in isolation. Once more he fell back on pious hope. The working class would remain by its very nature enlightened, progressive, tolerant. Somehow 'proletarian dictatorship' would escape the evils which other forms of dictatorship had always produced. Did Trotsky ever believe this? It seems unlikely. In the early days of doctrinal dispute he always preached toleration, despite his own sharp and wounding phrases. Lenin had an easier time of it. Both men understood the virtue of intellectual freedom. But for Lenin it was one of the many bourgeois virtues that he was

prepared to discard—confident that Communism would resurrect
it in a higher form. In just the same way he was ready to write off
the greatest artistic achievements of the past. The very wonder of
them was an embarrassment in the present. Trotsky could never
bring himself to renounce European civilization. He recognized
Russia's backwardness and resented being associated with it—an
attitude possible for a Jew, but repugnant even to Lenin. As the
net of intolerance drew tighter, as the European revolutions failed
and the Russian masses became increasingly discontented, Trotsky
grew more explosive.

His response was characteristic. At one bound he reached
totalitarianism in its most ruthless form. His own gifts betrayed
him. A dictator lurks in every forceful writer. Power over words
leads easily to a longing for power over men. Trotsky could
never resist a challenge. He wrote *The Defence of Terrorism* at
the height of his labours during the civil war; and he justified
the conquest of Georgia against the Social Democrats of
western Europe, though he had himself opposed it. Now in 1921 he
preached the militarization of labour and permanent dictatorship of
the Communist party. Lenin restrained him. But the weapons which
Trotsky forged then were soon to be turned against him by Stalin.
He was to purge his betrayal of freedom by many years of resistance and exile. The glories of his revolutionary triumph pale before
the nobility of his later defeats. The spirit of man was irrepressible
in him. Colonel Robins, the American military representative at
Petrograd, pronounced history's verdict: 'A four-kind son-of-a-
bitch, but the greatest Jew since Jesus Christ.'

19

THE GERMAN ARMY IN POLITICS

MR. GORDON CRAIG, of Princeton University, has written a fascinating book on the part played in German politics by the Army from its foundation by the Great Elector in 1640 to the disintegration of both Army and State in the defeat of 1945.[1] Most of it is based on well-known printed sources, though it is none the worse for that. Narrative is the lifeblood of history; and scholars err grievously if they think they have discharged the historian's task by writing articles or books of learned detail. Mr. Craig has also some new material which is worth special notice. He has had a free run of the German military archives which the Americans carried off to Washington in 1945. It is exasperating to reflect that the German naval archives were similarly carried off to London (where they still are) but that no British historian has been able to use them. Think what we might have done with them! We might, for example, have found out whether there was any truth in the stories of German acceleration which launched the great 'We want eight' naval scare of 1909. But British Government departments regard historians with suspicion and guard German secrets as eagerly as they guard their own.

Mr. Craig's 'plums' come from two periods when the Army was faced with a challenge from liberalism. The first is the years 1862–4, when Bismarck came to power. Everyone knows that Roon, as Minister of War, defended the Army from the attempts by the Prussian Chamber to determine its size and character. Mr. Craig shows from Roon's papers that he was also threatened from the other side by even more reactionary generals, particularly Edwin von Manteuffel, who wished to destroy the Prussian Constitution altogether. Bismarck certainly defeated the Chamber; but he and Roon also defeated Manteuffel, and their skilful diplomacy finally removed him from close personal contact with the king. Bismarck takes on a new appearance when he is shown as the saviour of the constitutional balance against liberals and generals alike. Indeed, though Bismarck always resisted parliamentary sovereignty, he

1. *The Politics of the Prussian Army, 1640–1945.* By Gordon A. Craig.

successfully asserted civilian authority (his own) against the
Prussian generals. The complicated structure of evasion and confusion which the German generals built up after 1871 was designed
to thwart none other than Bismarck. He was too much for them.
The elder Moltke was never allowed to influence policy. It needed
the feebleness of later Chancellors and the fickleness of William II
for Schlieffen to be free to dictate plans which made a general war
inevitable. In this sense William II and Bethmann were the true
'war criminals' of 1914.

The most substantial of Mr. Craig's revelations concern the
Weimar Republic. The papers of Groener, Seeckt, and Stresemann
are his principal sources. Here again much of the story is already
known. Other writers have described the pact between Groener
and Ebert, by which the Army agreed to defend the Republic on
condition that the Republic should protect the Army. Groener's
manoeuvres against the peace treaty are, however, new. When he
first read the terms he noted: 'The proposals will be contested all
the easier because they are so laughable.' He imagined that the
Germans would be allowed to take part in the negotiations and
that it would be easy to play on the differences between the Allies
—hence his secret discussions with an American representative,
Colonel Conger. His second, stronger card was to offer to the
victors a German alliance against Soviet Russia. His calculations
proved totally wrong; and it must be said in his honour that he
faced the duty of accepting the Treaty of Versailles. He told the
officers of the Supreme Command: 'I have undertaken great
responsibility by my action, but I will know how to bear it.'

After Versailles Seeckt organized the new force of 100,000 men
which was to keep the German Army alive for the future. Curiously enough the very limitation of the Army made Seeckt the most
independent and arrogant of all German generals. In a mass
army the rank-and-file were loyal to the symbol of the State—in
the old Army to the Emperor, after 1933 to Hitler. Seeckt's men
were pure 'legionaries' who looked only to their commanders. The
tragi-comedy of Seeckt's successors, from Fritsch to the 'resisters'
of 1944, was that they went on imagining that they could behave
like Seeckt when Hitler had really stolen the Army from them.
If the generals had come out against Hitler the troops would have
refused to obey them. This, and this only, is the truth about 'the
revolt of the generals'. Seeckt, however, could adopt an attitude of

F*

neutrality towards the Republic; he could even dream of making himself dictator. But in the end a civilian brought him down. Seeckt wanted to stake all German policy on an alliance with Soviet Russia; Stresemann balanced between West and East without committing himself decisively to either. When Seeckt opposed Locarno Stresemann got rid of him.

After 1928 the weakness of the politicians brought new opportunity to the generals—or perhaps imposed it upon them. Mr. Craig shows how Groener, now Minister of War, and his assistant Schleicher were the real makers of Bruening's Cabinet. They imagined that it would stand above party intrigue and give Germany 'strong' government. Groener wrote of Bruening: 'His attitude in Parliament towards the babblers is nothing short of an aesthetic pleasure. I have concluded a firm alliance with him.' And again: 'I have never known a statesman, Chancellor, Minister, or general who combined in his head as much positive knowledge and political clarity and adaptability as Bruening.' What ruined Groener was his attempt to suppress the S.A. Schleicher thought that he was 'keeping the Army out of politics' when he organized Groener's fall. Six months later Schleicher became Chancellor himself, only to fail still more catastrophically. He is often said to have tried to keep Hitler out of power. On the contrary, Schleicher regarded the return of Papen as a far greater danger and strained every nerve to create a Hitler Government. The ironical outcome was a Government which contained both Hitler and Papen—the Army's last gift to the German people.

There is a more general point. We often talk of 'Junker' generals and officers. Only half the officers were of Junker origin before 1914; only one in five after the First World War. The old Army, say before 1870, perhaps existed in part to defend the interests of the Junker landowners. The twentieth-century Army merely defended itself, like any other bureaucracy such as the Coal Board or British Railways. The more one studies Mr. Craig's book the more one reaches the conclusion that the faults of the German Army sprang less from the arrogance of its generals than from the weakness of the politicians. Bismarck kept the generals in order; and so did Hitler after him under very different conditions. If the Germans ever produce liberal statesmen of any guts the Army will give no trouble. As it is, the picture of German generals once more at Supreme Headquarters is bound to stir an anticipatory shudder.

20

HITLER'S SEIZURE OF POWER

NATIONAL SOCIALISM was based on fraud; and no fraud was greater than the legend that a seizure of power by Hitler took place on 30 January 1933. Certainly this day, on which Hitler became Chancellor, was the most important moment in his life and a turning-point in German history. But there was no seizure of power. That had been tried by Hitler at Munich in November 1923. It had failed; and he was determined never to repeat the attempt. There was an alternative path to power which he sometimes contemplated: that the Nazi party should actually win a majority of the popular vote and thus install Hitler as Chancellor by strict democratic choice. But this alternative, too, proved beyond him. The Nazis never received more than 37 per cent of votes at a free election for the Reichstag. The third path, and that which Hitler followed, was the way of intrigue; he would become Chancellor as the leader of a minority and would then use the power of the State to establish his dictatorship. The answer to the question how Hitler came to power is therefore to be found more in the actions of those German politicians who were not National Socialists than in those of Hitler himself. He waited; they decided.

The Weimar Republic always suffered from a multiplicity of parties. No single party ever possessed a majority in the Reichstag; and every German Government after 1918 rested on a coalition. This would have mattered less if there had been at least a majority in favour of the Republic; but this, too, was lacking after the first elections in 1919. The middle-class Liberal parties faded and disappeared. Only the Social Democrats remained a genuine Weimar party. The Nationalists welcomed anything that weakened the Republic; the Communists welcomed anything that discredited the Social Democrats. The Roman Catholic Centre party certainly took part in republican governments along with the Social Democrats; but it had no republican principles. It was a sectarian party, ready to work with any system that would protect Roman Catholic interests; and in the last days of the Republic it stretched out its hand to the forces of destruction, just as in the last days of the Empire it had turned to the republicans. Every party contributed to the fall of the Weimar Republic—the Social Democrats from timidity, the others with conscious ill-will. But none contributed with such cynicism as the Centre—indifferent to the Republic or even to Germany, so long as the Roman Catholic schools enjoyed their favoured position.

The failure to establish strong stable governments brought un-expected power to the President. The makers of the constitution in 1919 had intended to give him the position of monarch in a parliamentary state: choosing the Chancellor, but without inde-pendent authority in himself. The Chancellor was to be the heir of Bismarck, the true wielder of power. But the short-lived Chan-cellors never held this position. They were little more than parlia-mentary managers for the President. Even Ebert drew on his reserve of authority. Hindenburg, who became President in 1925, possessed it in greater measure and believed that his duty was to use it. Moreover, as the military leader of the World War, Hinden-burg both commanded the allegiance of the army and voiced its demands. The army was the one stable point of order in an un-stable society. It is a mistake to suggest, as some have done, that the army chiefs were bent on overthrowing the Republic. They would have attempted this only if the republican politicians had accepted permanently and sincerely the disarmament imposed upon Germany by the Treaty of Versailles; and none did so. The generals were willing to work with the Republic if it provided stable government. But this it failed to do; and the generals were ob-sessed with anxiety lest Germany's limited army, the Reichswehr, be called upon to intervene in civil strife. They did not make this civil strife, nor even welcome it. They were insistent that a civil solution should be found for it. That solution, they supposed, could only be strong government; and, since this was beyond the Republic, it must come in some other form. They were indifferent whether this form should be a presidial government (i.e., one resting on the authority of the President), monarchy, or dictator-ship. Their overriding concern was to keep the army out of politics.

There was another impulse making for strong government be-tween 1929 and 1933. These were the years of the great depression, which—starting in the United States—carried unemployment and

financial collapse across the world. Keynesian economics were unknown, at least among public men; and it was universally supposed
that, when men lacked the money to buy goods, the answer to the
crisis was to deprive them even of the little money that they had.
When, in the autumn of 1931, the British National Government
unwillingly abandoned the gold standard, and so stumbled on the
path to recovery, a former Labour minister exclaimed plaintively:
'No one told us we could do this!' His ignorance was universally
shared. The only solution proposed was the reduction of wages and
unemployment benefit; and for this a strong government was
needed. Moreover, in times of bewilderment and distress, men
demand authority for its own sake. They have no idea what should
be done, but they long for a commanding voice which will resolve
their doubts. Here again it is a mistake to suppose that Germany's
economic leaders were consciously set on overthrowing the
Republic or destroying the trade unions. They would have accepted
a republican leader if one had appeared with unquestioned authority
and self-confidence, just as Franklin D. Roosevelt was accepted by
the business leaders of the U.S.A. But they demanded strong
government from somebody; and they were rightly convinced that
the Republic could not provide it.

This, then, was the background of Hitler's rise to power. Far from
his hammering at a door which was long kept closed against him,
he was constantly being invited to enter by those within; and he
held back in order to increase his market value. Everyone assumed
that he would end up as Chancellor sooner or later. The real
problem in German history is why so few of the educated, civilized
classes recognized Hitler as the embodiment of evil. University
professors; army officers; business-men and bankers—these had a
background of culture, and even of respect for law. Yet virtually
none of them exclaimed: 'This is anti-Christ.' Later, they were to
make out that Hitler had deceived them and that the bestial nature
of National Socialism could not have been foreseen. This is not
true. The real character of National Socialism was exposed by
many foreign, and even by some German, observers long before
Hitler came to power. It could be judged from Hitler's writings
and his speeches; it was displayed in every street brawl that the
Nazi Brown Shirts organized. Hitler did not deceive the responsible classes in Germany: they deceived themselves. Their self-
deception had a simple cause: they were engaged in fighting the

wrong battle and in saving Germany from the wrong enemy. Hitler's hostility to Communism was his strongest asset. The Bolshevik peril in Germany had once perhaps been real: therefore anyone who was anti-Communist seemed to be on the side of civilization, and the Communists themselves fed this illusion by treating Hitler as their only serious enemy. 'Better Hitler than Communism' was the phrase which opened the way for Hitler first within Germany and then on a wider scale in Europe.

Further, the directors of German policy were obsessed with the struggle against the Treaty of Versailles. They regarded the disarmament clauses as a personal humiliation; and they genuinely believed, though without justification, that reparations were the cause of Germany's economic difficulties. They could not repudiate wholeheartedly a movement which raged against the Versailles system. Rather they welcomed it as an ally. Every advance of National Socialism strengthened the argument that Germany should receive concessions in foreign affairs—otherwise the National Socialists would get stronger still. And the argument was not without force. Can any English or French observer honestly maintain that reparations would have been ended or the Rhineland evacuated without the mounting shadow of Hitler? Even apart from questions of foreign policy, respectable Germans—especially army officers—were bound to look with favour on a movement equipped with uniforms and acting under military discipline. More than one general remarked: 'It would be a shame to have to fire on these splendid young men in their brown shirts.' Experience in other countries has repeatedly shown that the only answer to a Fascist party, with an organized private army, is to suppress it by force of law. The Red peril and the system of Versailles made it impossible to give this answer in Germany.

Even so, the lack of alarm among civilized Germans remains a strange puzzle. The explanation may perhaps be found in the taste which so many of them had for political intrigue. A country with a long constitutional history develops a political class. The politicians look after government. The generals and bankers and professors mind their own business. This has always been true in England; and it was largely true in the third French republic, despite an occasional political general. In Germany men were always coming in from outside; a political class never had a chance to develop. Even Bismarck was a gifted amateur, who knew nothing of politics until he started at the top. Of his successors as Imperial Chancellor, one was a general, one a diplomatist, one a civil servant. In the reign of William II generals like Waldersee and Ludendorff pushed into politics on one side; and business-men like Ballin or Rathenau pushed in on the other. The practice was maintained in the Weimar Republic. There was no true statesman in Germany after the death of Stresemann in 1929. Her fate was in the hands of amateurs, who mistook intrigue for political activity. Hindenburg, the President, was a retired professional soldier, a field-marshal over eighty years old. Bruening, who became Chancellor in 1930, was half scholar, half army captain, but never strictly a party leader. Papen, his successor, was a dashing cavalry-man of great wealth, with no political standing. Schleicher, the most influential of all, lived for intrigue and nothing else: claiming to represent army opinion with the President and the President's authority to the army, but in fact playing off one against the other. All four thought that they were a great deal cleverer than Hitler and that they would take him prisoner in no time. They never feared Hitler or took precautions against him. Indeed, the fact that he was a politician and the leader of a political party made them despise him, as they despised the other politicians. The Austrian generals of the old regime made much the same mistake when they came up against Bonaparte.

Intrigue took the place of politics when Bruening became Chancellor in March 1930. The previous republican governments claimed to rest on a majority of the Reichstag, even though the claim was not always justified. Bruening did not attempt to construct a parliamentary Cabinet. He relied on the authority of the President and ordered the Reichstag to vote for him, much as Bismarck had done in his great days. The Reichstag had not always responded to Bismarck's commands; it was even less likely to be overawed by Bruening. In July 1930 his measures were defeated; and the Reichstag was dissolved. Political theorists in other countries with a multiplicity of parties often lament that the executive cannot threaten parliament with dissolution. The German example shows that the remedy can be worse than the disease. General elections may provide a solution when they are contested by two strong parties. But the voter cannot be expected to solve the riddle that has baffled his leaders. A dissolution could have only one effect in the existing circumstances. The voters were told by Bruening, the Chancellor, that all the parties were equally factious and difficult. Many voters therefore turned to the political leader who said exactly the same. And this leader was Hitler. The National Socialist party had been an insignificant group in the previous Reichstag. It was inflated and artificially fostered by the repeated electoral campaigns of the two years that followed. How otherwise could the voters respond to Bruening's demand and return a Reichstag of a different character? If there had been no 'Bruening experiment', and hence no general election in September 1930; if Germany had struggled on with weak coalition governments throughout the great depression, the National Socialist party would never have won at the polls and Hitler would never have triumphed.

The election of September 1930 brought great gains to the National Socialists, and only slightly smaller gains to the Communists. It lessened Bruening's chance of achieving a parliamentary majority. Even now there was plenty of time for the forces of order and decency to unite against National Socialist barbarism. But Hitler's victory elated the political jugglers, instead of frightening them. They imagined that they could use the threat of National Socialism against the other parties in the Reichstag without ever being endangered themselves; and they even hoped that Hitler would be obliging enough to act as their agent. Bruening depended on the authority of President Hindenburg; but the President's term ran out in 1932. At the beginning of the year Bruening proposed a bargain to Hitler: Hindenburg's term should be prolonged for one or two years; then Bruening would resign, and the way would be clear for Hitler. Bruening's calculation was clear. Hitler was to perform a service now in exchange for a reward that might never have to be paid. Hitler's answer was equally clear: Bruening must be dismissed and a new Reichstag elected (with, no doubt, a larger Nazi representation); then he would support a prolongation of Hindenburg's term. In other words, he must have his price before he would perform his service. The negotiations broke down. A presidential election was held, with Hitler as candidate of the Nazis and the Nationalists, Hindenburg—absurdly enough—as the candidate of the Left, including the Social Democrats. Hindenburg was elected. The voters had rejected National Socialism; but they had not supported anything, except a figurehead of eighty-five. The problem of finding a strong government, based on a Reichstag majority, remained.

Bruening did not recognize this problem. He proposed to remain in office and to continue to govern with the support of the President and the Reichswehr. But this programme was rejected by the generals and, above all, by Schleicher, their political spokesman; they were determined not to be drawn into the conflict of parties. Bruening and Groener, his Minister of Defence, thought that they could now act against Hitler. On 14 April 1932 the Nazi armed forces were dissolved by decree. On 12 May Schleicher told Groener that the Reichswehr had no confidence in him; and the following day he resigned. A fortnight later, on 30 May, Bruening also resigned, on Hindenburg's order. The old man had been persuaded that Bruening was the sole obstacle to a deal with Hitler and so to a government with a democratic majority. The instrument chosen for this deal was Franz von Papen, a wealthy aristocrat of no sense, though much courage. Schleicher said of him: 'People sometimes say that Herr von Papen is frivolous. But that is what we need.' And Papen characterized himself when he asked an economist for a programme: 'I know nothing of economics, but I'll do whatever you suggest. I'm a gentleman-rider; and I'll jump, I'll jump.'

Papen, like Bruening, was a member of the Centre Party, though, unlike Bruening, he carried no weight in it. Schleicher did not understand this. He supposed that the Centre would support Papen and, with Hitler supporting him as well, the 'functioning Reichstag' would be made. This scheme at once broke down. The Centre insisted that Hitler must take real responsibility, not exercise influence behind the scenes; failing this, they opposed Papen's government. Hitler, on his side, demanded power; and he, too, continued in opposition when this was refused. Papen's was perhaps the weakest government that has ever ruled a great country—a Cabinet of elderly 'Barons' and no support at all in the Reichstag. This did not worry Papen. He was content to wait until Hitler came to heel. And Hitler also waited until Papen's difficulties swept him away. Both gambled on Germany's distress—the one a vain intriguer, the other the greatest demagogue of modern times. In June, Papen dissolved the Reichstag, not with any hope of getting support for himself, but solely as a demonstration to Hitler that he could wear him down. The Nazi election funds would not last for ever; and, besides, the voters might turn elsewhere if Hitler failed to achieve anything.

The election of 31 July gave Hitler his greatest success: 37·3 per cent of the votes cast. But he was still far from an independent majority, and the Nazi rate of increase was slowing down. In fact, as the next election showed, the tide had already turned. The bargaining of May was renewed. Hitler demanded full power; himself as Chancellor, other Nazis in all the key posts. It is true that he was prepared to include also some non-Nazis and asked only 'as much power as Mussolini got in 1922'. Papen and Schleicher were not well-grounded in current history. They only knew that Mussolini was dictator of Italy, and forgot the slow process by which he had reached that position. In any case, the analogy was revealing enough: however Hitler began, he, too, would end as dictator, and they were only prepared to employ him as their parliamentary agent. They offered Hitler the post of Vice-Chancellor, safely under Papen's control. On 13 August Hitler was summoned to appear before Hindenburg. The President rated him for the violence and illegality of the Nazi party. 'He was ready to accept Hitler in a coalition government . . . but he could not take responsibility for giving exclusive power to Hitler alone.' Hitler tried to repeat that he wanted 'only as much as Mussolini'. The fatal analogy roused Hindenburg's anger.

The interview of 13 August was the sharpest set-back that National Socialism ever received. Until then its prestige and the votes cast for it had been growing steadily. Hitler had spoken openly of the seizure of power and of the 'St. Bartholomew's night' that would follow. Now it was clearly established that the so-called national revolution could take place only with the permission of the President. And that permission had been refused. Papen's gamble seemed to be working. Many of the lesser Nazis lost heart. Some worried over their security as deputies; a few over the future of the party. Hitler's great triumph lay in the iron control which he managed to maintain over his party during the next few months. If it had once begun to crumble, he would have been left isolated in a very short time. It is in this sense that Hitler was brought to power by his gifts for leadership. The National Socialist party was never strong enough to force Hitler into power; but he never needed to look over his shoulder. The other politicians worried about their followers and their voters; and worry breaks a politician's nerve sooner or later. Hitler always assumed that his control of the party was unshakable—rather as Napoleon always assumed that he would win a battle, and therefore never wasted men in securing a line of retreat.

But for the moment it was Papen who went over to the offensive. On 12 September the Reichstag was again dissolved; and Germany was involved in yet another general election, in order to wear down the National Socialists. The results, which came in on 6 November, seemed to confirm Papen's calculation. The Nazis lost two million votes; their share of the total fell to 33 per cent and their deputies from 230 to 196. It was less encouraging that most of these votes were transferred to the Communists, who increased their representation to 100. Still, Papen hoped to repeat his manœuvre of August under more favourable conditions: Hitler should be offered office without power, under strict control, in order to save himself from further decline. On 16 November Hitler again refused. Papen swung over to his alternative line: he would show that no one was capable of producing a parliamentary majority, and would then transform his temporary dictatorship into a permanent one. Instead of again dissolving the Reichstag, he would govern without it. On 17 November Papen resigned, ostensibly to give Hitler his chance. The step was meant as a pretence; for Hitler could obviously not produce a Reichstag majority. He came again to Hindenburg, this time in a rather more friendly atmosphere. But the deadlock remained. Hindenburg would make Hitler Chancellor if he could offer 'a secure workable majority in the Reichstag with a coherent programme'. Hitler demanded to be made Chancellor on the same terms as Papen—governing, that is, on the President's authority. Hindenburg refused. With Hitler as Chancellor, the Cabinet would not be a presidential government, but a party dictatorship. The future was to prove him right.

Papen seemed to have played his cards correctly. He could now resume office without being open to the reproach of barring the way against a majority cabinet. On 1 December he went to Hindenburg with his plan: he would prorogue the Reichstag, proclaim a state of emergency, and govern by decree. If there was opposition from Nazis or Communists, he would crush it by force. But this was the very proposal for involving the Reichswehr in civil strife which the generals had always rejected. Schleicher opposed Papen's scheme, both as Hindenburg's military adviser and as spokesman of the army. Besides, he claimed he could succeed where Bruening and Papen had failed: he could provide a parliamentary majority.

He had been negotiating with Nazi leaders, such as Gregor Strasser, who were dissatisfied with Hitler's rigid line; and he believed, as well, that he could win the support of the trade unions. The Social Democrats, the Centre, and the dissident Nazis would give him a workable coalition. Hindenburg preferred Papen to Schleicher; and he authorized him to form a government.

But Schleicher soon carried the day. On 2 December the new Cabinet met. Schleicher produced a report from Major Ott of the General Staff, which asserted that the Reichswehr could not do what Papen wanted. The Poles might seize the chance of internal disturbance in Germany to attack her eastern frontier; and 'defence of the frontiers and the maintenance of order against both Nazis and Communists was beyond the strength of the forces at the disposal of the Federal and State Governments'. The Reichswehr was, no doubt, a limited force; yet it had managed to maintain internal order in 1920 and 1923, when the chance of Polish intervention had been much greater. There is little doubt that even now the Reichswehr would have been prepared to act if it had been against the Communists alone. But the Nazis, whatever their violence, were a 'national' element. This was the underlying sentiment of Ott's memorandum. Papen was still ready to face the risk, but his colleagues were reluctant, and Hindenburg still more so. He said to Papen: 'I am too old and have been through too much to accept the responsibility for a civil war. Our only hope is to let Schleicher try his luck.' Schleicher became Chancellor the same day.

His luck turned out to be a poor resource. He offered to make Strasser Vice-Chancellor; and Strasser was willing to accept. But he could not carry the Nazi party with him. Hitler forbade any bargaining with Schleicher; and Strasser lost his nerve. On 8 December he went off to Italy for a holiday. Hitler reasserted his domination over the party and determined once more to 'throw the whole party into the struggle'. Strasser's abortive revolt and failure actually strengthened Hitler's appeal to the propertied classes; for he could claim to have shaken off the extreme, Socialist wing of his party. Nazi finances were in a bad state. Even Goebbels had a feeling of 'dark hopelessness'. But Hitler's resolution was as strong as ever; and this time he was justified. Schleicher's feeble attempts at coalition had broken down. What is more, Papen—though out of office—continued to live next door to Hindenburg and to busy himself in political intrigue. He would have been less than human if he had not wanted his revenge on Schleicher; and while the latter had failed with Strasser, himself hoped to succeed with Hitler. On a more elevated plane, he could make out to be still pursuing the bargain with Hitler which had been everyone's object for the last two years. Papen and Hitler met, more or less secretly, on 4 January 1933. Papen, according to his own account, merely urged—in the most disinterested way—that Hitler should become Vice-Chancellor in Schleicher's Government. Schroeder, the Cologne banker in whose house the meeting was held, gives a different and more likely story. Hitler insisted on becoming Chancellor, though with Papen and his friends as ministers; in particular he did not ask for control of either the army or foreign affairs. Papen thought that he had performed the miracle: he had taken Hitler prisoner, figurehead of a respectable non-Nazi Cabinet. Wealthy Germans drew the same conclusion. Subscriptions began to flow into the Nazi funds. Goebbels noted: 'The financial situation has improved very suddenly.'

Schleicher did not realize that the position had changed. Once in office he thought, like Bruening and Papen before him, that he had only to issue orders for the crisis to disappear. It soon ceased to worry him that his political combinations collapsed. Gregor Strasser turned out to be a broken reed: he could not carry a single National Socialist with him. The Social Democrats and the trade unions were not won over. Like everyone else, they seem to have come round to the view that office was the best means of taming Hitler; and they still imagined that they could resist him if he attempted anything illegal. On the other hand, the extreme Right, though they distrusted Hitler, were alienated by the steps Schleicher had taken to conciliate the Social Democrats. The Reichstag was due to meet on 31 January. Its first subject for discussion was the *Osthilfe*—the subsidies to landowners in eastern Germany, which had involved many scandals reaching even to Hindenburg himself. On 28 January Schleicher had to confess to Hindenburg that he could not control the Reichstag; and he asked, as his two predecessors had done, for a decree dissolving it. This was the very policy of governing Germany by force which Schleicher had rejected when it had been put forward by Papen in December. Hindenburg liked Papen and by now disliked Schleicher. He refused the decree of dissolution. Schleicher then claimed that he could produce a parliamentary majority by negotiating with the

National Socialists. But this was exactly what he had failed to do during the last six weeks. Moreover, Hindenburg knew, as Schleicher did not, that Papen could do it more successfully. Schleicher was dismissed; and Papen was entrusted with the formation of a new government.

A single pattern ran through all the negotiations from the fall of Bruening, or even before, to the accession of Hitler. The President and his confidential advisers worked persistently for a coalition government, in which Hitler would provide the votes and would yet be held in check by his associates. There was never any attempt to build a coalition government which would exclude Hitler or the National Socialist party; and the delay came from Hitler, not from the side of the respectable classes. Now Hitler agreed to come in. It is impossible to say what led him to compromise. Perhaps he recognized that the Nazi tide was ebbing; perhaps he felt that the old order was now sufficiently weakened and would crumble of itself; perhaps the position of Chancellor, even under Papen's control, made the difference. More probably, his decision sprang from his unconscious sense of timing, just as a great general might find it difficult to explain why he flung in his reserves at the critical moment.

On 30 January Hitler became Chancellor. This was far from a seizure of power. Indeed, the forces of the old order imagined that they had seized Hitler. Though he was Chancellor, there were only three Nazis in a Cabinet of eleven; the two key posts of Foreign Minister and Minister of Defence were in the hands of non-political agents of the President; and Hitler could not see Hindenburg except in the presence of Papen, who was Vice-Chancellor. No arrangement could have been neater or more cynical. Yet it broke down within the first few days. What Hitler appreciated and his conservative associates did not was that, while the Nazi party was not strong enough to seize power when the forces of the State were hostile, it was strong enough to do so once these forces were neutral or on its side. Papen remarks regretfully that 'existing institutions and parties gave up without a fight'. What else could they do? They might have resisted the Nazis if the police and the courts were there to maintain order. They could no longer do so when the police were under Nazi control and when, therefore, the defence of democracy took on a revolutionary character. Again, Hitler had been crippled by the fact that he did not possess a majority in the Reichstag; this had driven him to accept Papen's terms. But once in office he could argue that a further general election would give him a majority; and, since this had been the object of all the negotiations, his demand for a dissolution could not be refused. This time Hitler supposed that he could indeed deliver the parliamentary majority which had hitherto evaded everybody. Once the National Socialists dominated the Reichstag, he could shake off Papen and the other elderly gentlemen who controlled him, and establish a Nazi dictatorship by law.

Hitler's calculation did not succeed. The election campaign was conducted with every weapon of Nazi terror; and the burning of the Reichstag building on 27 February enabled Hitler to declare the Communist Party illegal. Nevertheless on 5 March the National Socialists secured only 43·9 per cent of the votes. Even with the co-operation of the right-wing Nationalists they had only a bare majority—enough to control the Reichstag from day to day, but not enough to carry through any fundamental change in the constitution. Hitler, however, was set on an Enabling Law which would give him all the powers of a dictator. If the so-called democratic parties had held together, Hitler would have been driven to illegal action—or would have remained powerless. The Communists had been driven underground. The Social Democrats, though feeble in action, held nobly to their principles and voted against the Enabling Law, despite the threats of terror against them. The decision rested on the Centre, with its 102 votes. The leaders of the Centre were men of personal courage. But their party cared little for democracy; it was concerned only to secure the position of the Roman Catholic schools. It had a long tradition of doing this by intriguing with successive parties and governments; it had long lost the tradition of resistance which had once enabled it to defeat Bismarck. The Centre leaders were fobbed off with promises from Hitler in which they only half-believed; and on 23 March the Centre votes were cast in favour of the Enabling Law. These votes alone gave Hitler's dictatorship its legal character.

One barrier remained: Hindenburg's veto, and Hitler's promise that he would do nothing to override it. But Hitler, who had wooed millions of voters, did not find it difficult to cajole an old man, never mentally acute and now senile. Papen soon found that he was not needed when Hitler had his interviews with the President. He went on dreaming that some day Hindenburg would reassert his independence and that the Nazis would be over-thrown—again under Papen's direction. He waited patiently, as he had waited before. And fifteen months later he thought that his chance had come. On 17 June 1934 Papen delivered at Marburg the only public speech against the Nazi dictatorship ever made in Germany after Hitler's seizure of power. Even now his line was equivocal. His appeal was to Hitler to behave better, rather than to Hindenburg and the generals to overthrow him. In any case, Hitler was soon able to outbid Papen's feeble gesture. He, too, had his difficulties with the Nazi extremists—the leaders of the Brown Shirts who wanted to carry through a real social revolution now that their party was in power. He broke them in the blood-bath of 30 June. This seemed a guarantee to the generals that there would be no demagogic interference with the army. Hitler was already promising them rearmament on a great scale. Why, then, should they resist him for the sake of democracy or the constitu-tion? This would be the very interference in politics which they had always rejected.

On 2 August 1934 Hindenburg died. The army leaders were content that Hitler should take his place. Within an hour of Hindenburg's death, the office of President was merged with that of Chancellor; and Hitler became undisputed Head of the State. He kept his bargain with the army. For three and a half years it remained autonomous, standing outside politics and repudiating all responsibility for the Nazi terror. Early in 1938 Hitler overthrew this balance. He was now moving towards an aggressive war in Europe; and he could tolerate no independent authority. The army leaders were discredited by a series of personal scandals, some of them without foundation. Hitler dismissed those who stood out against him; made himself head of the armed forces, the Wehrmacht; and at the same time put his agent, Ribbentrop, in the Foreign Office in place of Neurath. By February 1938 the seizure of power was complete. It had taken Hitler four years to destroy legality in Germany by legal means.

If we look back over this wretched story, we see a man bent on success on the one side, and a group of politicians without ideas or principles on the other. Hitler was resolved to gain power. He did not know how he would do it, and he tried many means which failed; but he had an unbreakable purpose. The others were only concerned to strike a bargain with him. If there had been a strong

democratic sentiment in Germany, Hitler would never have come
to power—or even to prominence. He would have failed even if the
weak democratic parties had held together. He had two great
weapons. He could promise the generals a great army, if they let
him in; he could threaten civil disturbance, if they kept him out.
The promise was more potent than the threat. One can blame all
parties in turn. The Communists started the habit of violence and
disrupted the working-class front. The Social Democrats had lost
all ability to act and faith in their strength. The Centre would
bargain with anybody, even with Hitler. But the greatest responsibility lay with those who let Hitler in and established him as
Chancellor. Hitler recognized it himself. In 1938 Papen, then
German ambassador at Vienna, accompanied Schuschnigg to the
fateful interview at Berchtesgaden which ended Austrian independence. In the course of the argument, Hitler turned to Papen and
said: 'By making me Chancellor, Herr von Papen, you made possible the National Socialist revolution in Germany. I shall never
forget it.' And Papen answered with soldierly pride: 'Certainly,
my Führer.'

21

THE APPEASEMENT YEARS

THERE are no sensations to be found in the latest ragbag from the captured German archives.[1] The big questions of 1938 — Austria, Spain, Czechoslovakia — were covered in previous volumes. The present one rakes in all the routine business of diplomacy from Germany's neighbours to the Jewish question. Yet the volume is not without its importance. Hitler hardly appears; and we can therefore judge how Germany would have behaved as a Great Power if her old ruling class had gone its way without his interference. For this was the short period when Germany was once more unmistakably a Great Power, yet not clearly resolved on a war for the mastery of Europe. Mussolini's visit to Berlin in September 1937 was the symbol that the old anti-German coalition had dissolved; Hitler's occupation of Prague on 15 March 1939 the signal for attempting to prepare a new one. In the intervening period Germany could garner the fruits of appeasement.

German diplomacy had a clear pattern: to destroy the system of collective security and then to make adjustments of detail in Germany's favour. Every small country in turn was urged to detach itself from the League of Nations and from alliance with France, if it had one. Each was urged to rely on neutrality and on bilateral negotiations with Germany. As soon as it did so German pressure began to increase. The Poles were encouraged to depreciate the French alliance and to remove the question of Danzig from the League of Nations. Once they had done so they were faced in January 1939 with the demand that Danzig should return to the Reich. The Danes abandoned the League of Nations, only to find that German propaganda in North Slesvig increased. Belgium returned to her old neutrality; but the Germans then prepared to raise the question of Eupen and Malmédy. Lithuania was the most striking case. She was detached from reliance on Soviet Russia or the other Baltic States and then compelled to surrender Memel.

1. *Documents on German Foreign Policy, 1918–1945.* Series D, Vol. V. Poland; the Balkans; Latin America; the Smaller Powers. June 1937–March 1939. Stationery Office.

Indeed, she was only allowed to remain in existence as compensation for Poland if the latter surrendered Danzig and the Corridor. Farther afield, the Germans complained of Turkey's friendship with Great Britain and France, yet themselves evaded any recognition of her control over the Straits.

In south-eastern Europe Germany played off Hungary, Rumania, and Yugoslavia against each other—dangling concessions before each and forbidding at the same time any co-operation between them. Hungary, the most dissatisfied, was also the most sycophantic. The Regent Horthy said in December 1937: 'Regardless of his attachment to the beautiful Vienna of pre-war days, it was plain to him that Austria had to become German in the end, which would only please him.' Hungary fell out of favour with Hitler, because of her caution during the Czech crisis. He wanted her to go to war with Czechoslovakia. Then he, too, could have put the question 'on the territorial, instead of the ethnographic, point of view', and 'could have laughed in Chamberlain's face'. In other words, Czechoslovakia would have been dismembered, but on Hungary's initiative. Lacking this, Hitler still shrank from open aggression on his side. We have here the first convincing explanation of the contradiction between Hitler's intransigence at Godesberg and his acceptance of compromise at Munich. The Hungarian mine had failed to explode. Here, too, is the explanation why Rumania was treated gently in the autumn of 1938 and why even King Carol's dissolution of the pro-German Iron Guard went through without German expostulation. By the spring of 1939 the Hungarians had struggled back into favour; and the way was set for the dissolution of rump-Czechoslovakia as well as for the threat to Rumania which seemed to follow it.

It was a further sign of Germany's recovery as a Great Power that she began to play a part again outside Europe. In Latin America she could not make much headway against the influence of the United States, in spite of the large German colonies, especially in Argentina and Brazil. But opportunities were opening for her in the Near East. The Mufti of Jerusalem and King Ibn Saud both sought for German arms and German backing. Ibn Saud said in February 1939: 'He very well knew that all the British assurances of friendship are *lies*. . . . His aim is to free himself more and more from British influence in a manner that should not be too noticeable'; and he promised 'an attitude of benevolent neutrality towards Germany in case of a European war'. He wanted arms from Germany; but the Germans, 'in view of events in Europe which engage our full attention at this time', would not commit themselves.

The Germans did not need to go outside Europe to find friends. These documents confirm the equivocal role which Professor Burckhardt played as High Commissioner at Danzig. Though ostensibly the servant of the League of Nations, he seemed to aim at eliminating it from the Danzig affair and then to present himself as mediator between Berlin and Warsaw. What is more, he represented this as in line with British policy. He reported Lord Halifax as saying:

> What was now called liberal in England had nothing whatever to do with the old Liberals—the Whigs—who had probably all become conservative by now. The present liberals were very close to the Third International. . . . Lord Halifax had termed Danzig and the Corridor an absurdity. Separating a large province from the Reich had probably been the most foolish provision of the Treaty of Versailles. But since it had been done, it was, of course, difficult to alter. He was convinced, however, that such a change would have to come about through friendly negotiations between Germany and Poland. England, that is, the present Government, was quite prepared to play a mediator's role in such negotiations.

M. Burckhardt passed another interesting judgement on British politicians:

> Lord Halifax was in any case extremely just and well-intentioned, also regarding the colonial question. He honestly wanted to avoid a war. M. Burckhardt was not entirely clear about Chamberlain. Undoubtedly he also wanted to avoid a war, if at all possible. It was conceivable, however, that he had only postponed it at present because he considered that England was not strong enough.

The reader of these documents will acquit the German diplomatists of deliberately planning a large-scale war of aggression. Why should they? They were getting what they wanted without war; and there seemed no limit to what they could gain by this steady pressure. The world of peace and international order had dissolved. They had the same aims as Hitler's; only more caution. When Hitler set a faster pace on 15 March 1939, they had nothing to oppose him with except timidity. It is not surprising that they struggled helplessly along with him.

22

THE ALLIANCE THAT FAILED

THE failure to make an alliance with the Soviet Union in 1939 was the greatest setback for British diplomacy in the twentieth century. All our troubles from that day to this stem from it. What caused the failure? Were the Russians cheating all along, pushing up the British offers in order to reach an agreement with Hitler? Or were they driven into Hitler's arms by the belief, based on experience, that the British did not take the talk of alliance seriously? We shall not know the answer until some future generation sees the archives of the Kremlin; and perhaps not even then. But we are getting nearer. Hitherto we have relied on contemporary newspaper reports, to which have been added the German documents and Bonnet's somewhat selective memoirs. Now at last we have the record from the British Foreign Office;[1] only the discussions in the Cabinet are still lacking on the British side. These documents came out at a bad time. It had become established doctrine that the Nazi-Soviet pact caused the Second World War; and no one wanted to raise awkward questions that might shake this legend or disturb the moral unity of the western world. It was a symbol of 'the cold war' that the lesson of these Foreign Office documents was ignored and the documents themselves soon forgotten. The man in the street, so far as he reflected at all, continued to believe that the Russians had been offered an alliance by the West and that they had deliberately preferred to make a robbers' pact with Hitler.

Here is the story from the British papers, summarized in detachment. Like many stories, it begins at the point where it was also to end. The British Government had given guarantees at a moment's notice to Poland and Rumania. It occurred to them belatedly that there was no means by which these could be fulfilled. The Soviet Union would have to supply the aid if it came to fighting: but the British Government knew well that neither Poland nor Rumania would accept Soviet assistance. Unable to find any escape from this pit of their own digging, the British Government invited the Russians to do it for them. The Soviet proposal for a

1. *Documents on British Foreign Policy, 1919–1939.* Third Series. Vols. V–VII.

Four-Power declaration had been vetoed by the Poles; hence the British tried to commit the Soviet Union to a one-sided bargain. On 14 April they proposed that if any neighbour of the Soviet Union was attacked, 'the assistance of the Soviet Government would be available, if desired, and would be afforded in such manner as would be found most convenient'. On 18 April the Soviet Government replied by demanding a full-scale alliance with England and France for mutual assistance against aggression. This would not do at all. 'His Majesty's Government might be drawn into a war not for the preservation of the independence of a minor European state but for the support of the Soviet Union against Germany. On this issue opinion in this country might be seriously divided.' This was indeed exactly what the Russians feared.

The British beat around for a fortnight. They inquired of Poland and Rumania what arrangements these two countries would allow them to make with Russia. They also tried to invoke French diplomatic ingenuity. But the French let them down. On 3 May Bonnet revealed to the Soviet ambassador 'in the heat of conversation' that France favoured a pact of mutual assistance. On 9 May the British at last tried again: in view of the British guarantees to Poland and Rumania, 'the Soviet Government would undertake that in the event of Great Britain and France being involved in hostilities in fulfilment of these obligations the assistance of the Soviet Government would be immediately available, if desired, and would be afforded in such manner and on such terms as might be agreed'. Molotov had now become Commissar for Foreign Affairs (on 3 May). On 14 May he rejected the British proposal and demanded 'reciprocity': a pact of mutual assistance, a guarantee of all eastern European countries, and 'the conclusion of a concrete agreement as to forms and extent of assistance'. Once more there were discussions with France, Poland, and Rumania, and now with the Baltic states as well. On 27 May the British Government accepted the principle of mutual assistance, though dressed up—for the sake of public oipinion—with references to 'the principles of the Covenant of the League of Nations'. The three governments 'would concert together as to the methods by which such mutual support and assistance could, in case of need, be made most effective', but 'this rendering of support and assistance' was to be 'without prejudice to the rights and position of other Powers'.

Molotov at once rejected this proposal. It was 'cumbrous', 'no serious contribution', 'vaguely worded and referred to some distant future and unending conversations'; 'the Soviet Government wanted immediate and effective action'. On 2 June he again proposed a pact of mutual assistance, with guarantees to a number of named countries. This pact was to come into force as soon as the three States had made an agreement 'as to methods, forms, and extent of assistance'—in other words, a military convention. The British jibbed only at the Russian demand that any threat to one of the Baltic States should bring the alliance into action; and the Russians were to decide whether a State was threatened. This, the Foreign Office complained, would make the Russians 'the sole judge of what was a *casus belli* in the Eastern Baltic'. The British wished to keep this decision in their own hands; they would even put it into the hands of the Baltic States—anything to keep it from Russia. On 15 June they submitted a compromise. There should be immediate action by the three Allies if one of them went to the assistance of another State 'which had, by its own consent, received an undertaking of assistance'. There should be consultation only if one of the three 'should consider its security menaced by a threat to the independence or neutrality of any other European Power'.

Molotov rejected this on 16 June. Russia, he said, had been asked to join in guaranteeing Poland, Rumania, Greece, and Turkey. It would be 'a position of inequality, humiliating for Soviet Union', if Great Britain and France refused to join in guaranteeing the Baltic States. He therefore proposed to return to a simple defensive pact if one of the Allies were directly attacked. The British at once objected: 'Soviet Government would obtain the benefit of the guarantees we have given to Rumania and Poland without Great Britain and France receiving any reciprocal benefit on their side.' But this of course was already true. The British tried again. The alliance should operate in case of aggression 'which, being directed against another European State, thereby constituted a menace to the security of one of the three Allies'. On 21 June Molotov asked: 'Who would decide whether the menace constituted aggression?' Sir William Seeds, Ambassador at Moscow, answered: 'Nothing was said in our draft on this point.' Molotov therefore rejected the proposal.

On 1 July the British gave way. They agreed that the alliance should operate in case of aggression against 'another European

State whose independence or neutrality the contracting country concerned felt obliged to defend against such aggression'. Molotov demanded that the States should be mentioned individually in a secret list. The British agreed, but on condition that, if the Baltic States were named, Holland and Switzerland should be named also. Molotov refused: these two States did not recognize the Soviet Union. Further, he wanted to include 'indirect aggression', by which he meant 'an internal *coup d'état* or a reversal of policy in the interests of the aggressor'. The British found this 'completely unacceptable'. They suggested, however, that aggression 'is to be understood as covering action accepted by the State in question under threat of force by another Power and involving the abandonment by it of its independence or neutrality'. This was submitted to Molotov on 8 July and rejected by him on 9 July. He defined indirect aggression as 'action accepted by any of the above-mentioned States under threat of force by another Power or, without any such threat, involving the use of territory and forces of the State in question for purposes of aggression . . . and consequently the loss of, by that State, its independence or violation of its neutrality'. He further refused to include Luxembourg, which the French had tried to slip in, and would include Holland and Switzerland only 'if, and when, Poland and Turkey conclude pacts of mutual assistance with the U.S.S.R.'

There were again 'serious difficulties'. It would 'undermine our whole moral position in Europe generally'. The British stuck to their guns, or lack of them. On 17 July they again submitted their formula of 8 July and Molotov again rejected it, referring to the example of President Hacha of Czechoslovakia. The British agreed to drop Holland and Switzerland and proposed only that there should be consultation 'in the event of aggression or threat of aggression by a European Power against a European State not named in the list'. Molotov did not object to this, but he raised a new point. There must be a military agreement, and 'the political part would have no existence without it'. The French jumped at this proposal. They were ready to meet the Russians over 'indirect aggression' if they could get a military pact in exchange. The British still wanted to get their definition of 'indirect aggression' accepted before they would agree to military talks. This idea was put to Molotov on 23 July. He rejected it. Further political discussions without military talks would be 'a waste of time'. 'During military conversations outstanding political points could easily be settled.'

On 27 July the British agreed to military talks before the political agreement was settled. But they did not mean to give way over 'indirect aggression'—despite Bonnet's statement that the political agreement was initialled. On the contrary, with military talks in progress, 'we feel that we can afford to take a somewhat stiffer line in regard to the one point to which we have always attached capital importance'. It also occurred to them, apparently for the first time, that the draft treaty did not cover Danzig; moreover, unless they were careful, it might land them in guaranteeing the Soviet Union against Poland—which they certainly did not intend to do. A discussion with Molotov on 3 August showed that the conflict was still unresolved. The British would include indirect aggression only if the victim gave way 'under threat of force'; Molotov insisted on adding 'or without any such threat'. On 17 August the British sent to Moscow a mixed bag of alternatives, each designed to give the impression that they met Molotov's demand without actually doing so. There was to be 'threat of force, overt or covert', or 'pressure', or instead a reference to 'the action against Czechoslovakia in March 1939'—which came to the same thing. But as none of these proposals was put to Molotov, it is hardly worth dissecting them.

Meanwhile the military missions were proceeding slowly to Moscow by sea. They did not imply the decisive concession which the Russians perhaps imagined. Molotov had said that a military agreement must be made before the political agreement was concluded; the British were still determined to have a political agreement before taking the military talks seriously. The British mission was told: 'Until such time as the political agreement is concluded, the Delegation should go very slowly with the conversations', and 'until the political agreement is reached the Delegation must treat the Russians with reserve'. Out of the nineteen points of 'general policy' eleven specified subjects which the delegation should not discuss with the Russians or information which it should not give them. The military mission was, in fact, designed to keep Russia 'in play' during the critical weeks at Danzig which were now seen to be approaching. In this light, Annex IV of the instructions to the military mission is not without humour. It is entitled 'The Russian Character' and begins: 'The Russian is

G

suspicious by nature and a hard bargainer.' This wisdom was as profound as the rest of the negotiations.

The British military mission started with the cheerful assumption that 'agreement on the many points discussed may take months to achieve'. They were soon hustled out of their lethargy by the Russian insistence. Admiral Drax, the leader, had to confess that he had no proper credentials. He got them, though only on 21 August. The reservations were abandoned one after another; soon the Russians were being told everything of British and French plans —plans which indeed were far from reality as the events of May 1940 were to show. All this was a mere preliminary. On 14 August Voroshilov, leader of the Soviet delegation, asked the decisive question: 'Can the Red Army move across North Poland and across Galicia in order to make contact with the enemy? Will Soviet troops be allowed to cross Rumania?' The British and French were unable to answer. The talks were adjourned, never to be resumed seriously. No effective inquiry was ever made of Rumania; but the French did their best with the Poles, the British trailing along complainingly behind. The Poles, however, held out. Beck said: 'This is a new partition that we are asked to sign.' On 22 August the French tried a last trick. They offered to agree to the passage of Russian troops through Poland and Rumania without reference to the governments of these countries. With this offer the British were not associated. In any case it was of no use. Voroshilov wanted an assurance from Poland and Rumania, not from France. 'We do not want Poland to boast that she has refused our aid—which we have no intention of forcing her to accept. . . . Surely we cannot be obliged to beg for the right to fight the common enemy?' On the following day, 23 August, the Russians made their decision: they concluded the Nazi-Soviet pact. The British had remained firm to the end. They would leave the decision on peace or war to the Poles; they would not leave it to the Russians. Yet it was perhaps the Russians who won: for the Nazi-Soviet pact helped the decision towards war, even though it did not produce it.

The preceding summary contains one surprise, though by no means an unusual one. The documents reveal practically nothing that we did not know before. The account given by Sir Lewis Namier in *Diplomatic Prelude* was based almost entirely on contemporary newspaper reports—there was in 1946 little else for him to base it on. Nearly everything in his account is precisely accurate—not only in dates but even in the very phrases. Who made these elaborate 'leaks' to the press? No one has asked the question, let alone answered it; yet it must surely point to at least part of the explanation. The source can hardly have been the British Government. They were constantly embarrassed by these 'leaks' and driven by them from one concession to another. It must then have been the Soviet Government. For what purpose? Not to inform or influence their own people; Soviet public opinion could be manoeuvred at a nod as its reception of the Nazi-Soviet pact showed. The revelations were aimed at British opinion, or at western opinion generally. Again, for what purpose? The simplest explanation would be that the Russians genuinely wanted an alliance and believed, rightly, that they could get it only if public opinion forced the British Government on. They may have been playing a more elaborate political game. Convinced that they could never get sincere friendship from the existing right-wing governments, they may have been hoping for a political upheaval in both England and France which would bring the Left to power. Whether they would then have concluded an effective alliance with such governments or whether they would have sat back, more or less securely, as they did in the Spanish civil war, is a speculation too remote to answer. But it seems more likely that the Russians carried on these negotiations for the sake of their effect, whatever that might be, on British opinion than that they built up a façade merely to frighten Hitler. Of course there may be a much simpler explanation. The Russians always like to show that they are entirely in the right; and the 'leaks' may have been made solely for this reason. But it is almost inconceivable that they were resolved on the Nazi-Soviet pact all along.

The same point can be made in another way. If the Russians were merely concerned to alarm Hitler and to drag out negotiations until the critical last week in August, then the delays should have come from their side. But the opposite is the case. Here is the rhythm, British proposals on the one side, Soviet on the other:

British	Soviet	British	Soviet
14 April	18 April	1 July	3 July
9 May	14 May	8 July	9 July
27 May	2 June	17 July	17 July
15 June	16 June	23 July	23 July
21 June	22 June	17 August	

The contrast is startling. The Russians replied within three days, five days, six days; thereafter at breakneck speed, usually on the same day. The British took three weeks, twelve days, thirteen days, and then a week or more on each occasion. If dates mean anything, then the British were spinning things out, the Russians were anxious to conclude. There is other evidence of British reluctance. On 12 June Maisky invited Lord Halifax to Moscow, though admittedly 'when things were quieter'. On 21 June Chamberlain, questioned in Parliament whether 'the Russian Government had ever asked for the visit of a British Minister to Moscow', replied with a flat denial. The story of the military mission points the same moral. The British agreed to military talks on 23 July. Yet the mission did not reach Moscow until 11 August, only to reveal that it had no credentials. It would be plausible to deduce that the British, not the Russians, negotiated throughout with one eye on Hitler.

Yet this is probably not the explanation. Both sides wanted agreement, but they did not want the same agreement. The pattern of negotiations did not change despite the fog of phrases and trivialities. The Russians wanted a precise alliance for mutual assistance. The British wanted a promise of Russian aid 'if desired'. Each step by one side increased the suspicion of the other. The Russians had behind them the emptiness of the Franco-Soviet pact. After all, if Daladier and Bonnet had really been as keen on Soviet co-operation as they later claimed, they could have added a military convention to this pact without waiting for the British. The French aim seems rather to have been to put the odium of failure on the British; and the British certainly obliged them. The Russians remembered, too, the desertion of Czechoslovakia by Great Britain and France, and their own exclusion from the conference at Munich. Now they feared not for Poland, but for themselves. A German invasion of Russia, not any mere shifting of the European balance in Germany's favour, was their nightmare. All they were offered was the loss of such freedom of action as they still possessed.

The British did not share these Russian fears, and therefore could not understand them. It never crossed their minds that within twelve months the British Isles themselves would be threatened with invasion. The military mission were told that, if Germany attacked in the west, 'sooner or later, this front would be stabilized'. Hence the Russian demand for a direct alliance seemed to be irrelevant, and the Russian fear of attack through the Baltic

States an excuse for aggression. The British wished to keep the Russians dangling at the end of a string which only the British (or perhaps the Poles) could pull. Halifax defined British policy with his usual felicity: 'It was desirable not to estrange Russia but always to keep her in play.' Sir Edward Grey would have appreciated the fishing metaphor. But in 1914 Grey landed his fish. In 1939 the fish broke away, to the moral indignation of the angler. The British Government conceived alliance with Russia as a diplomatic manœuvre, not as a prelude to action. The Red Army was assumed to have no fighting value. Halifax held that 'the Red Army might be efficient for purposes of defence, but not for purposes of offensive operations'. There would be 'no point' in getting Soviet assistance if Poland and Rumania, who were ranked higher as military powers, then broke away. Moreover a mutual assistance pact 'would further infuriate Herr Hitler'. 'It would be said that—abandoning any further attempt to remain impartial—we were deliberately aligning for war between rival groups of Powers.' Italy, Spain, Japan would be offended; 'nor must it be forgotten that the Vatican regard Moscow even to a greater extent than Berlin as Anti-Christ'.

With many arguments for delay and few for decision, men who had long hesitated about everything now hesitated again. Mr. Strang, a member of the Foreign Office who was sent to Moscow for some obscure purpose (certainly not to conclude an alliance), wrote cheerfully on 21 June: 'I daresay we shall arrive at something in the end. When I say "in the end" I recall a remark of Naggiar's [the French ambassador] this afternoon that he will probably have reached the age limit and gone into retirement before I get away from Moscow.' The only argument for the alliance which the Foreign Office could think of was that foreign material could then be imported into Poland through Russia. But this could be done without an alliance; and in facr the Russians would have allowed it in September if the Poles had held out longer. There was a more general ground. 'It was essential, if there must be a war, to try to involve the Soviet Union in it, otherwise at the end of the war the Soviet Union, with her army intact and England and Germany in ruins, would dominate Europe.' Yet it never occurred to the Foreign Office that the Russians might make this calculation for themselves. On 8 May rumours of a Nazi-Soviet pact were dismissed as 'inherently improbable'. On 30 May Mr.

Kirkpatrick said: 'It would be a mistake to imagine that a Russo-German agreement could be so easily concluded as some people in Germany thought.' Lord Halifax telegraphed to Moscow on 28 July: 'There is no danger now of an imminent breakdown in the next critical weeks.' Ignorance reinforced complacency. Sir Orme Sargent, a high official of the Foreign Office, referred to Molotov in one letter as 'M. Momtchiloff.' A footnote adds: 'M. Momtchiloff was Bulgarian Minister in London.' A revealing slip of the pen. Momtchiloff or Molotov—what did it matter? They were both ministers of Slav countries, distant and unimportant.

Men project the dangers of the present into the future; they do not foresee the dangers that actually occur. Then, looking back, they imagine that they have been guarding against these all the time. In 1942 Stalin told Churchill that the Russians would have had to provide three hundred divisions, while the French provided one hundred and the British 'two now and two later'. This reflected the situation at the time of the battle of Stalingrad. It was not the decisive point for the Russians in 1939. The question of relative strengths was raised only casually and late in the day during the military talks; and then the Russians produced an absurd plan by which they would put into the field only as many divisions as the western Powers. The disagreement in 1939 was over policy, not over practical contributions. The Russians then did not fear a war in which they would bear an unequal burden; they feared a war which they would have to fight alone. Were their fears all that unreasonable? We know now that Hitler would not have been deterred from war by the conclusion of a Triple Alliance. He would have swept through Poland just the same; and would probably have inflicted great defeats on the Red Army. Would the British have stood by Russia to the death without the experience of Dunkirk and the blitz? Even now some, including Professor Butterfield, regret that Russia and Germany were not left to fight it out. That feeling was certainly much stronger in 1939. The Russian fears were exaggerated, but not groundless. They may have done the wrong sum, but at least they got its answer right. It was Soviet policy in 1939 which largely ensured that, when Soviet Russia was attacked, the western Powers were her ally.

British policy not only did the wrong sum; it failed even within its own terms of reference. The British were more anxious to keep Soviet Russia out of Poland and the Baltic States than to secure her aid against Hitler. They did not secure her aid; they also did not keep her out of Poland and the Baltic States. The only thing saved from the wreck was their reputation; to this Englishmen attach much importance. The Soviet leaders have never recovered in the eyes of their western admirers the moral superiority which they forfeited by making the Nazi-Soviet pact. The members of the British Foreign Office concerned with the Anglo-Soviet negotiations all rose to the highest positions. Respect for their abilities has survived even the revelation of the most incompetent transactions in British history since the loss of the American colonies. The minister responsible has done best of all. Many Foreign Secretaries have remained subjects for controversy. No one has been found to question the wisdom of Lord Halifax, K.G., O.M., G.C.S.I., G.C.I.E., D.C.L.

23

FROM ISOLATION TO WORLD POWER

THE lives and reminiscences of British ambassadors fill the shelves of nineteenth-century libraries. They are all much of a pattern — some confidential correspondence, polemics over dead issues, and the small-change of anecdotes. American ambassadors do not wait for a biographer. They hire an historian to put their papers in some sort of order and add a few comments in the footnotes. The result is a mound of undigested raw material, not a book; and, since the great questions of American foreign policy are fought out in public, revelations are lacking. The collected papers of Mr. Joseph Grew[1] are even drearier than Cordell Hull's *Memoirs*, which have hitherto carried off the palm for heavy going. But they illustrate in a unique way the breakneck speed at which the United States has passed from isolation to being the centre of the world.

When Mr. Grew entered the diplomatic service in 1904 his only task was to look after American trade and to observe, with aloof amusement, the fantasies of European courts. He ended in 1945 as Under-Secretary of State, with all the world shaped by his decisions. In between he had attended the peace conference at Paris in 1919; watched the making of peace with Turkey in 1923; and served as ambassador to Japan in the decisive ten years before Pearl Harbour. He had also fought hard, and not unsuccessfully, to make diplomacy a professional service instead of a preserve of the spoils system.

The picture of the imperial courts at St. Petersburg, Vienna, and Berlin before 1914 deserves to be read as historical evidence, though there is little on high politics. When war came Mr. Grew was in Berlin. He recorded: 'We all believe here that the war was carefully cooked up by Russia, England, and France.' Though he now repudiates this judgement with dismay it was shared by many Americans and helps to explain much of the confusion of later years. He remained in Berlin until America entered the war in 1917, but there is little new here on the struggle between Bethmann

1. *Turbulent Era.* By Joseph C. Grew. Edited by Walter Johnson. Hammond Hammond. 2 vols.

and the German generals. Nor does his account of the Paris
Peace Conference add more than a few footnotes. He brings out
well the improvised muddle in which everything was conducted.
In November 1918, Lloyd George thought that one week would
be enough 'for the conference itself'. Balfour remarked, with his
usual detachment: 'Five years ago we entered upon this war in
order to end war and now we are entering upon this peace in
order to end peace.' The spectre of Bolshevism haunted the conference; and the statesmen rattled through one treaty after another
in the belief that, when peace was made, Bolshevism would fade
away of itself. This belief is still a substitute for policy in many
quarters.

In Paris the United States was a principal: in Lausanne in 1923
only an observer. Negotiations there curiously anticipated diplomacy in the Near East after the Second World War. The Turks
played off Great Britain against Russia and emerged independent
of both. Mr. Grew sympathized with the British and disliked the
Russians; but he was not prepared to let American interests be
jeopardized by any British gains and before the conference ended
he was urging the Turks to resist Curzon's pressure. In much the
same way, as ambassador to Turkey later, he wanted the Turks to
be independent of everybody—a solution possible only when crisis
was far away. For it never occurred to him at this time that
America might have to protect the independence that she was
generally recommending.

In 1931 Mr. Grew went to Tokio; and the core of his book deals
with his sustained attempt to urge a realistic Far Eastern policy
on the American Government. He wished America to build up its
military strength; then she should strike a practical bargain with
Japan for the security of her own interests. Neither side of this
advice was followed. The United States remained too weak to
impose any effective barrier on Japan; at the same time she damned
Japanese policy and refused to consider any compromise. In 1937
Mr. Grew noted after Roosevelt's 'quarantine' speech: 'I felt my
carefully built castle tumbling about my ears.'

He soon rebuilt it. He held that American economic pressure
would compel Japan to seek a compromise, and, in the summer of
1941, believed that the time for this had come. He argues strongly
that when Konoye, the Japanese Prime Minister, proposed a meeting with Roosevelt this was a genuine bid for a lasting settlement.

G*

His urgent messages were ignored in Washington. Did Roosevelt and Hull believe that they could compel Japan to surrender everything? Or did they think that a Japanese attack was the only way of forcing the American people to give up neutrality? We are still in the dark. Perhaps there is no rational explanation. Future historians may have to say that America stumbled into world power by accident. But Mr. Grew's narrative is a reminder that in 1941 the resources of diplomacy were not exhausted; they were pushed aside, perhaps deliberately, perhaps from obstinacy.

In 1944 Mr Grew became Under-Secretary of State; and he was one of the first to advocate resistance to Soviet policy. He wrote on 19 May 1945: 'A future war with Soviet Russia is as certain as anything in this world can be. . . . As soon as the San Francisco Conference is over our policy towards Soviet Russia should immediately stiffen, all along the line.' For this reason he advocated, unsuccessfully, a generous offer to Japan, so as to keep the Soviet Union out of the Far Eastern war; and he succeeded in keeping the Emperor as ruler of Japan.

There is another illustration here, even more striking in its way, of how the United States grew into world power overnight. On 30 April 1945, Yugoslav forces occupied Trieste. President Truman telegraphed to Winston Churchill: 'I wish to avoid having American forces used to fight Yugoslav forces or being used in combat in the Balkan political arena.' But, on 10 May, President Truman 'had finally come to the conclusion that the only solution was to clear Trieste. He realized that this was a reversal of his former position but that developments were such that it left no alternative.' Marshal Tito, in fact, withdrew his forces ten days later. Soon after, Mr. Byrnes, the new Secretary of State, started out on another attempt to get on friendly terms with the Russians, and Mr. Grew left government service. But in that casual sentence over Trieste he had discovered the key to American policy thereafter: 'Developments were such that it left no alternative.'

24

STUMBLING INTO WAR

BRITISH policy reached its moment of decision in September 1939. Hence our interest is in the road which led from Munich to Danzig. But for the Americans these were still far-off events which concerned them little. Even 'the phoney war' might almost have been fought on another planet. Messrs. Langer and Gleason called their previous volume on American foreign policy *The Challenge to Isolation*; and though the destroyers-for-bases deal, with which the volume ended, implied that isolation was over, America's entry into the Second World War was still more than a year away. Their new volume[1] covers this period, when the United States stumbled into war, and so into world power.

They have used all the most secret papers, including the private notes of Mr. Morgenthau, Mr. Stimson, and President Roosevelt himself; and they repeat the claim that their book 'is in no sense a work of official or even semi-official history'. Certainly they often pass harsh verdicts on the muddle of American policy. But their independence is a little formal. Both writers, according to the preface, returned to government service in 1950; and it must have involved complicated feats of personal adjustment to decide when they were acting as independent historians and when as government servants. Even with its reserve their book establishes itself at once as the leading authority for the period.

In September 1940 President Roosevelt and his advisers still doubted whether Great Britain would hold out. Mr. Hull remarked: 'This whole darn thing is hanging in the balance.' They anticipated having to fight alone against both Germany and Japan, and were concerned only to buy time. The result was words without action. Messrs. Langer and Gleason write scathingly at one point: 'When it came to a showdown the Government invariably fell back on words and demonstrations.' Again, 'The Greeks derived no material benefit from the sympathy and generous impulse of the President and the American people'. And they quote the Chinese

1. *The Undeclared War, 1940–41.* By William L. Langer and S. Everett Gleason.

saying, 'There is much noise on the stairs, but no one enters the room'.

The worst moment came in the autumn during the Presidential election campaign, when Roosevelt was driven to pander to the voters' belief that it was easy 'simultaneously to advocate increased aid to Britain and avoidance of war'. Yet this was not conscious deception on Roosevelt's part. It seems clear that even he thought the two could be reconciled. Later, in May 1941, Hopkins surmised: 'The President is loath to get into this war.' There was, of course, the complication that while Roosevelt wished to defeat Hitler and was reluctant to fight Japan, Hitler refused to be provoked and the Japanese pushed relentlessly forward.

Hitler held the initiative even when he had failed to invade Great Britain. The decisive check came perhaps in the late autumn, when he failed to attack Gibraltar. Or perhaps our authors (one of them an old advocate of America's Vichy policy) exaggerate the importance of this. British and American policy remained curiously out of step. The Americans wished to conciliate Pétain and were contemptuous of Franco. The British had no faith in Vichy and much in Franco's obstinacy.

Similarly the two governments had difficulty in co-ordinating their policy towards Soviet Russia. In October 1940 the British offered Stalin fulsome terms in exchange for a genuine neutrality; the State Department bargained more ruthlessly. But in the spring of 1941 the Americans tried to buy Stalin with machine tools, and the Foreign Office complained of their softness. Even when Hitler invaded Russia there was no clear agreement. The State Department regretted Winston Churchill's eagerness for a Russian alliance until its reserves were swept aside by Roosevelt, who always had more faith in Russia than his advisers. The present authors destroy the legend that Great Britain and the United States missed the chance of imposing rigorous terms on Soviet Russia — such as the freeing of the Baltic States — in exchange for their alliance. On the contrary, they had the greatest difficulty in evading Stalin's demand that they should recognize the Curzon (or Molotov-Ribbentrop) Line and all his conquests of 1940 before he would condescend to make an alliance with them. With the German armies at the gates of Moscow this toughness had a certain grandeur.

Lend-Lease was, as our authors show, the decisive commitment.

Decisive not only for the United States but also for Great Britain, who therewith surrendered her sovereign independence. The authors complain that the American people were ready at this point to go faster than Roosevelt; but they would not actually go to war. Even the Atlantic Charter did not move them. The Charter was incidentally a by-product of the Atlantic meeting. The real purpose of the meeting was to co-ordinate supplies and naval strategy. But the Americans had been alarmed by Keynes's prophecy that 'the post-war world economic structure could only be one of closed economics'. They wished to tie Great Britain down to a liberal economic system, not to make a declaration of principles against Hitler. Roosevelt had a solution of his own for the post-war world. Everyone should be disarmed except the United States and, grudgingly enough, Great Britain; then plebiscites should be held almost everywhere—even in Allied countries—under Anglo-American supervision. It is difficult to see how the Soviet Union fitted into this picture. Presumably it was to be exhausted by the war against Hitler.

Roosevelt and his advisers wished to avoid war against Japan but not at the price of surrender. Their aim was peace in the Far East, but on America's terms—an impossible contradiction. Our authors destroy the claim that there was any lost opportunity for peace with Japan in the summer of 1941. The Japanese would not have settled for anything less than permanent domination of China. Yet the American Government did not consciously manœuvre Japan into war. The Americans believed almost till the last moment that Japan would give way. And they feared that a Japanese attack, if it came, would be directed solely against Singapore and the Dutch East Indies. Then what would be the reaction of American public opinion? An attack on American territory 'seemed senseless'. Roosevelt and his advisers forgot Pearl Harbour. 'This tragic oversight may be a classic instance of human frailty, but it provides no evidence whatsoever to support the thesis that the President or any other responsible American official courted a Japanese attack on the Pearl Harbour base in order to enable them to lead the country into the European war by the Pacific back door.'

25

MAN OF AN IDEA

ONE of Frank Horrabin's illustrations for Wells's *Outline of History* is called Tribal Gods of the Nineteenth Century, Symbols for which men would die. There they stand in a row: John Bull in masculine isolation and four females classically draped—Britannia, la France, Germania, Kathleen na Houlihan. Every statesman invokes them; some take them seriously. But after the ringing phrases and the emotional dedication, statesmen have to turn to practical affairs. Bismarck has to manufacture his majority in the Reichstag; Churchill must consider the figures of aircraft production; Clemenceau reckons how long it will take for the American transports to cross the Atlantic. Logistics determined the hard battering of two world wars. The Tribal Gods were pushed into the wings. Yet they, too, represented a reality. Without them the conflicts would have been senseless, indeed could never have been kept going. The Tribal Gods will reward a worshipper if he is single-minded enough. General de Gaulle is the proof of it. That mystical symbol, France, made him a world figure; and in return he brought abstract France to life, if only for a brief period.

His book[1] is called *War Memoirs*; but the Second World War in the ordinary sense takes a small place in it. The pressing question for de Gaulle was how to restore France to greatness, not how to defeat the Germans. One can understand the impatience of the British, and the contempt of the American Government. Pressed for men, harassed by shipping losses, they had no time to conduct the war according to the protocol of an imaginary French sovereignty. Roosevelt could have borrowed Stalin's phrase about the Pope and have asked it of de Gaulle with more devastating effect: 'how many divisions has he?' The men of Vichy had the same standards. Weygand has recently put the case for them in a plaintive little book.[2] They were trying to maintain French administra-

1. *War Memoirs*. By Charles de Gaulle. Vol. I. *The Call to Honour, 1940–1942*. Collins. *Documents*. Collins.
2. *En lisant les mémoires de guerre du Général de Gaulle*. By General Weygand. Paris: Flammarion.

tion and to rebuild the fragments of an army. De Gaulle's heroics, they thought, would only bring new disasters on France. Weygand, Churchill and Roosevelt sent up a common chorus: let de Gaulle help against the Germans with his few followers and neglect political claims. This refrain did not shake de Gaulle. The defeat of Germany would be meaningless for him unless France was present on the day of victory in all her greatness. And he achieved the miracle. France was restored as a Great Power in 1945 thanks to de Gaulle alone, though whether to her advantage or anyone else's is still an open question.

The note is struck firmly in the first paragraph: 'France cannot be France without greatness.' This sets the tone of the book as effectively as Proust's announcement that he used to go to bed early. Most memoirs serve one of two purposes. Either they give a picture of the man, or they record the events in which he took part. Not so the memoirs of General de Gaulle. The human being behind the stern, unbending front never emerges for a moment either in the text or in the photographs. In one of these, indeed, the general is smiling. But it is a political smile: he is shaking hands with a member of the Home Guard. The human being in de Gaulle was of no account, least of all to himself. Napoleon and Trotsky wrote of themselves in the third person in order to assert their individualities more dramatically. The 'I' of de Gaulle is an equally effective disguise, but in the opposite sense. Apart from France he did not exist, and would not wish to exist. He said so himself in argument with Churchill: 'If I do not represent France, why speak to me?' This was the secret of his success, as of his later failure. He could be reduced to nothing; therefore he was relentless in demanding all. Other political leaders could be cajoled or threatened; they might see practical advantages or recognize practical dangers. De Gaulle knew only one rule of conduct: 'limited and alone though I was, and precisely because I was so, I had to climb to the heights and then never come down'.

He withdrew not only from humanity but from events. His book does little to illuminate the course of the war; and even when the lights are turned on, they produce unusual effects. Not that de Gaulle's memoirs are untrue or misleading. But they are not about the Second World War, as it was experienced by millions of men, high and low, in every belligerent country. They are not even about de Gaulle, as others experienced him. Consider the first two chapters which cover the period until the appointment of Pétain as Prime Minister on 16 June 1940. They show de Gaulle seeking to inspire resolution in Reynaud, proposing offensive manœuvres to Weygand, weighing up Huntziger as a possible commander-in-chief, and finally leaving Bordeaux in calm resolution. 'There was nothing romantic or difficult about the departure.' Others failed to notice the hero in the making. There are innumerable French memoirs on the period before the armistice; de Gaulle's are the only ones to suggest that he played a serious part. Weygand has remarked, probably truly, that he himself was too preoccupied to listen to strategical rhapsodies from a junior general. Sir Edward Spears has drawn a very different picture of the departure: de Gaulle sheltering in the dark behind a pillar, making bogus appointments to conceal his plans for departure, and finally being pulled into the aeroplane as it left the ground. No doubt things happened much like that, though later estrangement may have sharpened a line or two. Yet the historical truth is here a matter of feeling, not of events. Once de Gaulle had become France, he had to hold his head high from the beginning. He became France as he crossed the Channel; and he has never cast himself since for any other part.

Like most legends, the legend of de Gaulle presents itself as all of a piece. The leader arrives in London; he assembles a few devoted followers; and this force continues to grow until, at the climax of this volume, the Fighting French cover themselves with glory at the battle of Bir Hakeim. The real story seems to have been more varied, though equally heroic. When de Gaulle first came to London, he did not realize that he would be alone. He supposed that the colonial governors would continue their resistance; and his own task was to be the representative of France in London only in the sense of being her ambassador. The governors obeyed the orders of Vichy with one outstanding exception. Even then de Gaulle thought that his isolation would be temporary. He anticipated that all Africa would turn against Vichy, despite the governors. Instead the expedition to Dakar ended in failure. This was the real turning-point of de Gaulle's career. Not only was he alone. His warmest adherents, Churchill and Spears, doubted his effectiveness. Spears showed reports from London that 'de Gaulle, in despair, abandoned by his partisans, dropped by the British into the bargain, would renounce all activity'. De Gaulle adds:

I, in my narrow cabin, in a harbour crushed by the heat, was com-
pleting my education in what the reactions of fear could be, both among
adversaries taking revenge for having felt it and among allies suddenly
alarmed by a set-back.

He did not weaken. From this moment he set out to embody 'the
image of a France indomitable in the midst of her trials'. This was
'to dictate my bearing and to impose upon my personality an attitude I could never again change'.

Until Dakar, de Gaulle and the British Government both
assumed that his movement would soon bring large concrete
advantage to the allied cause. After Dakar, de Gaulle had few
assets, and these were more or less stable. Equatorial Africa sent
colonial troops which performed miracles of valour at Bir Hakeim;
France itself provided some centres of intelligence, though hardly
a resistance. De Gaulle was left willy-nilly to fight a different war,
the war against the allies; and there is nothing to suggest that he
fought it with any reluctance. Roughly half the present volume
deals with this absorbing struggle. No doubt something real and
important was at stake, if only for de Gaulle. Yet in retrospect it
provides material for comedy. There was first the struggle for
followers. The British Intelligence Services were eager to kidnap
every fresh arrival from France, and would assert cheerfully that
de Gaulle and the British were the same thing. In the dark winter
blitz of 1940–1 British and French agents dodged and manœuvred
for 'bodies' as mercantilist powers used to dispute over skilled
craftsmen. Then, on a higher level of farce, comes the war over
Admiral Muselier. He was accused of treachery on the basis of
forgeries so crude that only M.I.5 could have been taken in by
them; released after a crisis of international magnitude; then
became a rebel against de Gaulle; and was finally confined by the
British on de Gaulle's request. It must have been puzzling for
Churchill to decide whether de Gaulle was asking to have a Free
Frenchman released or imprisoned.

This was small beer compared to the conflict over Syria. There
must be something in the Near East which deprives men of their
common sense. How otherwise explain the long-standing British
craze for the Arabs, even at their Egyptian stage of decay? Why
should England and France have quarrelled over Syria even as
allies, ever since the Crusades? Everyone behaved badly in the
Syrian affair. Dentz, the Vichy general, outdid his government in

collaborating with the Germans; the British authorities first neglected Syria and then blamed de Gaulle for the consequences of
their own mistakes; and de Gaulle claimed to liberate Syria,
though it turned out to be impossible for him to do so. The story
has all the futility which makes men dismiss diplomatic history as
trivial. It had important personal consequences, however. De Gaulle
and Spears were permanently estranged; as were many British and
French officials in the Middle East. But, of course, it amounted to
little in the long run. Both Great Britain and France have been
pushed out of the Arab countries; and the events in Syria merely
determined the order of their going.

There was a similar dispute when the British acted in Madagascar
without de Gaulle's approval; and a tremendous row with Washington when he ordered Muselier to liberate the islands of St.
Pierre and Miquelon solely because the American Government had
forbidden the operation. De Gaulle was indeed relentless in asserting himself. Did the British commander in the Middle East plead
that he had no transport with which to move French troops from
Syria to the North African battlefield? Within twenty-four hours
de Gaulle had approached the Soviet Ambassador in London and
offered to send a French army to Russia. The same superb assurance served de Gaulle well with the Communists. He makes out
now that he welcomed them in order that France should be for
once united. Did he not also welcome their assistance against the
British and American Governments? The Communists no doubt
thought that they had captured him. They were wrong: he had
captured them and will go down in history as the only man who has
ever outwitted Communists on their own ground.

The whole makes a strange story, a triumph of the human will
over material circumstances. Was there any sense, any use in it?
So far as winning the war goes, not much; nor can it be said that
present-day France has profited from the Gaullist epic. De Gaulle
was the servant of an idea, not a statesman, still less a politician.
He appealed to others of the same kind—novelists, anthropologists,
perhaps most of all to foreigners who loved France from afar. The
France he worshipped meant little to the Frenchmen who lived there.
Still, an individual defying the world and succeeding in his defiance,
however briefly, will always inspire admiration until the rule of the
masses submerges us. The story of de Gaulle has, maybe, little to
do with the Second World War, but it is magnificent all the same.

26

THE TWILIGHT OF THE GOD

THE writing of contemporary history is often dismissed as an impossibility. We stand too near the events that we seek to record and are too deeply involved in them to make a detached judgement. Moreover, men in public affairs know how to conceal their springs of action and appear to the world made up like any film star. Yet the trained historian should be able to break through this crust to the reality beneath. Many of the actors are still living; and the historian has some chance of discovering the answers, if only he can devise the right questions—more chance, it would seem, than if he ransacks a casual heap of documents. Given the historical temperament, the contemporary world can yield results as good as any other. Time does not always bring detachment; and an historian might well feel himself more engaged in the controversies of Luther than in those of Hitler. Dislike and contempt may be dangerous if they dominate the historian's mind. Yet the example of Gibbon is there to show that they need be no barrier to a work of genius.

All the same, the British intelligence officer who was given the task in September 1945 of discovering the circumstances of Hitler's death could not have been expected to produce a masterpiece. The inquiry might well have been barren. The witnesses, even if found, might have had little to tell. Moreover, intelligence reports, however dramatic their evidence, do not usually produce a dramatic story, as other attempts to describe Hitler's death bear witness. Our times are packed with tremendous themes which have never been exploited. The great Renaissance tragedy of Mussolini's end, for instance, remains unwritten. Hitler's fate, too, might never have got beyond the intelligence files. But the intelligence officer happened to be Mr. Trevor-Roper, an Oxford historian who had already proved his merit in a biography of Archbishop Laud; and what was more important, a man of confident judgement, anxious —as every great historian must be—to reach a wide audience and capable of giving events their true historical setting. The British Intelligence Service got more than they bargained for. Mr. Trevor-

Roper certainly accounted for every detail in Hitler's last days; but he also produced, almost by accident, the wisest and most profound analysis of the third Reich and so implicitly of German civilization.

His book is a model judged simply as a work of detection. In fact it eclipses the fictional efforts in this vein which are said to be the favourite reading of intellectuals. Every statement is grounded on fact; and a long introduction to the second edition showed how these facts had been arrived at. The dank gloom of Hitler's bunker might have been expected to remain for ever obscure; the last political writings of the Nazi leaders hopelessly entangled. Thanks to Mr. Trevor-Roper, the opposite is the case. Few stories in history are known more accurately or more fully. We can follow Hitler's every act until the 180 litres of petrol consumed him; and we understand the manœuvres of Himmler, Goering and Bormann more clearly than those of most democratic leaders. There is one flaw to prove that Mr. Trevor-Roper is human. He has not accounted for Hitler's ashes or bones. He guessed that they had passed into the possession of Artur Axmann, the Nazi youth-leader. But his guess came too late. Axmann was in American hands; and their intelligence officers, tardily 'jealous of Mr. Trevor-Roper's success, would not allow further questioning. Axmann vanished—perhaps with the bones, perhaps without them. For, as Mr. Trevor-Roper suggests, Hitler's remains may have disappeared in the general ruin of the Chancellery garden. Apart from this, no mystery remains. Even if the participants who fell into Russian hands are still alive, they would have nothing new to tell. We shall never know for certain whether Bormann died during his attempt to escape. Only his reappearance could disprove it.

The original object of the inquiry was to prove beyond all doubt that Hitler was dead. This object was successfully accomplished. No false Hitler will ever make a plausible claim to survival. But the political calculation behind the inquiry miscarried. The British authorities sought to kill National Socialism by proving that Hitler was dead. Instead they provided the Germans with a scapegoat for all their crimes and failures. There seemed no disloyalty in loading on to a dead Hitler the full responsibility that he had claimed when still alive. German generals blamed him for the defeat. German politicians blamed him for the policy of aggression and racial extermination. Far from being an act of desertion, suicide turned out to be Hitler's greatest service to the German people. He was guilty. Therefore they could be acquitted. This was far from Mr. Trevor-Roper's verdict. With artistic skill and perhaps some artistic exaggeration, he built up Speer as the one man of supreme ability among Hitler's supporters and showed how his detachment from political responsibility made him 'the real criminal of Nazi Germany'. Speer was the symbol of all those other devoted Germans who did their duty while Hitler drove to triumph through fraud and blood.

Speer could at least claim that he considered the Germany that would follow Hitler's defeat and sought to preserve it. The other Nazi leaders never thought of Germany's future, but much of their own. This was the most extraordinary of Mr. Trevor-Roper's extraordinary discoveries. Germany was falling to pieces; the allied armies were on the point of joining hands; the Russians were in the suburbs of Berlin. Yet every Nazi leader was obsessed with the ambition of seizing the succession as soon as Hitler would commit suicide. None of them except Speer dared to criticize or oppose him; but all longed to step into his shoes. Goering was the first to claim his place as the constitutional heir. Himmler was not far behind. Bormann discredited them both with Hitler and ensured their excommunication. Yet he, too, imagined that he could continue to wield power from behind the throne even when Hitler was dead. Only Goebbels, with what Mr. Trevor-Roper rather fancifully calls his Latin clarity, recognized that they were nothing without Hitler and clung to the dead leader's chariot-wheels by committing suicide in more modest form. Mr. Trevor-Roper calls this atmosphere of rivalry and intrigue 'Byzantine'; but the parallel is not exact. The story of the Byzantine empire was punctuated by an endless series of rebellious generals and successful challengers for the imperial throne. A Byzantine emperor could expect to be murdered or dethroned; few went to a voluntary suicide. Nothing like this happened at Hitler's court. He would have reigned for ever if it had not been for the victory of the allied armies.

This is the central problem of Mr. Trevor-Roper's book, as it must be in any book devoted to Nazi Germany. Why should Hitler have been for so long the undisputed master of a great nation? He had no originality of thought or of expression. His oratory to

the masses was no more remarkable than that of any other demagogue. His eyes were glazed and dull, his grasp soft, his voice
toneless. He looked well preserved and even youthful until the
middle of the war. Then time caught up on him. His whole left
side trembled; his senile face twitched. He moved like an auto-
maton. His mental powers had crumbled to vanishing-point. Often
he could not follow a discussion or even articulate clearly. Yet even
now he remained the sole master. Generals obeyed the directions of
his lunatic strategy. The most ruthless and ambitious politicians
were helpless before him. Indeed one has the feeling that Hitler
could have pulled Germany into an abyss of utter destruction, if
he had not at the end lost interest and destroyed himself. There
indeed may be found the answer to the mystery. The Germans
have always lacked certainty and self-confidence. Hitler possessed
these qualities and gave them to others. He never doubted even
in 1923, or in the dark days at the end of 1932. The Germans
wanted orders. No one has ever known so well as Hitler how to
give them.

The Germans were never devoted to Hitler. Mr. Trevor-
Roper's account makes this clear. The clerks and orderlies in the
bunker put a dance-tune on the gramophone when they heard that
Hitler was going to commit suicide; and everyone up to the highest
ranks smoked in a relaxed way as soon as the suicide had actually
taken place. Hitler was Germany's voice of conscience. The
Germans were sometimes impatient at this voice or regretted its
existence; but they had to obey it. And Hitler on his side had
equally little devotion to the German people. He often doubted
whether they deserved him; and when their failures of 1945 confirmed his doubts he withdrew proudly from the stage. Goebbels
may have meant the last scenes in the bunker to found a legend and
to prepare for a Nazi resurrection. Hitler had no such projects. He
did not believe in a future life either in this world or the next. He
had walked the earth as a god; and now he wanted the destruction
of Valhalla. The only delight of his last days was to topple others
from their pedestals before crashing down himself. It would be
an exaggeration to say that this was the end that he had always
expected; but it was no surprise to him.

Mr. Trevor-Roper has written in this book and elsewhere of 'the
mind of Adolf Hitler'. This is better than to treat him as an illi-
terate vulgarian or even as an adventurer pursuing personal power.

Hitler's ideas can be reduced to a system with a pedigree and rational consequences. But it is a risky business. Even Mr. Trevor-Roper has had to plump for a system and lays down that for Hitler the attack on Russia was more important than anything else. But could Hitler have exercised his superhuman sway if he had been merely a mouthpiece of Professor Haushofer's geopolitics? Of course the Germans succumb easily to this or any other rubbishy generalization about the course of history. But they succumb only enough to add the system to their stock of platitudes and grievances. Hitler had more than mind. He had vision. It was no doubt a detestable vision—ranging from total destruction to an earthly paradise where every German ate cream buns—but vision all the same. The sons of petty officials often have fantasies; Hitler differed in turning these fantasies into reality. This gave him supreme power. Perhaps gods can only destroy themselves. But if the voice of reason can contribute anything to weaken them it has spoken through Mr. Trevor-Roper.

No one cares now about Germany's bid to conquer Europe. Few care about the fate of Adolf Hitler. In the present situation of international politics both are better forgotten. Mr. Trevor-Roper's book would be forgotten along with them if it merely solved the riddle which he was originally set. But it transcended its subject. Though it treated of evil men and degraded themes, it vindicated human reason. In a world where emotion has taken the place of judgement and where hysteria has become meritorious, Mr. Trevor-Roper has remained as cool and detached as any philosopher of the Enlightenment. Fools and lunatics may overrun the world; but later on, in some future century, a rational man will rediscover *The Last Days of Hitler* and realize that there were men of his own sort still alive. He will wish, as every rational man must, that he had written Mr. Trevor-Roper's book. There are not many books in our age of which that could be said.

27

DEMOCRACY AND DIPLOMACY

Every diplomatist dreams of independence. In an ideal world, he imagines, he would be pitted against the representative of a rival power as in a game of chess. He would be free to make his moves without anyone at his shoulder suggesting other moves or even forbidding the moves that he would like to make. Then, he supposes (quite wrongly) he would always win. But this ideal situation has never existed. Not only do spectators comment and interfere. In the diplomatic game 'of chess the very pieces have a will of their own and rush over the board in unexpected directions. Kings and queens have always insisted that the player of the game is their servant, not the other way round. Bishops announce that they take their orders, not from the player, but from someone who is not in the room at all. Knights develop absurd points of honour. Nowadays, worst of all, the pawns assert the rights of 'the common man', and insist on having the moves explained to them before they will move at all, and then often move in quite a different direction. The diplomatic player abuses his pieces, declares that foreign policy is impossible in a democracy, and refuses to accept responsibility for the outcome. He expects to lose; and he remains disgruntled even when he wins.

This is not a new problem. At most, the problem is presented in new terms. No diplomatist has ever enjoyed a completely free hand. Perhaps Richelieu could really do what he liked; but that was in days so far off as to be by now legendary. No other foreign minister could rattle along according to his own inclination. Every royal master had whims of his own—antiquated prejudices, family ties, fragments of knowledge to which he attached exaggerated importance. Which of the old masters could count on getting his own way? Certainly not Talleyrand, whose ideas were constantly overruled by Napoleon. Nor Metternich, who had the greatest difficulty in drawing his emperor Francis into action of any sort. And least of all Bismarck, who admitted that William I caused him more trouble than any foreign power. These great men sometimes cheated their employers; but for most of their careers

they were absolutely dependent on decisions of slow-witted, suspicious monarchs they had to cajole. And yet they succeeded,
though not as completely as they liked. If our present-day diplomatists say that foreign policy is impossible in a democracy, that
is their fault, not the fault of the people. Diplomatists are the
servants of the state. In a democracy they exist to serve the needs
of the people; the people do not exist to serve theirs.

Those who conduct foreign policy always resent this. They like
to make out that foreign affairs are a mystery; and they really
believe it. Diplomatists live in a world apart. They spend much of
their time in foreign countries; and even at home they move in
artificial surroundings. Few of them have experience of ordinary
life. Indeed, diplomatists of different countries—even, say, of the
United States and Soviet Russia at the present day—have more in
common with each other than with other citizens of their own
countries. They worry over details of procedure; run after fragments of gossip; and are bewildered by many things which are
obvious to the plain citizen. For instance, the ordinary Englishman
realized that Hitler was a nasty man when many of our great diplomatists were still trying to appeal to his better nature. The diplomatist wants to deal with foreign affairs as an abstraction, free
from principles, emotions, or ideals. This is called 'realism', con-
centrating on 'the national interest', and so forth. It is nothing of
the sort. The hydrogen-bomb, let us say, is real. But the dislike
of the British or American citizen for political intolerance is
equally real. Writing off general principles is not realism. It is
merely idealism standing on its head. And this, contrary to the
diplomatists' belief, is not a position of strength—especially when
their heads are not particularly good.

Diplomatists know more about foreign affairs, and therefore
claim to judge them better. Even their superior knowledge is
doubtful—they are often surprisingly ill-informed. In any case it is
a great mistake to suppose that knowledge of itself brings understanding, still less wisdom. The men who succeed in this world are
not those whose heads are stuffed with facts, but those with a
native shrewdness and an ability to make the right decision by
instinct. The gardener with 'green fingers' does better than the
man whose shelves are crammed with horticultural books. This is
true in business; it is true of the great inventors; it is equally true
in the world of states. The people may seem ignorant and narrow-

minded when taken as individuals. But they possess a collective wisdom which nearly always judges right. If I ever had to direct British foreign policy I would sooner do it after listening to conversations in a public house than on the advice of the experts in our Foreign Office. Democratic assemblies are not all that far removed from the saloon bars. That is their strength. They fail when they try to set themselves up as experts and to deliver a more informed verdict.

The advocates of professional diplomacy will answer that the collective wisdom of the people is a piece of mysticism—like the Holy Alliance, 'sound and fury, signifying nothing'. I don't think so. After all, the people have a vital stake in the right conduct of foreign affairs. They pay the bills; they fight the wars. If a diplomatist makes a mess of a job he is merely moved to another capital. If the people let things go wrong they get killed, and the taxes go up. They certainly have to bear the responsibility. It is only right that they should make the decisions. In old Europe the budding statesman studied the personal characteristics of the monarch whom he was going to serve. Nowadays the diplomatist is encouraged to despise the people and seeks for tricks by which he can dodge their control. He would do better to find out what sort of foreign policy a democracy wants and then try to translate this into practical terms. The people in their collective wisdom tend to be either much better or much worse than they would be as individuals—usually much better. Democracies have been swept into wars of unprincipled aggression, such as the Spanish-American War of 1898 or the Boer War in 1899. But even then they demanded a moral motive and had to be convinced that they were discharging a civilizing mission. The people can succumb to panic, though not worse than the neurotic panic of William II or Ludendorff in 1918. But they are also capable of a sustained idealism quite beyond any individual ruler; and a foreign policy which refuses to appeal to this idealism will fail.

The great majority of mankind are not dominated by self-interest. Of course they want a decent living for themselves and their families; they want reasonable security and a quiet life. But they are not driven on by an insatiable appetite for power or even for great wealth. The men who have these appetites come to the top as political leaders or as captains of industry. They would find very few willing to change places with them; or rather few willing to pay the price which changing places with them would involve. Therefore, when the people are called upon to sacrifice their quiet life for an active foreign policy or, still more, in war, it is useless appealing to them on grounds of self-interest. This is the very cause which they have rejected unconsciously as the motive for their private lives; they will reject it equally when it is put forward as the basis for foreign policy. When George Kennan writes that 'our national interest is all that we are really capable of knowing and understanding', or when Hans Morgenthau calls his book *In Defense of the National Interest,* he strikes the one note which alienates democratic opinion. Let the people get it into their heads that a policy is selfish and they will not follow it. There was perhaps a case in terms of profit-and-loss for holding the Persian oil-fields and the refinery at Abadan by force in 1950. But no British Government dared make that case to the British people. Even those who wanted to use force had to assert that we were discharging a great civilizing mission which was much to the benefit of the Persians themselves. Now a Conservative Government has won universal approval by making an agreement which the Persians find satisfactory.

A democratic foreign policy has got to be idealistic; or at the very least it has to be justified in terms of great general principles. If the people are to exert themselves they must be convinced that what they are doing is for the good of mankind and that a better world will come out of it. The 'realists' smiled at 'the war to end war' (First World War) and at the hopes for a lasting peace in the Second World War; but these wars could not have been kept going without these appeals. Once tell people that they are fighting only for their properties or their lives and they will discover that there is an easier way to do it—to surrender. France had more 'realist' diplomatists than any other country and this realism went deeper. This is the basic reason why France surrendered in 1940, and why most Frenchmen accepted the policy of the Vichy Government. A realist foreign policy must always end at Vichy—cautious collaboration with the aggressor. When the people go wrong it is not from selfishness or materialism, but because they have got their moral values wrong. For instance, American 'isolationism' in the 1930's did not rest on selfishness. It sprang from the conviction that the First World War had been a crooked conspiracy of armament manufacturers and that it served no moral purpose. Once the

American people discarded this belief isolationism was dead; and the few isolationists who still survive are not the most selfish Americans, but the most obstinately idealist—though perhaps the most mistaken.

In exactly the same way, the British failure to resist Hitler before 1939 sprang from moral confusion, not from cowardice. It is now becoming the fashion in England to argue that the long series of retreats from 1935 to 1938 was caused by our military weakness; and Chamberlain is praised for buying time at Munich. My recollection is different. The British people were told over and over again by their most idealistic advisers that Germany had been hardly used. Reparations, one-sided disarmament, the peace settlement of 1919 were condemned by liberals and the Comintern alike. I can remember when I first visited Prague, in 1928, thinking how backward it was and how Dresden and Vienna were more civilized and democratic. For the vast majority of British people Hitler's demands seemed justified, however evil Hitler was in himself—otherwise they would have opposed him despite the risk. The military experts may have held that we were too weak to go to war when Hitler reoccupied the Rhineland in 1936. That was not how the question presented itself to public opinion: English people felt that the Germans had the right to reoccupy their own territory, and that was all there was to it. The debate over supporting Czechoslovakia in 1938 was conducted entirely in moral terms; and in fairness to Neville Chamberlain it should be said that he stuck to these terms—he never used the argument of military weakness by which he is now defended. The Sudeten Germans were supposed to have a justified grievance; the Czechs were supposed to be in the wrong. Those of us who wanted to stand by Czechoslovakia lost not because the country was short of fighter aircraft or radar defence. We lost because we could not undo in six months twenty years of moral propaganda in favour of Germany. But the moment that Hitler destroyed his moral prestige by occupying Prague in March 1939 the British people were determined to oppose him; and nothing could have stopped them.

It is one thing to say that democratic opinion is usually right; quite another to say the same of democratic statesmen. The almost universal pattern of democratic countries is the lack of faith in the people shown by those who are supposed to be leading them. The prototype of democratic statesmen is the revolutionary of 1848 who was seen trailing after a crowd and who said: 'I am their leader; I must follow them.' Democratic statesmen have excused their failures again and again by asserting that the people would not have stomached a stronger policy, though in fact the experiment of offering the stronger policy was never tried. How are the people to appreciate the hard truth when their leaders go on assuring them that all is well? The failure of Great Britain and France to rearm against Hitler is always held up as the warning example. But the people were never given the chance to judge this issue. Stanley Baldwin, who determined British policy, believed that he would lose a general election if he advocated great armaments. The British people were therefore told that Great Britain was stronger than Germany and that, in any case, Hitler was not dangerous. Baldwin won the general election of 1935; but even then he did not rearm. At every stage the British Government was driven forward by public opinion, not held back. When I woke up to the German danger in 1936 (rather late in the day) I wanted the Labour party to come out for great armaments and uncompromising resistance to Hitler. I was told that this would lose the next general election. Instead the war came. There was no general election; and Winston Churchill, the only man who had advocated resistance to Hitler, was swept into supreme power.

Recent American history teaches the same lesson. Franklin D. Roosevelt may have been ahead of public opinion in 1937; but those detached historians, William L. Langer and S. Everett Gleason, insist that he was a long way behind it in 1940. During his campaign for re-election he inserted—against the advice of his closest colleagues—the sentence: 'Your boys are not going to be sent into foreign wars.' His subsequent difficulties were not forced on him by public opinion; they sprang from his own desire to have it both ways. Messrs. Langer and Gleason refer to 'the mental confusion which had made it so easy for the American people simultaneously to advocate increased aid to Britain and avoidance of war'; and they add: 'The only conclusion which voters were logically entitled to draw from the campaign of 1940 was their right, on the very highest authority, to persist in incompatible courses of action.' The behaviour of Baldwin and Roosevelt may be reduced to a general proposition. When a democratic leader is faced with the choice between remaining in power and telling the truth to the people he will follow the course which he thinks will keep him in power. We may add a further proposition: the choice is wrong, even for him, in the long run. Baldwin became so unpopular that in 1940 he dared not visit London—'they hate me so'. Roosevelt's historical reputation was redeemed only when he was forced into war against his previous pledges, in 1941.

The people judge soundly on great issues. They cannot be expected to determine tactics. In diplomacy they are impatient with formality and delay; in war they expect fleets and armies to be in two places at once. The experts—whether generals or diplomats— are doing their right job when they translate the will of the people into practical terms. They err when they try to substitute a will of their own. The people lose faith in the cynical exponents of the practical; and they turn in disillusionment to those false prophets—the whole-hogging idealists. It is tempting to argue that, since it pursues idealistic aims, foreign policy should be uncompromisingly idealistic all the time. We went to war to free Poland; therefore every country in the world should receive a democratic constitution straight away. We dislike methods of violence and hate war; therefore all wars must be immediately forbidden. The common man knows that there is a difference between right and wrong, between black and white. That is his strength and his virtue. His weakness is to suppose that there is only black and white with nothing in between. He is impatient with the suggestion that they shade into each other or that there is something to be said on both sides. Such arguments seem to him 'expediency'. They savour of the 'realism' which he has rightly rejected. The idealists play into his hands. They too know little of the practical difficulties; they too want a ready-made answer; they too are exasperated when an ideal, once formulated, is not immediately achieved —and even more exasperated if its moral superiority is challenged. And in their impatience they advocate the victory of idealism by the most violent methods.

The League of Nations and the United Nations roused the idealists in this way. Both organizations rested on the dogma that war between nations must cease. This moral purpose was their sole justification. As an ultimate goal, it represents the only foreign policy which a democratic public opinion can applaud. But how can we move towards this ultimate goal? By seeking to limit and to end such wars as occur? Or by blowing up every little war into a big one? The idealists gave the second answer. The man in the street had too much common sense to follow them. Though he needs an abstract principle for which to fight, he also needs to be convinced that some practical issue is at stake. The Abyssinian crisis of 1935 was the outcome of this contradiction. The idealists wanted to assert the prestige of the League of Nations. The man in the street had a shrewd idea that it did not matter whether Italy conquered Abyssinia — or Abyssinia conquered Italy. The worst of all possible outcomes followed. The League of Nations was ruined; and Abyssinia was ruined also. Indeed, Abyssinia would have preserved some of its independence if there had been no League of Nations. There was something wrong with an international organization against war which could protect its members only by making war universal.

The United Nations was supposed to have more modest aims. Hence the veto which its creators deliberately put into the hands of the founding Great Powers. No action could be taken without their unanimous permission; therefore, it was thought, no great war would be possible. Russia's temporary absence from the Security Council in 1950 gave the idealists their chance. They set out to do in Korea what they had failed to do in Abyssinia. They would make war on war; and they cheerfully faced the risk of world war for an issue that was not in itself worth war at all. Had not the American chiefs of staff themselves proposed withdrawal from Korea before the invasion started? We got the war, but not the reward. Korea was not liberated; it was devastated and, in the end, partitioned, just as it could have been at the beginning. There were many practical reasons why the forces of the United Nations failed to achieve complete victory in Korea. But the basic reason was that this victory could be won only at the risk of general war; and the people would not run this risk for a question that did not matter in itself.

The people temper their idealism with common sense. They will make sacrifices for an ideal cause; but they have to be convinced that the ideals are genuine and that the sacrifices will bring commensurate rewards—for others, if not for themselves. The British and, later, the American people were so convinced in regard to Hitler. They believed that he was wholly evil and that liberation was a real boon to the peoples of Europe—as anyone who saw them in the first days after 1945 must have recognized that it was. They do not hold these beliefs so clearly about Soviet Communism.

They detest the political tyranny of Communism; but they also think that it has brought great social gains. They may be wrong in this belief, but it is widespread. It can be found not only in the speeches of Labour politicians, but in a recent book by the correspondent of a Conservative newspaper, the *Daily Telegraph*. Liberation from Hitler seemed a worthy cause, even though it meant restoring the systems of government and of society which had existed before Hitler's conquest of Europe. Liberation from the Communists does not seem a worthy cause, if it means putting back the systems (now no doubt exaggeratedly blamed) which the Communists overthrew. Popular opinion has a confused hope that the Communists will become less tyrannical if they are left alone. It believes that prosperity ruins dictatorship; and therefore, perhaps absurdly, pins its faith to the economic success of Communism.

The confusions and hesitations of the West spring from the attempt of the idealists to drive the people too fast and too far. The people will ride out on a Crusade. They have done it before; and they will do it again. But they cannot go crusading all the time, particularly when they are not convinced that good will follow. It is not enough to prove that Communism is evil; we have also to show a better alternative. Every anti-Communist is an asset for Communism; for he implies that Communism is the only positive value. Faith, not resistance, made the Crusades. Lacking this faith the people relapse into cynicism and indifference. But it is not the cynicism of the 'realist' diplomat. The people are as sceptical of realism as of everything else. It is a cynicism of negation, of indifference, if not of despair. Railing against democracy will not remove this cynicism. Constitutional changes will not alter the character of democratic foreign policy. Everyone in private life strikes a balance between self-interest and high principle. The people want the same in public affairs. They will never support a policy which thinks of 'the national interest' alone; nor will they sacrifice themselves, and others, for an idealism which does not count the cost. It is for the leaders, not for the people, to find a solution. The professional diplomats must have ideals; and the idealists must have some common sense.